THE HURRICANE PORT

THE HURRICANE PORT

A SOCIAL HISTORY
OF LIVERPOOL

ANDREW LEES

MAINSTREAM
PUBLISHING

EDINBURGH AND LONDON

To my father, brother and son

First published in Great Britain in 2011 by
MAINSTREAM PUBLISHING COMPANY
(EDINBURGH) LTD
7 Albany Street
Edinburgh EH1 3UG

ISBN 9781845967260

A catalogue record for this book is available
from the British Library

Printed in Great Britain by
Clays Ltd, St Ives plc

1 3 5 7 9 10 8 6 4 2

Acknowledgements

I wish to thank my wife Juanita for her indulgence over the six years it took to write this book and my daughter Nathalie for drawing the maps of Liverpool and providing valuable advice on photograph selection. Liverpool is truly a matriarchal city despite its tough shell.

My thanks go to Bill Campbell, my publisher, and the editorial team at Mainstream, particularly Ailsa Bathgate and Alex Hepworth, who ironed out many ambiguities and redundancies, Graeme Blaikie for his invaluable help with the logistics and also to my last editor Graham Watson, who made the necessary elisions painless.

The poets who have written about Liverpool and the films of Terence Davies have been rich influences. The library at the Athenaeum in Church Row, Liverpool, is a font for the arcane.

Much of this book was written with tears in my eyes in Café Valencia in Marchmont Street, not far from Euston Station. I thank the proprietors for their interest and rare Cuban coffee.

The people of Liverpool whether departed or in residence have inspired this book. I hope that they will not feel that I have betrayed their trust or distorted their truths and that I still love their city.

On the banks of a large river close to the sea there lies an empty port rich in aspiration and false pride. At the beginning of the nineteenth century, desperate families came here in their thousands to embark on journeys into the unknown. Those who were left in the wake of the hurricanes have learned to survive with their defiant dreams, unshakeable faith and sentimental redemption songs.

Contents

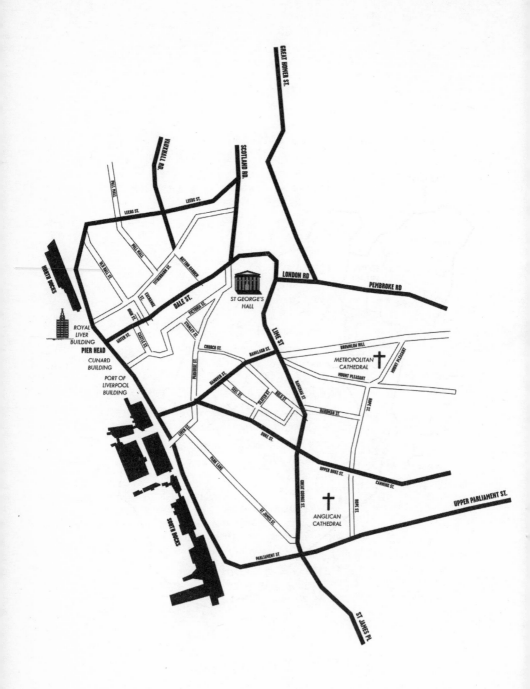

Liverpool's main streets and the docks in the mid 1960s.

Liverpool's districts and their relation to St Helens.

Preface

My father brought me from St Helens to this bustling two-tone port where gulls spiral up in narrow gaps of grey between the coal-black buildings. On one of those typically overcast, lowering Liverpool afternoons, we looked out from the edgeland onto the great river. My father told me he could see a sugarloaf rising out of the water and a flotilla of cutters drifting far out in the rain. The river seemed full of dark seafaring secrets as we discussed the possibility of hidden contraband in the holds of empty ships. We were both running away to sea but couldn't quite sever the umbilical cord that tied us to the shoreline.

Behind us lay the dead weight of Lancashire, with its shaking cornfields, wrecked alders, smothering gloom and forgotten family quarrels. At the top of Water Street we stopped, and between the first skyscrapers saw the *Queen Mary* ghosting towards the Irish Sea and on to the Cape of Good Hope. The streets around the Exchange were always full of hurrying, purposeful men with money to burn and an eye for profit, who talked to us as if their lives depended on it. In the rookery of streets leading up from the docks, warm-hearted women ruled the roost and spoke to me as an equal. However, even here, in the very heart of town, one sensed the seductive pull of the Atlantic. Furtive comings and goings at the Gorée terminus, secret love affairs at the end of the line and tearful farewells at the Pier Head were part and parcel of this shifting city.

My mother was the one left to tell me that we would soon be leaving St Helens for a better life in Leeds. She was desperate to escape coal, glass and the pungent steaming waters. Smut on privet and a river full of cadmium held no attractions for a young mother. The neon glow, which lit up the sombre sky and stained her washing, had made her lose weight and miscarry.

All at sea in West Yorkshire, I started to read books in an effort to understand this discontinuous presence, which forced me to measure my life by the passage of imaginary freighters. Liverpool was now a sealed envelope away rather than a short bus ride but I was unable to move on. Much later I started to haunt the port's seven streets looking for old familiar faces and hoping to hear the reassuring accents of those swaggering democrats. I tried to recapture vivid moments of childhood through chance encounters with comedians, guitarists and dancers, but each new visit revealed only the scents of their shadows and more washed-up corpses, tall stories and shipwrecks left from the last hurricane. In desperation, I ran away on Mondays, carrying no luggage and heading for cheap waterfront hotels with forgettable names where I could listen, uninterrupted, to the music of the waves at night. Yet even in Gdansk, New Orleans and Shanghai, I was fleeing landfalls, trying to turn back the clock and rescue lost memories.

This book is born from a need to be included and an inability to move on. There may be some honest lies hidden within its pages, but its sea lanes are suspect and the connecting bridges rickety. Each of its chapters has grown out of headlines of the sort seen after hurricanes. Little by little I have come to realise that the irregular rhythms of Liverpool cannot be separated from the ocean and that her history is joined with the Gulf Stream currents and the arrival of darkness. It is a tryst for all those fellow tide travellers who see their lives as a passage back to their home port . . .

Henry the Navigator

I will leave for Pasárgarda
There you have everything
Another civilisation
With a safe-proof system
To prevent conception
Automatic phone booths
Alkaloids on demand
Good-looking whores
With whom to romance
And when I am sadder
Sadder beyond any hope
When at night I have
A desire to kill myself
–There I am the friend of the king–
I will have the woman that I want
In the bed that I will choose
I will leave for Pasárgarda.

> Extract from 'Vou-me Embora pra Pasárgarda',
> from *Libertinagem* by Manuel Bandeira (translated
> into English by Francisco Cardoso)

On sultry autumn afternoons, as the last burned leaves of the idle healing ash tinkled into the culverts, my father and I left the suburban drives, passed 'The Towers' and the decaying, spectral piles of the last Victorian cotton brokers. A rustic lodge, a boating lake, the statue of the boy who never grew up and the bluebell Field of Hope were the nearest we ever got to a rural ride. It was there among the trees that I first felt the mysterious sorrow of this lost city.

I am back in Sefton Park now, where the Palm House is wearing a sullen face, its incongruity temporarily flattened by the charcoal-grey flannel sky and a gentle south-westerly wafting in from the sea. Two whippet-faced lads from a 'corpy' in the Dingle are half-heartedly kicking a tennis ball on one of the grand lawns. The kites are up behind the boating lake, and the Fairy Glen herons are on the prowl. An everyday necklace of alyssum and lobelia and a swathe of damp-velvet northern sod stand between the footpath and the jaded presence of Christopher Columbus. The wild adventurer's plinth pronounces, 'The discoverer of America was the maker of Liverpool.'

In the shadow of the city's acclaimed hero stands the forgotten bronze of the pious celibate Prince Henry the Navigator, fifth child of King John of Portugal; maternal grandson of John of Gaunt, 1st Duke of Lancaster; and the scourge of the Moors. If he is remembered at all in Liverpool, it is through the romantic name of a champion racehorse sired by Kingmambo, brother of Queen Cleopatra and winner of the 2,000 Guineas. Prince Henry's swarthy face is open and gentle, but he is clad in chain mail under a tunic decorated with castles and fleurs-de-lys. His right hand holds a mighty longsword, while his left lies on his thigh, his knee flexed to allow him to rest his left foot on a piece of rock. The history books paint an elusive and contradictory portrait of a nobleman who behaved more like an entrepreneur and who, despite his mixed European blood, was a staunch patriot. He was heroic, inquisitive, charming and open to suggestion but possessed a resolute determination. It is claimed he never quite shook off the domineering influence of his English mother, Philippa, who after her arrival in Lisbon likened the Portuguese court to a sewer and is said to have left it resembling a nunnery.

Under the flag of the White Cross with its five symbolic wounds of Jesus, Henry's captains sailed to the Berber coast to defend the faith, capture Ceuta and prepare Portugal for her long push south. His country's future would depend on the exploration of new worlds out in the darkness. The visionary young prince made it his business to talk to everyone who knew the ways of the sea. He hired foreign mathematicians and cartographers for his naval observatory built on the sacred promontory of Sagres at Cape St Vincent and had consultations with his astrologer to divine the unknown. He also expanded Lagos, 20 miles to the east of Sagres, for the construction of high-quality ships.

The Medici Portolano atlas, a fourteenth-century Italian chart, had identified mysterious lands far out in the Atlantic, and soon Henry's caravels, with their Arab lateen sails, were pressing further and further out from the Pillars of Hercules, colonising Madeira and then the Azores. The dusty harmattan wind blotted out the sun, and the doldrums becalmed his vessels under a burning sky in the Green Sea of Darkness, and held up progress. It took a decade for his sailors to pass Cape Bojador, the headland on the northern coast of the Western Sahara known to the Moors as 'The Father of Danger'. Once the Portuguese navigators had rounded the shoulder of Africa, they made fast progress to the Cape of Storms (the Cape of Good Hope), where Henry hoped to trap the rampant Moors in a gigantic pincer movement by joining forces with the mythical Christian kingdom of Prester John.

Antão Gonçalves, a captain on one of those expeditions, returned to Portugal with nine Muslim captives of mixed Arab and African blood who claimed to be a proud race unfit for bondage. Adahu, a well-travelled noble Tuareg chieftain, informed Henry that in the interior of the Dark Continent lived the accursed progeny of Ham, son of Noah, who had fathered the children of Africa. He also enthused over the opulence of Timbuktu. Very shortly after Adahu had been taken home, Captain Nuno Tristão returned to Portugal with a full boatload of African slaves he had obtained in trade with a number of tribes along the coast of Cabo Blanco, the vanguard of the millions who over the next four centuries would lose their lives for the sweet taste of rum and sugar. On their arrival in the Algarve port of Lagos, they were herded into a field and described by Zurara in his *Chronicle of the Discovery and Conquest of Guinea* as:

> A marvellous sight, for amongst them, were some white enough, fair enough, and well-proportioned: others were less white, like mulattos: others again were as black as Ethiops, and so ugly, both in features and in body, as almost to appear . . . the images of a lower hemisphere.

Prince Henry received the statutory 'royal fifth' of the proceeds from the sale of the slaves on behalf of the Church, giving thanks that he had saved so many souls for God and that he could use the money to finance further journeys of discovery. Some months later, some of the Tuaregs left Portugal again in a ship captained by Gonçalves and were exchanged on the Río de Oro for black slaves, gold and ostrich eggs. Before his death on the Algarve in 1460, Prince Henry's navigators had proved that it was possible to sail and survive in tropical seas and establish lucrative trading links with Black Africa. His enthusiasm for navigation inspired his academy graduates Da Gama, Diaz and Cabral to epic voyages that redrew the Atlantic shorelines, forged new trade routes and ultimately joined east with west.

A century after Henry the Navigator's caravels reached Cape Bojador, 138 daub cottages and the ramshackle tower of Lyrpole weathered the plague years and the Great Storm. The settlement's few merchants sold Bolton fustian, calico, inkhorns, quicksilver and madder in the streets on Saturday. Her serfs laboured on the Norman barons' estates and welcomed the Childe of Hale on market day. A lone ferryman piloted tanners and glovers across the tidal pool to the Great Heath. Her craftsmen found employment as skinners, pursers and shoemakers, working with Irish hide, while a few adventurers were away at sea, fishing for herrings, trading in Galway or working the crossings. A coaster carried linen to the Palatinate of Lancashire and North Wales. Drogheda was a fortnight away, and the Basque ports of Portugalete, Bilbao and Bermeo two months by sea. Twelve ships loaded with salt, iron and cotton were little Lyrpole's meagre dowry.

Plantains and dock now undermine the base of Henry's plinth. The engraved epitaph acclaiming him the Protector of the Studies of Portugal and the father of Atlantic exploration has faded. The Liverpool jazz crowd and wedding-reception guests who approach the Palm House from those same deserted suburban drives of my childhood have all but forgotten this remarkable Lusitanian visionary who banished the unknown terrors of the deep and opened up the possibility for a tiny fishing hamlet in the north-west of England to become one of the world's great ports.

Bagaceira

If I give you sugar, will you give me
Something elusive and temporary?
If I give you sugar, will you give me
Something elusive and temporary?
We've got a signal to leave you alone
Alone's where we leave you and alone's where we find you
If I give you sugar, will you give me
Something elusive and temporary?

'Sugar' Ladytron

A cup of tea with two sugars was my mother's little helper, and at Speakman Road the tea ceremony became linked with peace offerings and consolation. We celebrated in sugar and used it as a token of our affection. My rewards were fudge, aniseed balls, pear drops, treacle toffee, pineapple chunks, Jujubes, clove rock, Uncle Joe's Mint Balls, liquorice sticks and dolly mixtures. We made sugar butties for elevenses, smeared syrup on toast, and mixed cocoa and molasses in sherbet bags. Tate & Lyle's Mr Cube was a friendly face around town, sugared butterballs were said to cure colds and a spoonful of sugar helped the medicine go down. Once rationing was finally over, sugar became an affordable, essential everyday intoxication, a source of stimulation and fulfilment much more glamorous than brown bread. In 1963, 'Sweets for my Sweet', a Drifters cover by the Searchers on the Pye label, hit the charts. The Mike Pender, Chris Curtis and Tony Jackson nasal harmonies and the chiming twin six-string guitar accompaniments confirmed to me there was no single Merseybeat:

Sweets for my sweet, sugar for my honey
Your first sweet kiss thrilled me so,
Sweets for my sweet, sugar for my honey
I'll never ever let you go.

It says in a book that I am now reading in Leeds Public Library that in

1625, on his way home from Brazil in the *Olive Blossom*, Captain John Powell landed on a limestone coral atoll in the Lesser Antilles that had already been cleansed by the Portuguese of its Arawaks and Caribs. The island was dominated by rainforest but had dense shrub and grassland in the north and east, and large stretches of pristine mangrove and bearded fig close to the sea. The crew erected a cross on the west coast of the island in a place they christened Jamestown (now Holetown) and after dining richly on the pigs left by the Spaniards set sail for England.

British colonisation of the Caribbean soon followed Captain Powell's return, and by 1655, the pioneer Barbados farmers had largely moved away from tobacco, cassava, ginger, indigo and cotton cultivation to plant the rapacious 'sweet bamboo'. Two hundred British families, backed by London and Bristol merchants anxious to extend their commercial portfolios, now owned half of Barbados, deforestation was almost complete and nearly 90 per cent of the island's 100,000 acres was under cultivation, much of it to sugar. Eleven parishes had been delineated and local government was in the hands of the Episcopalian vestries.

Some of the neophyte British planters visited Brazil to learn about cane cultivation, and in *A True and Exact History of the Island of Barbadoes*, Richard Ligon describes their first attempts at sugar cultivation:

> At the time we landed on this island, which was in the beginning of September 1647, we were informed partly by those planters we found there, and partly by our own observations, that the great work of sugar making was but newly practised by the inhabitants there. Some of the most industrious men have gotten plants from Fernambrock, a place in Brazil, and made trial of them at the Barbadoes, and finding them to grow, they planted more and more as they grew and multiplied on the place, till they had such a considerable number that it was worth the while to set up a very small ingenio [sugar mill], and so make trial what sugar could be made on that soil.

'Fernambrock' in Ligon's account is likely to refer to the state of Pernambuco in Brazil, and on their visits to Olinda ('the beautiful place'), the captaincy's main settlement, the English overseers did not fail to notice that the large profitable plantations depended on the forced labour of African slaves.

British ethnocentrism and an aversion to mixing between the races deterred many of the first planters from using black labour, despite the commercial advantages, and in the early years the farms relied almost totally on 'indentured' white servants who, in return for a free passage and an opportunity to buy a strip of land, bound themselves to work for the plantation owners. Many of these poor yokels, some of whom had been spirited away from a semi-feudal England, ended up in a situation that amounted to little more than slavery. The Irish and Scots expelled by Cromwell's ethnic-cleansing programme were also 'Barbadosed', with their numbers swelled by 800 West Country supporters of the 1st Duke of Monmouth, sentenced by Judge Jeffreys at the Bloody Assizes to transportation to the new colony. This motley crew of disgruntled and often rebellious 'Red Legs' and 'Black Irish' toiled for a generation on Britain's dunghill, where many succumbed rapidly to yellow fever or dysentery.

The virgin shoots of the thirsty grass sprouted after several weeks and within eight months it grew to two and a half metres in height. After several harvests, cane fields were often permanently abandoned. Field slaves used machetes to cut down the Creole cane, oozing with sweet sap, to be taken by horse- and ox-drawn carts to 'Dutch mills' powered by water, wind or ox. It was then passed several times through the presses, and once all the glutinous elixir had been expressed from the stalks the sticky liquid trickled down gutters into the tayches (open copper pans) of the boiler house. The bagasse husks were piled in mountainous rotting heaps to be used as fuel and manure while the syrup stewed in the feverish, heady heat of the roasting room. White lime was sprinkled into the tayches to assist the thickening and cleansing of the brew. The excremental mud and floating detritus were skimmed off and added to the heap of bagasse. After continuous simmering and stirring, the brown crystals were separated out and the residual viscous molasses was distilled as rum or sold off as bricks of low-class sugar. Once the muscovado had cooled and been weighed, it was packed in hogsheads and transported by schooner from Speightstown and Holetown to the big ships waiting in the favourable waters of Bridgetown harbour. The Brazilian anthropologist Gilberto Freyre described the plantation culture as a 'bagaceira', after the shed where discarded cane fibre was left. Colloquially in Portuguese, the term refers to rubbish, marginalised riff-raff or waste produced by an oppressive monoculture. Out of brute force and exploitation came an exotic sweetness and intoxicating romance, but this decaying fermentation came to be associated with death, violence and destruction. A horrible loneliness came with the cutting of cane that left deep scars in the soul.

The plantation owners built two-storeyed wooden mansions (often referred to as 'The Big House') with jalousies to keep out the tropical rain and redundant hearths and fireplaces to remind them of England. Most of the properties followed a similar design, although their sizes varied. The central part of the residence was composed of a spacious pine-floored dining room and salon filled with mahogany furniture. There was a narrow room on either side of the house: one used as the lady's sun lounge and the other the master's study. From the veranda to the gates wound an elegant drive lined with casuarina trees, bougainvillea, frangipane, flame trees, oleanders and hibiscus. Rose and herb gardens added the fragrances of rural England, while the numerous Anglican chapels kept the planters in touch with God in this heathen, faraway land.

Some of the 'masters' made large fortunes and lived gluttonous and profligate lives, dining on capons, mutton, turtle doves and rabbit, all washed down with the best claret. Most were anti-Catholic, pro-Commonwealth who, as Charles Kingsley put it in *Westward Ho!*, considered this new land to be the 'very garden of the Lord', which 'neither Spaniard, cannibal or other evil beast' could enter.

With the financial and technological resources made available to the planters by the 'New Christian' Portuguese and Spanish and Jewish sugar makers who had fled Brazil in 1654, Richard Ligon's conviction that Barbados would never usurp Olinda's pre-eminence in the sugar trade was now open to question. Warfare between the Portuguese and the Dutch in Pernambuco had disrupted Brazilian sugar production and created a golden opportunity that the English plantation owners had been quick to seize. Many, like the Anglo-Dutch militia captain James Drax, returned to England as rich men, and the fortunate families who owned the cane fields came to look on them as veritable gold mines.

At any one time, up to twenty Dutch and British vessels would be moored off Bridgetown waiting to load sugar and rum. Barbados's relative isolation, her encircling coral reefs and the difficulties of sailing against the trade winds gave the island a degree of immunity from French and Spanish attack. Thirty-six forts were built on the west and south coasts to protect the island from invasion so that by the end of the seventeenth century Barbados had become a mature windmill-based sugar-exporting economy presiding over an archipelago of molasses sprinkled over the surface of the Caribbean Sea. Some of the English and Scots Protestant planters who had been awarded land confiscated from the native Irish by the British government in the new plantation of Ulster would travel home on the returning ships.

Liverpool was still a small growing port, four days away from London by road, with the nearest stagecoach service stationed sixteen miles away at Warrington. Its 36 narrow and crooked oil-lit streets were full of Dissenter and Quaker merchants who had fled north to escape the Great Plague. A flourishing Exchange had been built on eight pillars, and from the impressive tower one could see the Isle of Man. The town was surrounded by hedgerows of briar and honeysuckle extending out, through meadows, to the pretty villages of Wavertree, Edge Hill and Everton.

It was from here in 1666 that the *Antelope*, a diminutive ship of 60 tons' displacement, headed out with linen, shoes, nails and coal on a long voyage that took her far beyond Ireland and the town's most distant trading horizons of Portugal and Spain. A year later she re-entered the mouth of the Mersey to rapturous celebration, loaded with a rich cargo of sugar cane from the Barbados plantations. Liverpool now firmly grasped that there was a new world of opportunity far beyond the Irish Sea as it worked with its satellite partners in Dublin, Cork and Drogheda to ship beef, herring, horses, linsey-woolsey, Kendal cotton, pork and butter to the West Indies. Some of Lancashire's undesirable and unloved mendicants, orphans and prisoners would soon join the Bristolian, Irish and Scots slaves in the fields, allowing a new breed of Liverpool ship captains to establish business links in the Americas.

Liverpool's first sugarhouse employed just 15 men and produced a modest 200 tons a week. Bullocks' blood, known as 'spice', coagulated as the raw sugar reached boiling point and entangled the sugar scum. After repeated separations, the golden liquor was strained off. The mixture of crystals and syrup was then run into heavy clay cone moulds and allowed to cool for several days. Residual syrup was drained through a plug in the narrow end of the mould. The colour of the conical loaves was improved by water percolation and they were then put out to dry. These crystalline rocks, often weighing 150 lb each, had to be splintered into small pieces by the town's grocers using specially designed crushing appliances. The chunks of sugar were too large for domestic use, and customers used decorative sugar nippers and tongs to splinter the crystalline mass into shards suitable to sweeten tea. Despite its modest beginnings, the sugarhouse was profitable, and one of its owners, Daniel Danvers, a resident of Red Cross Street, became the largest ratepayer in town, entitling him to become a Freeman and an eligible suitor for the apothecary's attractive daughter Sarah Pemberton, from Moore Street.

Molasses soon turned eighteenth-century Liverpool into a sugar daddy and a rum place, and came to signify far more than salt or spice. The white gold rush would corrupt taste buds and contribute to an exotic botany of desire.

Across the water, south of the black-treacle pond and the morass of modern Dublin, stands the Great Sugar Loaf of Wicklow, rising in the mists. Much further west and to the south, the Pão de Açúcar guards the mouth of Guanabara Bay, the legendary pointed cone of the Tamoios and Tupinambás; the butter pot of the French; the bulbous sentinel at the mouth of the January River, sighted by Gonçalo Coelho and his cosmographer Vespucci on New Year's Day 1502; and the cenotaph for the misery of Brazil's north-east. The white, sugary sand of Leblon stretches out its stranded hand, and the ochre of the almond trees and the old lamps light the quiet streets in the shadow of the rock. These are sweet memories of a different but familiar face. I can still buy tarry treacle in a tin on Tithebarn, the last dregs of an imperial commodity that helped glue Liverpool together and give me a sweet tooth. Sugar still transforms bitterness to sweetness, intoxication to revelation, and torment to pleasure. It is still ecstatic, soothing and lubricious, and on Thursday nights in the Alma de Cuba bar a sweet, tropical sickness lingers when the night gets long.

Gorée

Beware and take care of the Bight of Benin.
There's one that comes out for forty goes in.
Nineteenth-century Liverpool sea shanty

A golliwog once sat at the foot of my cot, next to Pinky the teddy bear. This scary bed partner had been inspired by a nineteenth-century children's book by Florence Upton and her mother Bertha:

Then all look round as well they may
To see a horrid sight!
The blackest gnome
Stands there alone
They scatter in their fright.

Dressed in scarlet trousers and a blue jacket and bow tie, my golliwog had ebony skin, thick red lips, wild frizzy hair and large, laser-beam-white eyes. I admired his mischievous chivalry but could never quite love him. Later I found golliwog sportsmen on the lids of Robertson jam jars and for a while wore the prized metal badge on my lapel.

I didn't meet a black boy until I was seven. His name was Tony Dibb. Our teacher asked us what we wanted to be when we grew up. When it came to Tony's turn, I piped up that I thought he would be great as a coalminer. I was put outside the classroom and told off by the headmistress. After that, I became friendly with Tony, who was regarded at school as a curiosity. Somebody taught me 'Eeny, meeny, miny, mo; Catch the nigger by his toe; If he squeals, let him go; Eeny meeny miny mo.' I didn't understand what it meant until a boy told me Tony was the 'nigger in the woodpile'.

At home, I was encouraged to rescue black babies from limbo. None of those Saturday matinees helped. All they showed me were terrifying Zulus with knobkerries charging valiant English soldiers, or howling war-

23

painted cannibals dancing round cooking pots. Sunday night was a time we got together as a family to watch *The Black and White Minstrel Show*, in which Al Jolson lookalikes and pretty white girls sang traditional chain-gang Dixie ballads. One day, my taciturn grandfather came out with this ditty he had learned from his father:

> Oh, there was an old darkie called Uncle Ned
> But he died long ago, long ago
> And he had no wool on the top of his head
> In the place where the wool ought to grow
> So lay down the shovel and the hoe
> And hang up the fiddle and the bow
> No more hard work for Poor Old Ned
> And he's gone where the good niggers go.

I was taught nothing about the slave trade at school but as I entered my teens a few black families were arriving in the Chapeltown and Harehills areas of Leeds to do the jobs and live in the houses no one else wanted. I had discovered the music of Ben E. King and Little Richard, but Afro roots didn't show through. The second black boy I met was Gilbert Browne, who was an ace at table tennis. 'Wog' felt like an insult for 'Wily Oriental Gentlemen' and 'Pakis', rather than Gilbert. At school, some people called him 'Rastus', while others preferred 'coon'.

A few years later, David Oluwale, a victim of police harassment, was pulled out of the River Aire on Warehouse Hill. A year after that, the local gentry, the Lascelles family of Harewood House, sold their last plantation in Barbados.

Apartheid stirred my conscience, but I had still not grasped that slave labour was inseparable from mercantilism and monopoly, nor indeed that Liverpool had been built on its proceeds. Later, once I learned the dark secret, I tried to justify the morally indefensible by blaming the African chiefs and a few unscrupulous merchants from out of town. I also half believed that the Liverpool cartels had saved the captives from a miserable life of bondage in the cesspits of West Africa. I argued that most of those 'ordinary' people who had drifted into the city looking for work had toiled like slaves themselves and led lives that were only marginally better. I didn't realise that, although it was not my fault, I was a racist and that golliwogs were an unwitting symbol of racism. Belated apologies don't really help and are not demanded, but I need to understand the horrible truth of the diaspora if I am to fathom my attraction to this city by the sea.

The high attrition rate of the indentured servants and the unslakeable demand for sugar in England led ineluctably to the arrival of the first black slaves in the British Caribbean. Large rowing boats called 'lighters' transported them from slave ships anchored in Carlisle Bay to the Bridgetown waterfront. At the sound of a drum, the buyers would charge into the pens where the Africans were kept and, with a great deal of clamour and shouting, try to apply their tally to the slaves they wanted to buy.

In 1700, the *Liverpool Merchant* arrived in Barbados with a cargo of 220 Africans. Terrified and exhausted, they were auctioned on the Careenage for £4,239. The same year a second Liverpool boat, the *Blessing*, set off with the following instructions to the captain:

> We order you with the first fair wind and weather that Presents to make the best of the way to King-sail in the kingdom of Ireland where apply yourself to Mr. Arthur Izeik merchant there, who will ship on board you such necessary provisions and other necessaries you shall want for your intended voyage and . . . with the first fair wind and weather make the best of your way to the Coast of Guinea . . . where dispose of what of the cargo is most proper and purchase what slaves you can . . . I hope you will slave your ship easy and what shall remain over as above slaving your ship lay out in teeth which are there reasonable – when you have disposed of your cargo and slaved your ship make the best of your way to the West Indies . . . if you find the markets reasonable good sell there, if dull go down Leeward to such Island as you shall see where dispose of your negroes to our best advantage and with the produce load your ship with sugar, cottons, ginger if to be had . . . and make the best of your way home . . .

The *Eliza*, under Captain John Dunn, also arrived in Barbados that year, unloading 71 slaves at the market. The Liverpool traders began to promote the island as a veritable paradise with slavery as part of the natural order of things, a legitimate activity that would bring prosperity to the port and a realistic expectation of happiness for the supposedly backward, heathen savages of the 'Dark Continent'. Despite Liverpool's entry into the 'rough trade', in 1720 most of the 150 English Guineamen leaving for Africa still departed from the southern ports of London and Bristol.

Each plantation in Barbados now covered between 60 and 100 acres, and local custom rather than law was used to control the slaves. They were listed as the chattels of the planters and were despised and feared by their white owners, who were now outnumbered three to one. Scantily clad and half-starved, the slaves were forced to work in the fields 18 hours a day in groups of 50, guarded over by a mulatto slave-driver. Exhausted, they slept on hessian sacks on earthen floors in cramped wooden- and mud-hut barracks thatched with sugar cane and plantain leaves; many were dead within a decade of enslavement.

Some of the plantation owners were cruel, sadistic men who took pleasure in the torture of what they saw as expendable property. Their slaves were manacled and immobilised with ankle shackles and neck collars and imprisoned in dark outhouses guarded by callous henchmen. Some were muzzled with iron masks to prevent them drinking rum; others were gagged and bound, hoisted into the air and flogged to within an inch of their lives. Rebels were boiled alive or nailed to the ground and burned in front of jeering audiences. Gelding and the amputation of half a foot with an axe were not uncommon.

It was not too long before one in five vessels leaving the Landing Stage in Liverpool was involved in the rough trade of the middle passage. By sending their ships around the north of Ireland, the Liverpool merchants were able to minimise the risk of attack from French privateers and keep down insurance premiums. Their captains were known for their lower charges, faster turnaround times and greater willingness to take risks than their London and Bristol counterparts. The liberal use of ship's apprentices also kept their costs competitive and allowed them to sell their 'prime Negroes' at £5 less than their competitors. The Isle of Man provided a ready haven for contraband and tax evasion.

Over the next 50 years, more and more armed slavers with good honest names such as the *Rebecca*, the *Brookes*, the *Enterprise*, the *Lively* and the *Prudence* left the Old Dock and sailed down the Mersey heading for the Gold Coast and the Niger Delta. These three-masted square-riggers with copper-sheathed hulls were powered by the action of the sea winds on their broad flax canvas sails. Their fundamental design had changed little since the pioneering Atlantic voyages of Vespucci, Pinzón and Cabral, but they were faster over the water. Each boat was fitted with a good depth of hold and high wooden sterns, which permitted the swivel guns mounted on the quarterdeck to be trained on an enemy ship's waist. They were also reinforced with a strong width of beam, thickened round the rails to prevent any leaps for freedom by the desperate slaves.

Each Guineaman had a captain, two mates, a supercargo, a ship's surgeon, a handful of craftsmen and around fifty rough-and-ready sailors. The crew was largely composed of the scum of Liverpool: habitual drunks, ex-convicts, moral degenerates and social misfits. Procuring a crew for a slave mission was not straightforward, and many men had to be lured aboard. The captain's labour agents, or 'crimps', would drag unsuspecting landsmen who were down on their luck into the waterfront taverns. There the conspiratorial publican would ply them with grog, indicating their rising debt with chalk marks on the wall. By the end of the night, those who refused to settle up were labelled as jailbirds and threatened with prison. Eventually the 'friendly' sailor thief would suggest a solution: the man could sign an 'article of agreement' to clear his debt. Some crews also contained a few disgraced or lovelorn landlubbers and the occasional idealistic adventurer who had signed on voluntarily. Swedish, East Indian and Portuguese seamen were also recruited on the Liverpool ships. Many of the sailors bound for Africa were guilt-ridden and ashamed, and did everything in their power to conceal the nature of their voyage from their family and friends. Fortunately for the captain, there were also some penniless and able old salts that could be depended on in the many crises that arose on the long journey south.

The captain, usually a man in his 30s, together with the 'ship's husband', oversaw repairs and detailed the preparation needed to ensure a profitable trip. Once at sea, the captain ruled with an iron fist. Ruthless, arbitrary bullying was the preferred method of control. Too much familiarity with the crew could fatally diminish authority and encourage mayhem and mutiny. As an early show of strength, the sailors' chests, which contained their few worldly possessions, were often burned or destroyed. The captain would then sometimes select an easy target, such as the ship's black cook, for corrective attention from the mate's cat-o'-nine-tails. The sailors were slashed with knives, tortured with marlinspikes and thrown into irons for the most minor offence. Prison was considered by some to be heaven compared with life on board a slaver. The motto 'We're all in this ship together' kept the Guineamen afloat.

One in five sailors lost his life from green contagion, a few more died in brawls and the odd sea dog ended up in the cooking pots of Gabon. Under firm instructions from the merchant princes, the captain judged the life of a 'white slave' to be more expendable than that of one of his prized black cargo. The slave ships were a concentration of human misery. It was a hard, unforgiving world of chronic abuse. Dog ate dog, kindness was a weakness and decency was in very short supply. Dicky Sam, in his 1884 book *Liverpool and Slavery*, described the horrors of the slave ship: 'The captain bullies the men, the men torture the slaves, and the slaves' hearts are breaking with despair.'

Life was not much better back on land, where the town's illiterate paupers lived from hand to mouth under constant fear of hell and damnation, with few surviving beyond their 40th birthdays.

Slavery was well established in the Dark Continent long before the first Liverpool boats arrived, so it was relatively straightforward for the town's merchants to piggyback onto the existing commercial networks developed by the Portuguese, Dutch and Spanish. The slaves were bought from African kings in the notorious 'canoe houses' of Bonny and Old Calabar and from the dreaded island entrepôt of Gorée. Antera Duke, a leading Efik trader based at Duke Town, in the Bight of Biafra, kept a diary in which he described how he helped to 'slave' twenty Liverpool Guineamen over a three-year period from 1785. On arrival at Seven Fathoms Point, the slave ship would fire her cannon before she headed slowly up the Calabar River. Duke, dressed in waistcoat and breeches and sporting a gold-laced hat, would be waiting on shore to greet the captain and his officers with liberal quantities of *mimbo* (palm wine) and 'plays' of communal singing and native dancing. Many of the business negotiations were finalised on board ship with a tea ceremony and the traditional exchange of *dashee* (presents).

The Liverpool supercargo's bartering commodities consisted of the popular coarse, striped and coloured *annabasses* ('Guinea cloths') from Manchester, muskets and gunpowder, Yorkshire woollens, rum and tobacco from the colonies, Staffordshire clay pipes, and beads and pewter trinkets. The unit of currency was the 'bar' or 'piece', originally iron strips brought from England. These were exchanged for African muscle, yams for the middle passage, elephants' tusks and gold dust. The finest specimens of teenage black manhood sold for £80 a 'carcase' in the Bridgetown slave market. Despite the wastage from disease and suicide, many thousands of Africans completed the long journey to spend the rest of their lives toiling on the West Indian and American colonial plantations. Antera Duke, with the adopted customs of an English gentleman, became an influential member of the Efik Leopard Society. He organised the ritual sacrifice of slaves, democratically presided over village disputes and even oversaw the decent burial of Edward Aspinall, a slave-ship captain.

The rapacious Liverpool 'buckos' soon struck out from the traditional enclaves to make new links in Gabon, Sierra Leone, the Cameroons, Congo and Angola. Some of the slaves had been kidnapped and others were prisoners of war, while black relatives or superiors sold a small number on. As the ship captains grew in confidence, they looked for ways of cutting out the hard bargaining of the cunning African chiefs by increasing the use of gangmasters and dodgy agents. This practice led to mounting coastal tensions and the eventual colonisation of the heart of Africa. Men like Yellow Henry, the pirate admiral Lemma Lemma and the Brazilian émigré, the Chacha of Ajudah became important and respected trading partners. There were now two more Liverpools in the world: one on the St Paul River in what is now Liberia and the other on the Rio Pongas in Guinea. Both were nefarious slaving centres and popular destinations for the Guineamen.

The slaves were manacled two by two and packed like spoons, one next to another, so that each slave had less room than he would have had in a coffin. If fine weather prevailed, the slaves were chained on deck, but during storms or at the first sign of dissent the men were shackled below in the stinking, putrid holds. Captain Thomas Marshall of the *Black Joke* flogged a malnourished nine-month-old infant to death and forced its distraught mother to throw the child overboard. The women were easy sexual prey for the crew, and the captain would take several black wives to live with him in his cabin. Every morning and evening, the slaves were brought on deck and fed with raw yam and horse beans and then made to jump in their chains either to the sound of their own sad death songs or to the morbid reels of the sailors' fiddles. If the 'black cattle' were reluctant to perform for the leering crew, they would be subjected to the stinging bite of the cat-o'-nine-tails. This ritual was euphemistically referred to on board as 'dancing' and was claimed to provide exercise, minimise the risk of hunger strikes and calm homesickness.

At night, the slaves would wail and cry out as their broken dreams reminded them of a lost happiness. The 'subhuman cargo' was occasionally dumped lock, stock and barrel overboard for insurance purposes. Sick or dying and rebellious slaves were also jettisoned, while a few managed to jump to their own deaths in the shark-infested sea. The slave ships resembled gruesome slaughterhouses full of misery, filth and blood. Between 1710 and 1810, a quarter of a million Africans were transported to Barbados. Families were split up, and the only permitted recreations on the plantations were dancing and drumming. Those of inferior stock who remained unsold were left to die on the beaches. Dr Thomas Trotter, ship's surgeon on the *Brookes*, described the auction of slaves as a 'scramble', and Olaudah Equiano, the Nigerian abolitionist and former slave, relates the sad spectacle of the Bridgetown waterfront in his autobiography:

> On a signal given (as the beat of the drum), the buyers rush at once into the yard where the slaves are confined, and make choice of that parcel they like best. The noise and clamour with which this is attended, and the eagerness visible in the countenances of the buyers, serve not a little to increase the apprehensions of the terrified Africans.

A year after they set sail from the Mersey, the Liverpool slave boats, enriched with the scents of the Americas, would arrive back at Salt House and Queen's Dock stashed with coffee, ginger, cotton, tobacco, nutmeg and sugar cane. Elephants' teeth, ginger gum, coconuts, indigo and tortoiseshells were among the fabulous treasures unloaded on the quayside. These precious cargoes were sold off, the bills of exchange discounted and the profits divvied up between the Liverpool cartels. Ballast and light freight were also transported from the Caribbean in the slave ships, further increasing the margins of profit.

Liverpool grocers, tallow chandlers, drapers – and even the clergy – had shares in the slave trade. In 1792, 131 Liverpool ships were cleared to carry 40,000 slaves from Africa to the New World, compared with a mere 42 from Bristol and a paltry 22 from the capital. Through the commercial nous of her Nonconformist merchants, a once humdrum and nondescript port in the north-west of England had become the acknowledged capital of the Atlantic slave trade. In the town's heyday, seven large firms controlled more than half her slaving enterprise, with her mayor and thirty-seven of the forty-one members of Liverpool council actively involved. Despite the inherent risks and narrow profit margins of slavery, the accrued wealth was so great that it could later be claimed that the Industrial Revolution was financed by its proceeds.

A small number of male slaves were sold on the steps of the Liverpool Custom House. Some were from the Gold Coast Fante tribe and had been used on the homeward voyage as competent replacements for sailors who had deserted or died; others represented a 'payment in kind' for the captain. Auctions also took place in the coffee houses of Water Street and at a warehouse on what became known as 'Negro Row', in Liverpool's South Docks. Captain Robert Syers advertised for sale 'a very fine negro girl about eight years of age' and, three years later, 'a fine Negroe Boy of a sober, tractable, humane Disposition'. Black children were often bought as playthings and toys for rich ladies, who placed adverts in the papers such as the following, which appeared in *Williamson's Liverpool Advertiser* in 1756: 'Wanted immediately a Negro boy. He must be of a deep black complexion, and a lively humane disposition with good features, and not above fifteen, nor under twelve years of age.' The town's slave sellers also became bounty hunters when 'their property' absconded, and newspapers would offer rewards for any information about black runaways.

In spite of wartime destruction, the Gorée still survives behind the Three Graces, and, 200 years after Wilberforce, slavers are still at work in Liverpool. On 5 February 2004, Lin Liang Ren, a young Snakehead gangmaster and blackjack gambler, left Liverpool in an old white van crammed with Chinese cockle pickers bound for Hest Bank, on Morecambe Bay. As the wind whipped up and a hard rain sheeted down, these 21 illegal immigrants, most from Fujian Province, were trapped by the high tides and quicksand and drowned on Warton Sands. There were seventy more, working for a pound a day, banged up in four rented properties in the Kensington area of Liverpool. These people are trapped in a twilight world, bought and sold like commodities and controlled by violence.

Derek Wragge Morley's book *The Ant World* provided me with further insight. The large blood-red ant is a rarity in England, living in small nests of 1,000 workers, forming clustered communes of 20 or so intertwined nests. When its numbers get low, or rapid expansion is demanded for new projects, black ant slaves and their eggs are captured. It seems that even the ant, with its reputation for industry and teamwork, resorts to exploitation.

There are pimps at work who imprison and murder teenage sex slaves, and cruel families who exploit women to toil as helots. There are the starved, the imprisoned and the sexually violated, who keep the prices down and are forced to forfeit their passports. African children are still sold on and sometimes sacrificed, and young women in fear of juju priests forced to sell their bodies. The city is full of enslaved addicts living in West Derby concentration camps, and dejected rejects who are paid to stay at home and remain hidden.

The ant queen was dead, absolute sovereignty was lost and the shrinking workforce no longer knew what to do with itself.

The Old Firm

There is only the fight to recover what has been lost
And found and lost again and again: and now, under conditions
That seem unpropitious.

Extract from 'East Coker' by T.S. Eliot

By the middle of the eighteenth century, Liverpool's population had expanded to 20,000 (of whom 2,000 were freemen) and the town was second only to London in the tobacco and sugar trades. The new docks were receiving vessels from trading partners in Norway, Rotterdam and Oporto. Commerce was controlled by a tightly knit Protestant and Dissenter oligarchy of about twenty families, and four of these owned private carriages. Most were successful slavers, and the most upstanding of all was Foster Cunliffe, a tobacco magnate originally destined for the Church who had left Lancashire's rural rides to seek his fortune in Liverpool. He became adept at exploiting 'damaged' Potomac Oronoco weed and as a consequence managed to avoid Customs duty on more than a quarter of his Virginia tobacco imports. In partnership with the town's bailiff Richard Norris, brother of one of Liverpool's Members of Parliament, Cunliffe commissioned three or four Guineamen a year to sail to West Africa, and from the proceeds was able to hold three large fields to the north of the town.

Cunliffe and another merchant, Richard Gildart, started to reorganise their businesses by reducing the turnaround times of the warehouse cargoes and establishing stores in America run by factors for the sale of linen and wrought-iron goods. They continued to ship indentured and convict servants as well as sell African slaves to the Virginian planters on the Eastern Seaboard. These initiatives gave them an advantage over their competitors and an increasing share of business with the region around Chesapeake Bay. Between them, the Gildart brothers and Foster Cunliffe & Sons transported more than 4,000 slaves to Chesapeake in 31 voyages, and Cunliffe and his family owned shares in 26 vessels trading with West Africa.

Cunliffe was regarded as a stubborn and humourless man, but he had gained respect in Liverpool for his sense of civic responsibility and philanthropy. He was a sponsor of the Blue Coat School, had been elected Lord Mayor of Liverpool on three separate occasions, and before his death succeeded in securing his son Ellis's election to Parliament and to the Presidency of the Liverpool Infirmary. In the chapel of St Peter's Church in Woolton village, there is a memorial plaque that describes Foster Cunliffe as follows: 'A merchant whose sagacity, honesty and diligence procured wealth and credit to himself and his country, a magistrate who administered justice with discernment, candour and impartiality, a Christian devout and exemplary.'

Ellis Cunliffe's predecessor at Westminster was John Hardman ('The Great Hardman'), another successful Liverpool slaver and shipowner, who died in 1755 at the age of 92. Cunliffe would later lose his seat to the Jamaican planter and slave owner Richard Pennant, who chaired the West India Company and later invested part of his fortune in quarries in Snowdonia. A list compiled in 1752 of 101 Liverpool merchants trading to Africa included 12 who had been or would become mayors of the town. These Freemen met regularly in male-only clubs like the Ugly Face Club and the Noble Order of the Bucks, and under the influence of the best rum would hatch new conspiracies and debate the social issues of the day.

Another of Liverpool's elite traders was the grocer William Whaley, who every year sent his slave ship the *Saint George* to the Bight of Biafra to barter for slaves. William Davenport, a youth from a privileged Cheshire family, was apprenticed to Whaley, and towards the end of his training started to dabble in the rough trade by buying shares in some of his mentor's exploits. Shortly after he had been made a freeman, Davenport established his own trading partnerships with a number of other well-connected young associates in Drury Lane, just 100 yards from the Exchange. Over the next 35 years until his retirement, he would be involved in 163 Liverpool slave ventures. He invested the modern equivalent of £10 million and, although returns fluctuated wildly, he was able to average a profit of about 10 per cent per annum, making him one of the most successful Liverpool slavers of his generation. Two voyages of his ship the *Hawke*, in 1779 and 1780, made an exceptional 100 per cent net profit of £13,000.

With the help of his business partners, Thomas and William Earle, Davenport imported glass beads from Livorno, Silesia and Prague that would comprise up to half the value of the cargoes on his ships going to the Gulf of Guinea. Cowrie shells from the Maldives, knives from Holland, guns from Birmingham, copper manillas from Wigan and Warrington, cotton fabrics from Manchester, silks from India, and West Indian rum were other commodities used by his captains to barter for slaves. His two main trading posts in Africa were Old Calabar and a new entrepôt, Cameroon, 50 miles to the east. Many of his boats sold slaves to the newly developing plantations of Dominica and Grenada. Davenport never married, shunned local politics and the limelight, and after his retirement lived in modest circumstances in Mathew Street.

A popular saying of the time was that one was either 'a man of humanity or a man of Liverpool'. Cunliffe and Davenport and their breed rarely set foot outside their green and pleasant homeland, letting the dirty work of the slave trade fall squarely on the shoulders of their young ship captains. These strong-willed and shrewd pillars of society succeeded in sanitising their lucrative commodity while vehemently denying any wrongdoing. They rarely lost an opportunity to publicly assert that they were honest, God-fearing tradesmen who were diligent to the welfare of their crews and human cargo. The merchant princes contended that they were on a mission to rescue 'unfortunate negroes' from a life of misery in the heathen jungles of Africa. They argued that the profits from the Africa trade were integral to Liverpool's growth and that slaves were essential to put sugar into English teacups. They also had a number of influential supporters, including the naval hero Lord Rodney and the diarist James Boswell, who wrote that to abolish the slave trade would be extremely cruel to the African and would 'shut the gates of mercy on mankind'. In his poem 'No Abolition of Slavery, Or The Universal Empire of Love', Boswell wrote:

> The cheerful gang!—the negroes see,
> Perform the task of industry,
> But should our Wrongheads have their will,
> Should Parliament approve their bill,
> Pernicious as th' effect would be,
> T' abolish negro slavery,
> Such partial freedom would be vain,
> Since Love's strong empire must remain.

For most of these God-fearing Protestants and Nonconformist burgesses, the Ten Commandments were open to interpretation: 'Thou shalt not steal' did not apply to the enslavement of foreigners, and 'Love thy neighbour' seemingly did not extend to 'heathen' black men. The business plan was to 'Get slaves, honestly, if you can, And if you cannot get them honestly, Get them.' The motto on the Liverpool coat of arms, *Deus nobis haec otia fecit* ('We owe all this to God'), could be applied just as well to the fate of the slaves in the plantations waiting to be bludgeoned into Christianity and, two generations later, to the wretched Irish peasants forced from their homeland by famine.

In 1757, the port was struck by a severe hurricane, which blew down windmills, toppled the spire of St Thomas's Church and sank five vessels in the Mersey. Tornadoes and floods wreaked further damage, but in spite of these setbacks the shared values of her merchants and the cohesiveness of the civic authorities ensured that the town's phenomenal growth would continue unabated.

The proceeds of the slave trade had made Liverpool a prosperous place for her merchants. The professional confidence and strong sense of local identity of her old families allowed the town to outflank her rival, Bristol. Handsome buildings, like the Bluecoat Chambers and the Theatre Royal, had been built in her long, straight streets, with fashionable shops sprouting up in Castle Street and Red Cross Street. Liverpool was now connected to most of the towns of the kingdom, with the Golden Talbot in Water Street being the house of call for the London stagecoach. Dale Street, full of inns, blacksmiths' forges, saddlers' shops and stables, had become the main entrance into the town. Some of the most influential merchants lived and had their counting houses in gabled two-storey detached houses with back gardens in Lord Street, Hanover Street, Church Street and Duke Street. The Old Dock was bulging with ships flying flags of many nations. There was a new Custom House, and the Stanley Tower stood strong at the bottom of Water Street. Retired sea captains looked over the market gardens onto the Mersey from their pleasant homes in the gentrified villages of Kirkdale and Everton. A lonesome chapel standing at the crossroads of Windle, Ecclestone, Parr and Sutton, surrounded by woods and windmills, would later mark my birthplace.

Throughout the slave boom, Liverpool continued to expand and develop her expertise in privateering, the legalised piracy that licensed armed merchant vessels to attack and capture foreign shipping. The Letter of Marque, which authorised attack, was easily obtained from any post office and was carried by most of the Liverpool ships on the off-chance they had the good fortune to stumble upon some profitable and vulnerable foreign brig. By far the biggest prize ever taken by a Liverpool privateer was the East Indiaman *Carnatic*, plundered by the slave captain and merchant John Dawson of the *Mentor* in 1778. On board was a box of diamonds valued at £135,000, the proceeds of which allowed the *Mentor*'s owner to build Carnatic Hall (later Mossley Hall), a grand mansion used (until its demolition) as a storehouse for the Liverpool museums.

In the 1807 municipal election, Sir Banastre Tarleton, born in Castle Street to a wealthy Aigburth family who owned a number of slaving vessels, including the *John* and the *Swan*, campaigned under the banner of 'Church and slave trade forever'. After leaving Oxford University and frittering away a proportion of the family fortune, he volunteered for military service in America. Although his first campaign to suppress the Revolution resulted in failure at the Siege of Charleston, he soon distinguished himself on the battlefield and became renowned for his sangfroid and swashbuckling style that were to earn him the nickname of 'The Butcher' from his troops. He helped capture General Charles Lee and was promoted to Lieutenant Colonel. He then played a leading part in the brutal massacre at Charleston and the taking of Philadelphia for the British in the War of Independence. For many years, he lived with the actress Mary 'Perdita' Robinson, the former mistress of his friend the Prince of Wales, who helped him write some of his most strident anti-abolitionist speeches.

In less than a century, Liverpool's princes of commerce financed about 5,000 slave ships, and a large proportion of the population had become indirectly dependent on the 'Triangle of Misery' for a living. These oligarchs who had built Liverpool into a thriving and opulent town with sea baths, gardens, bowling greens, a playhouse and a tree-lined walk with bowers for ladies, firmly believed that Africans for whom slavery was a natural state were lazy thieves. Through their good offices, thousands of souls had been saved from the hell of the Dark Continent.

Negro Row

Never seen
a man
travel more
seen more lands
than this poor
path-
less harbour-less
spade.
Extract from *Rights of Passage*
by Edward Kamau Brathwaite

At Yorktown in 1781, the 'invincible' Redcoats were routed by a rabble of American rednecks, and when the end came the 'thin red line' was composed largely of Negro cannon fodder. The American Revolutionary War destabilised the Virginia plantations, with some of their chronically abused slaves electing to remain loyal to the mother country in return for promises of freedom. Several thousand of these displaced and defeated 'Black Loyalists' fled Charleston and Savannah to make a new life outside the United States. According to the *Book of Negroes* most headed for the northern wastes of Nova Scotia, but some ended up on boats bound for the Mersey and the Thames. On arrival at Liverpool, many were incarcerated in prison hulks moored on the river or were forced to beg on the streets.

As a response to this crisis some liberal philanthropists established a 'Committee for the Relief of the Black Poor'. One of these was Scarborough-born Henry Smeathman, a businessman known to his friends as 'Mr Termite' or 'The Flycatcher'. After four happy years of entomological research on the Banana Islands, off the coast of Sierra Leone, under the protection of the Liverpool slaver James Cleveland, Smeathman then set sail to the West Indies, where he attempted unsuccessfully to eradicate the cane-ant epidemic using the blubber of large whales. He finally returned to England, where he led a harmless and marginal existence lecturing to the Royal Society and other learned London institutions on the behaviour of termites. By 1783, he was heavily in debt and was forced to flee England for France, where he would witness the Parisian balloon ascents and passionately espouse his ideas of black repatriation to Benjamin Franklin, the representative in Paris of the newly independent American states. His studies on ant and plantation society in the tropics and the caste system of termites had convinced him that the 'St Giles Blackbirds' could be successfully resettled in Africa. Inspired by the Montgolfier brothers, he then set about designing an aerostatic flying machine with wings, which he hoped would fund his scheme.

Smeathman set before the Lords of the Treasury a 'Plan of Settlement', with the intention of creating a harmonious community considered congenial to the black man's constitution, close to the Sierra Leone River, a few miles from the slave entrepôt of Bance Island. Each of the new settlers would be allowed as much land as he could cultivate and be liberated forever from the white man's chains. Smeathman described this region in glowing terms:

> Pleasant scenes of vernal beauty, a tropical luxuriance, where fruit and flowers lavish their fragrance together on the same bough! This Elysium would provide the new settlers with produce that could successfully compete with the 'riches of the East'.

While racially mixed marriages started to increase in England, many in authority viewed the presence of 5,000 destitute black people on the streets of Liverpool, Bristol and London as a threat to moral standards. Smeathman's plan was greeted with considerable enthusiasm by London's coffee-house society, particularly when it was shown to cost £14 per capita. It also received backing from several slave owners and from the apologist Edward Long, who saw it as a humane form of ethnic cleansing. The veteran abolitionist Granville Sharp was also adamant that, provided slavery was eradicated, Sierra Leone could become the 'Province of Freedom' for the black poor.

The Committee for the Relief of the Black Poor also unanimously supported Smeathman's plan, and with Sharp's backing it received government approval. To cynics it looked like an act of political expediency rather than the imaginative vision of an altruistic and well-meaning scientist. Editorials appeared in the newspapers drawing an analogy with the proposed penal settlement in Botany Bay. It was assumed that this scourge of wretched black beggars would jump at an opportunity to return to their long-lost homeland. Some of the Black Loyalists were attracted to the plan and made contact with Smeathman at his 'Office for Free Africans' in Cannon Street. However, once the details of the plan became apparent, there was fear and an almost unanimous reluctance to sign up. Even the threat by the Committee for the Relief of the Black Poor to withdraw the Loyalists' bounties failed to change their minds.

Ship captains had started to bring a few Africans back to English ports as early as the sixteenth century, and with the help of benevolent patronage a small number rose to positions of influence in eighteenth-century London society. These included Ignatius Sancho, the former butler to the Duke of Montagu, who had been born on a slave ship, and the ex-Ibo slave Olaudah Equiano, who, after several periods of enforced slavery and extensive voyaging, had settled in London. These self-educated black intellectuals joined forces with the white abolitionists to try to persuade the English government of the inhumanity of slavery. Equiano was appointed the Commissary of Provisions and Stores for the repatriation venture, and acting on his assurance about 500 Loyalists and black poor eventually agreed to return to West Africa. No sooner had this agreement occurred than Smeathman died, after which serious consideration was given to repatriating the beggars in the Bahamas or New Brunswick rather than on the Grain Coast.

The *Belisarius*, the *Atlantic* and the *Vernon* were prepared at Blackwall with the intention of sailing to West Africa before the arrival of the seasonal torrents. As a result of unforeseen delays, no more than 250 Black Loyalists and their families had boarded the ships by the end of November. Equiano became concerned that the settlers waiting to be transported were being treated no better than slaves in the West Indies. The government ignored his concerns about the inadequate housing and clothing, and he was relieved of his post. Meanwhile, conditions on board the moored vessels were appalling: corrupt officials continued to siphon off the small allocations of provisions, while children died of malignant fever as the ships waited in port. Demoralisation and apprehension increased among these unloved patriots, who now suspected they would be diverted to the new penal colony at Botany Bay.

The fleet did not finally sail down the Thames until February, making arrival in the rainy season inevitable. Almost immediately, the Royal Navy escort ship *Nautilus* ran onto a sandbank in the English Channel and the

Vernon's topmast came down, forcing the ships to seek haven in Torbay. On 9 April 1787, the ships set sail again with a total of 309 Loyalists, 59 white wives, 41 black wives and their surviving children on board. At the last minute, a few white colonists and their families also boarded the ships in the hope of a better life away from England. Conditions on board marginally improved when cattle, food and water were brought on ship at Tenerife, although 35 of the passengers would eventually lose their lives during the month-long voyage. Nevertheless, the chaplain described his ship as 'a happy ark, enjoying the sweets of peace, lenity and almost uninterrupted harmony with the odious distinction of colours forgotten'.

HMS *Nautilus* arrived in Sierra Leone on 10 May and anchored in Kru Bay. The captain's first and overriding concern was to rename the estuary St George's Bay and claim it for the Crown. Its local name, Romarong ('the haunt of the wailers'), where the Koya Temne tribe would go to weep during storms, would prove much more apt for the new colonists. King Tom appeared on the shore in a flowing robe, gold-trimmed hat and ruffled shirt, accompanied by a harem of voluptuous wives bedecked in lavish taffeta and turbans. After a 13-gun salute, Captain Thompson declared his intention to buy a substantial piece of mountainous woodland territory that sloped down from the harbour and to rename it the Province of Freedom. The wily king, who in fact had no authority to sell the land, acceded without hesitation, realising that the English were actually asking for permission to dump their black passengers and allow them to complete their unhappy circle. Instead of the beautiful woods, groves and hills described in Mr Termite's Plan of Settlement the exhausted families were greeted by putrefying mangrove swamps and fetid mud banks. Twice a year, Romarong was covered with brown sludge and brine pools, rendering it barren except for a few desolate paddy fields.

The seasonal deluge and tornadoes continued for a few weeks after the Loyalists arrived, adding to their sense of desolation. They had used all their meagre provisions and had been forced to sell their tools and clothes to the slavers on nearby Bance Island. By the time Captain Thompson and the *Nautilus* departed in September, 122 of his passengers had died in the new settlement named Granville Town from malaria, bilious complaints and other pestilences. Disillusionment had grown from the outset, forcing some of the survivors, including the white chaplain and Harry Demane (whom Granville Sharp had rescued the previous year from a slaver bound for Jamaica), to move to Bance Island, where Demane joined his former oppressors. He later became a successful slave agent. A few families held on in Granville Town and managed to live amicably with the local tribes, but they remained vulnerable to the depredations of King Tom and the Bance Island slavers.

Back in England, Granville Sharp hoped that the imminent abolition of slavery would force the government to come to the aid of the settlers, and in the nick of time the store ship *Myro*, loaded with supplies, was dispatched to help the remaining 120 beleaguered colonists. A treaty securing the long-term future of Granville Town was then agreed with the higher authority and ruler of the region, King Naimbanna, and trading started with the local tribes.

In 1789, Captain Henry Savage of HMS *Pomona* was ordered to sail to the Grain Coast to distribute copies of Dolben's Bill to the slave agents. As soon as they anchored in St George's Bay, the officer and his crew were besieged by the free settlers and the slavers, who looked to the Crown to uphold their grievances. Abraham Ashmore, the governor of Granville Town, complained to the captain that the residents were being abducted and sold by the slavers in Bance. The agents, on the other hand, complained that the new settlers were thieves and rogues who threatened the success of their triangular enterprise.

Both parties, however, shared the opinion that King Jimmy, who had succeeded King Tom, was an unscrupulous despot. Captain Savage demanded the reprobate come to parley on the *Pomona*, but the new Koya Temne leader refused. Savage was forced to send his men to a village to the west of Mount Auriol, where stray gunfire from a jumpy midshipman's musket led to a thatched roof going up in flames. Within minutes, the whole compound was ablaze and the sailors fled back to their vessel in blind panic. Over the next few days, the crew fired salvos at the shore while King Jimmy's men shot at anyone trying to land in search of water. After several weeks, a pact was agreed and the *Pomona* sailed away. Having become jealous of the new colonists' control of the waterfall, King Jimmy took his revenge with the support of a slaver called Bowie. He ordered the settlers to leave Granville Town then razed the village to the ground. In 1791, when the surgeon Alexander Falconbridge returned to set up the St George's Bay Association, only 64 of the original colonists were still hanging on.

Despite this catastrophe, Granville Sharp arranged for 1,000 more Black Loyalists stranded in the barren wastes of Nova Scotia to join the few survivors. Under the wise governorship of Lieutenant John Clarkson, brother of the abolitionist Thomas Clarkson, these new Canadian settlers successfully established a new community close to the original site of Granville Town. Six hundred runaway Ashanti Maroons from Trelawny Town in Jamaica were the next group to arrive, and slowly and with great difficulty, a viable colony began to take root.

In 1790, the first fair-trading system was set up with the newly formed Sierra Leone Company, and some of the survivors from Granville Town helped to facilitate new commercial links between Africa and Liverpool. Following the abolition of slavery, the settlers' numbers were further swelled by soldiers from the disbanded Second and Fourth Divisions of the Barbadian and Jamaican West India Regiment, and 86 African Americans who arrived on the *Mayflower of Liberia* from New York. In 1829, a further 85 slaves from Barbados were transported as convicts to Sierra Leone but were freed soon after arrival. The largest of all the repatriated groups was made up of West African 'recaptives', slaves who had been rescued from slave ships between 1807 and the 1860s. These men, made up of Yorubas, Ibos, Ashantis, Fulanis and Angolans, created Freetown and spread Christianity and their distinctive Krio language throughout West Africa.

The displaced black patriots and black poor who had avoided the Flycatcher's master plan and declined to travel to London continued to colonise Liverpool's Negro Row. A small, free and ignored black community had grown up around Upper Pitt Street, a narrow thoroughfare laid out in 1765 in honour of William Pitt the Elder. This area was also the home to the children of African chiefs and the disowned mixed-race progeny of Liverpool's Barbados plantation owners and English traders on the Gold Coast. Some of these men worked as crossing sweepers, entertainers and sellers of halfpenny ballads. Amos, Charles, Cole, Nelson, Snowball and Wilson, the surnames of the early black families in Liverpool, can be traced today in Charleston and Freetown. Despite the liberal influence of the 'white Jacobins', a leprosy of racial hatred persisted and repatriation of African seamen remained firmly on the political agenda. A few blacks were still being auctioned in coffee houses and on the steps of the Custom House, and some former slaves were put to work as coachmen, servants and maids in the grand mansions of the former Royal Chase of Toxteth. Many shops in Liverpool still sold branding irons, handcuffs, leg shackles, thumbscrews and the dreaded speculum used for force-feeding in the sugar lands.

The invisible, ignored people of Pitt Street and Granville Town were engaged in a war over the nature of their own reality. Poor, well-meaning

Smeathman had not grasped the tensions created by one-way tickets. He should have known that ants put into another nest die or are killed rapidly. These landless, alienated hybrids, wounded by loss and abandoned by empire builders, straddled a three-legged stool in the mid-Atlantic. They were trapped between past and present, never quite engaged in any confrontation and incapable of ever again fully reclaiming their African heritage.

The narrator of Joseph Conrad's *Heart of Darkness*, written in 1899, warns that Charles Marlow's story will not be the average sea yarn in which 'the whole meaning lies within the shell of a cracked nut'. Europe wants to rule the world and build oppressive empires under the guise of civilisation, and, if need be, will achieve this by domination and extermination of those with darker complexions and flatter noses. Marlow describes the black people in the labour camp in King Leopold's Congo:

> They were dying slowly . . . nothing but black shadows of disease and starvation . . . lost in uncongenial surroundings, fed on unfamiliar food, they sickened, became inefficient, and were then allowed to crawl away and rest.

The ivory hunter Kurtz, a charismatic, self-styled god of the natives, represents the unacceptable face of colonial Europe. Marlow considers that life in deepest Africa has brutalised Kurtz and exposed a savage, selfish soul beneath a thin veneer of urbanity. On the other hand, a Russian trader who meets Marlow at the Inner Station feels that Kurtz has freed himself and enlarged his mind and is no longer subject to the same moral judgements applied to Europeans. On his deathbed, the ivory hunter hands over a bundle of personal belongings, including a broadsheet on how to civilise the black savages. On the back page, there is scribbled a note in his hand saying 'Exterminate all the brutes.' Kurtz's dying words before he is buried in a muddy hole are, 'The horror! The horror!'

It seems to me that Conrad had not given the African a voice in his gripping story and that the tropical rainforest where 'The Company' made its profit differed little from dehumanised eighteenth-century Liverpool. Macgregor Laird's vision would soon make the Mersey a tributary of the Congo, and from the lucrative proceeds Liverpool's Old Firm would construct the Second City of the Empire.

The Athenaeum

'There is no God,' the wicked saith,
'And truly it's a blessing,
For what He might have done with us
It's better only guessing.'

'There is no God,' a youngster thinks,
'Or really, if there may be,
He surely did not mean a man
Always to be a baby.'

'There is no God, or if there is,'
The tradesman thinks, ''twere funny
If He should take it ill in me
To make a little money.'

Extract from *Dipsychus, Part I*
by Arthur Hugh Clough

Towards the close of the eighteenth century, the consciences of some of England's gentlemen began to be pricked by the inhumanity of transporting people against their will. The Religious Society of Friends – the Quakers – set up a committee to demand the abolition of the slave trade, while Thomas Clarkson, an Anglican clergyman and friend of William Wilberforce, risked the wrath of merchants and plantation owners by hanging around the Liverpool taverns and dockyards, appealing to sailors for evidence of the hardships on slaving vessels. The problem for men like Clarkson – labelled a 'white Jacobin nigger' for his efforts – was that there was little documentary evidence of what was happening, and without it, the case against slavery would always be his word against that of the politically savvy merchants. A country that prided itself on a commitment to liberty was practising a double standard.

The autobiography of the former slave Olaudah Equiano provided a rare account of slave-ship conditions:

> The closeness of the place, and the heat of the climate, added to the
> number on the ship, which was so crowded that each had scarcely
> room to turn himself, almost suffocated us . . . The shrieks of the
> women, and the groans of the dying, rendered it a scene of horror
> almost inconceivable.

Finally, after 7 years and 35,000 miles of risky campaigning, Clarkson
managed to accumulate a collection of damning written testimonials from
sailors; he also acquired a horrifying armoury of shackles, collars and
speculums bought from the shops on the Gorée Piazza. The Liverpool
merchants made a distinction between what was morally acceptable at
home and what was permissible 'beyond the line'. As long as the two
worlds did not converge, they saw no problem, and the ledgers and
almanacs had managed to dehumanise the cargo on the ghost ships. The
slavers despised Clarkson, and one night a gang of eight men, two or three
of whom the abolitionist had spotted earlier in the King's Arms,
manhandled him and tried to throw him off the Pier Head.

In his supplications to Parliament, Clarkson handed out a plan of the
Brookes, which showed how 482 slaves had been packed into her narrow
holds for the 6–8-week transportation. Clarkson later stated that this
document had made 'an instantaneous impression of horror upon all who
saw it'. The *Brookes* had been commissioned in 1781 for the Liverpool
slaver Joseph Brooks. It was a heavy Guineaman weighing 297 tons, with
14 scuttles carved into its side to ventilate the lower decks. It made 10
successful voyages in the Triangle of Misery and transported 4,000
Africans, with an average mortality rate per voyage of 11 per cent, to the
New World. On taking his campaign to France, Clarkson was informed
by Necker that the diagram of the *Brookes* could not be shown to Louis
XVI because it would offend the king's sensibilities. In Manchester, on the
other hand, Clarkson received considerable support and was able to collect
20,000 signatures in support of abolition. He was backed by John Newton,
a former Liverpool slave-ship captain and tide surveyor. Newton had been
ordained in his late 30s but, despite his religious conversion, remained
haunted by his memories of the horrors of slavery. From his Anglican
Olney Parish, he would later compose 'Amazing Grace', beloved of
Christians and all supporters of human rights.

Others too were making a stand. The women of Britain started a campaign to boycott West Indian sugar. Once it gained momentum, it began little by little to erode some of the prejudices of the English towards black people. The potter Josiah Wedgwood joined the Abolitionist Committee and produced a cameo depicting a chained slave on his knees framed with the words 'Am I Not a Man and a Brother?' This was inlaid into gold snuffboxes and set into bracelets and lockets.

In 1803, a French ship called the *Jeune Amélie*, bound for the Orient with a cargo of sugar, indigo, spices and muslin, was captured by the *Kitty*. Refitted by her new owners, Henry Clarke and George & Robert Tod & Co. of 32 Red Cross Street, she sailed for Africa in February 1804 under her new name, the *Kitty's Amelia*, in the company of two other ships, the *Laurel* and the *Urania*. Three days out, a French man-of-war attacked them and casualties were sustained, but by October the ship had arrived safely back in Liverpool from Havana with sugar, cowhides and timber. In December, the 380-ton vessel, with its 16 guns, was on its way back to the Congo River accompanied by the *Thomas* and the *Juno*. During the middle passage to St Kitts, a plot was hatched by the crew to mutiny, but it was foiled by the captain. Three of the conspirators jumped ship to the HMS *Saint Lucie*, accusing Captain Nuttall of irregularities relating to the transportation of his cargo of slaves, which forced him to remain for five months in the Caribbean in order to clear his name.

The *Kitty's Amelia* then sailed from Saint Bartholomew under the command of the first mate, Thomas Forrest, arriving in Liverpool in November 1805 with sugar and cotton. Captain Nuttall resumed captaincy and sailed again for Bonny in May 1806. By this time, the owners were becoming anxious about the future of the slave trade following Wilberforce's Abolition Bill and urged the captain to return with all haste. On 5 August 1806, a letter notified Nuttall that the bill had been passed, thus precluding further voyages to Africa. He arrived in Barbados in October and then proceeded to Trinidad after beating off attack from a French privateer. The West Indian waters were swarming with fast-moving, heavily manned French sloops. Nuttall was forced to remain in the Caribbean yet again, and Thomas Forrest brought the *Kitty's Amelia* back to Liverpool with a cargo of ivory, palm oil, hides, cotton, coffee, indigo and sugar.

Although slavery had been abolished, clearance for one final slaving voyage was obtained. In July 1807, the *Kitty's Amelia*, now captained by the one-eyed Manxman Hugh 'Mind Your Eye' Crow, left the Landing Stage. The ship returned to Liverpool from Jamaica the following year with beeswax, palm oil, elephants' teeth, Madeira wine, rum, sugar and coffee. Crow claimed in his diary that a deputation of former slaves came to the ship in Kingston and chanted 'God bless Massa [Master]!' He wrote:

> I always took great pains to promote the health and comfort of all on board by proper diet, regularity, exercise and cleanliness, for I considered that on keeping the ship clean and orderly, which was always my hobby, the success of our voyage mainly depended.

By the time Hull-born Tory Member of Parliament William Wilberforce's Abolition Bill was finally passed by Parliament in 1807, *Gore's Directory* contained 246 pages of affluent Liverpool merchants. The rough trade had provided rich pickings, and a fair proportion of the banking system and textile industry was underwritten by the profits of slavery. The town's population had exploded from 18,000 in 1750 to 75,000. Almost 2 per cent of the nation's income came from slavery and its feeder industries. It was hardly surprising, therefore, that no fewer than 64 anti-abolition petitions had been submitted from Liverpool to the Houses of Parliament.

Liverpool's main stakeholders dominated the social and political life of the town, became its mayors and councillors, and gave their names to its streets and thoroughfares. A few of Liverpool's more enlightened men – such as William Roscoe, the Presbyterian son of a Mount Pleasant publican; the Rathbone family, who had made their money from timber; the blind poet and revolutionary Edward Rushton; and the Quaker reformer and packet-steamer owner James Cropper – selflessly supported Wilberforce. In 1809, Roscoe and his supporters in the Liverpool Society for Promoting the Abolition of Slavery rescued nine black slaves from a Portuguese ship docked in the port after they had been impounded in the bridewell as surety against the vessel's outstanding debt. When the enraged captain learned that his cargo of 'black gold' was to be set free, he took an armed detachment to the gaol but was repulsed by the other prisoners. The slaves were then bailed by Roscoe's friends and eventually liberated. This small group of Liberal abolitionists wrote broadsheets, attended meetings and defended themselves bravely against the wrath of the traders. Despite their strong resistance, most of the Liverpool merchants had come to terms with the inevitable and had moved on to even richer commercial pickings.

Although the blame for the cruelty of the slave trade had been laid firmly on the shoulders of the sea captains, the reality was that most were doing no more than carrying out the orders of their masters. Some, like John Newton and the former ship's surgeon Edward Rushton, became active abolitionists after witnessing the carnage and horror of a slaving voyage at first hand. Major General Tottenham provided written evidence to Parliament on the atrocities in Barbados. In reply to the question, 'Did it appear to you that the slaves in the British islands were treated with mildness or severity?' he replied:

> I think in the island of Barbados they were treated with the greatest cruelty. I will mention one instance . . . About three weeks before the hurricane, I saw a young man walking the streets in a most deplorable situation – he was entirely naked – he had an iron collar about his neck, with five long spikes projecting from it. His body before and behind his breech, belly and thighs were almost cut to pieces with running ulcers in them, and you might put your finger in some of the weals. He could not sit down, owing to his breech being in a state of mortification, and it was impossible for him to lie down, owing to the protection of the collar round his neck . . . the field negroes are treated more like brutes than human beings.

Following the emancipation of slaves in Barbados, the Bajans made up the following song:

> Lick [beatings] and lock-up [jailing] done wid,
> Hurrah fuh Jin-Jin [Queen Victoria];
> Lick and lock-up done wid,
> Hurrah fuh Jin-Jin.
> God bless de Queen fuh set we free,
> Hurrah fuh Jin-Jin;
> Now lick and lock-up done wid,
> Hurrah fuh Jin-Jin.

Freedom came at a price: the former slaves were now forced to wander from plantation to plantation carrying their shelters on their backs and looking for work, while the poor white slave-drivers were completely surplus to requirements and hid away in caves deep in the countryside. Some of the former slaves took to living in dwellings carved out of the coral, and coolies recently brought in from India were given their jobs. The insatiable British appetite for sweetness continued, and the 'nigger yards' were now home to black indentured servants working 20 hours a day.

Back in Liverpool, trade with West Africa was far from over. Macgregor Laird, Greenock merchant and African sentimentalist, harboured a Christian dream of opening up West Africa for commerce. Laird travelled on the paddle steamer *Alburkah*, built in his Birkenhead shipyard, to the confluence of the River Benue and the River Niger and was one of only nine of the forty-eight Europeans on board to return alive to Liverpool two years later. He never returned to Africa but, backed by a group of like-minded investors, he formed the African Steamship Company, and the first 'iron ships' started to arrive on the River Niger to buy palm oil in 1835.

The Liverpool merchants realised that there would be considerable advantages in offering additional perks to their African partners. In exchange for business favours from the chiefs of the Windward and Gold Coasts, Laird offered to 'soften their sons' manners' in England. This provided him with an opportunity to indoctrinate the young future leaders of Africa into the British way of doing things and at the same time strengthen commercial links between Liverpool and Old Calabar. The enthusiastic African kings naively entrusted their princes to unscrupulous white agents, and some of these young black aristocrats never arrived at the Salt Dock. The younger brothers of King Abandozan from Dahomey (now in Benin), for example, were sold into slavery in Demerara and were only returned to Judah (Ouidah) after the forceful intervention of the incensed Laird and his associates.

By the middle of the nineteenth century, there were at least 100 African children being educated into the ways of the English in Liverpool schools. Some of these, together with a handful of 'rescued' educated slaves, returned to Africa to live privileged existences and assist the 'English chiefs' with their trading operations. White traders in the Dark Continent regularly remarked on the excellent English spoken and written by their black business partners. Others amongst these Africans married and remained in Liverpool, joining a small band of slaves who had earned their freedom by working on the African ships. Laird's vision was starting to establish enduring cultural and social exchanges between West Africa and the port of Liverpool.

At the municipal elections of 1806, the increasingly crowded town tried to reinvent itself. The reviled 'humanity man' Roscoe and his gentlemanly mercantile coterie of Whigs were elected with a strong majority. Inspired by the Italian Renaissance and the Medici princes, the largely self-educated Roscoe strove to find aesthetic nourishment within the brutal materialism of his home town. William Rathbone, William Earle and Thomas Bolton, all men born into wealthy Liverpool merchant families, became the Unitarian flag bearers of a new spiritual vision that would enhance civic pride by linking commerce with culture and civilisation. In this new age of enlightenment, the Jacobins began ambitious programmes of health and education reform and tried to break down the entrenched and destructive religious divide. Unfortunately for Liverpool, these Liberals lacked grass-roots political clout, and it was not long before the door was left agape for yet another round of opportunistic, hard-nosed Tory paternalism. The notion of creating a 'Florence of the North' proved little more than a pipe dream, and some of their worthy initiatives, like the foundation of the Liverpool Mechanics' School of Arts, were considered by some Corporation members as a dangerous institution which could incite the poor to insubordination. In 1844, Charles Dickens gave his support to these noble aspirations with a reading at the Mechanics' Institute accompanied by piano solos from Christiana Weller. A number of impressive Italian palazzos were built on the seven streets to reflect the power of the city's merchant princes. The Hargreaves Building, built in 1859, became the headquarters of Sir William Brown, a leading American merchant, and it was from here that his son-in-law Hargreaves ran the Liverpool arm of his transatlantic operation. To recognise the importance of the Americas to the company, figurines of Isabella I, Columbus, Pizarro, Queen Anacaona, Vespucci, Cortés and Bermejo were carved above the third-floor windows.

The political shrewdness of Liverpool's businessmen, with the help of the eloquent and charismatic Antrim-born cleric Hugh M'Neile, led to a rapid, inevitable and lasting defeat for the historian Roscoe and his aesthetic, pie-in-the-sky dreams. The Liberals had been careless in their attention to detail in relation to several important local issues and in the end had remained a stunted force. The derided intellectuals were forced to lick their wounds in the Newsroom, Gore's bookshop, the Lyceum Library and the Athenaeum, and bemoan the fact that Liverpool still had no centre for higher thought. Only the forward-thinking poet Arthur Hugh Clough, born the son of a cotton merchant at 74 Rodney Street, kept Roscoe's epic vision alive.

Despite the prevailing ingrained philistinism in the town, Thomas Carlyle, the Scottish satirist and historian, who regularly visited Liverpool, formed a favourable impression and after his first visit wrote:

> I found time to be impressed by the seeming efficiency of the
> inhabitants; they appeared to me to be remarkably go-ahead people.
> Streets, streets, streets! Market places, theatres, shops. I confess
> amazement at the preponderance of public houses . . . As I observed
> comparatively little insobriety, I considered that many of these places
> relied on foreign seamen for their trade . . . a gratifying thought
> because I rather like Liverpool and its people.

Liverpool was now back in the hands of a small group of ultra-
Conservative, Corporation, king-and-country families who, over three
generations, had made fortunes from the profits of slaving and
mercantilism. These men had little time for poetry and read very little.
The town was changing fast. The abolition of slavery had tilted Liverpool
away from local manufacturing and towards global commerce. Her few
industries were on the decline, and the craftsmen from the pot and silk
houses were making way for an influx of casual workers employed to shift
cargo and build ships. The 'Cast-Iron Shore' on the south side was being
pulled down and replaced with a waterfront dominated by docks.

The names of the abolitionists and the slavers are represented in the
streets through which I idle today. Cunliffe Street is a narrow cut-through
between Dale and Tithebarn, above Moorfields and below Cheapside.
The printers and sugarhouse that once gave it some function have long
gone, and it is now a rat run. I turn right at Vernon and again at Tithebarn,
making my way towards Islington. As always, I am armed with a notebook
and an eye for the concealed. Around the university, there are plenty of
lively and happy white, Indian and African students, but a degree of
segregation is obvious in the groupings. I mooch down London Road and
Prescot Street towards the sadness that is Kenny (Kensington). Three
masked gunmen had recently burst into a flat in nearby Edinburgh Road
and shot Asif Bashir in the legs. A few white lads with hoods are dealing
drugs in the run-down Victorian-terraced streets, and there is a new Indian
restaurant called Akshaya. Liverpool is so empty during my walks that,
despite the regular homicides, I rarely feel threatened these days. I hurry
on to Edge Hill, with its last few Georgian houses, vacant plots and empty
railway station. I walk down Binns Road, named after a doctor and
abolitionist, and into Crawford Way. I turn left at Pighue and take the first
exit at the roundabout to Rathbone Road.

Many of the white people I have talked with on these pale streets still think that all black men have enormous phalluses and great rhythm, and distrust 'those cheating Pakistanis' who work hard and can't speak English. This is, of course, not just an antiquated Scouse viewpoint, because every major institution in England still has ingrained racial prejudice. Cunliffe was Jekyll, and Rathbone Hyde. One could not have existed without the other. Most poor whites in Liverpool are still sidelined from the gravy train of Cunliffe and have started to see themselves as a problem. The black minority in a white ghetto search in vain for a new, decent, fair-play Rathbone to protect them and help them start to belong.

Landfall

The big ship sails on the ally-ally-oh,
The ally-ally-oh, the ally-ally-oh.
Oh, the big ship sails on the ally-ally-oh,
On the last day of September.
Traditional Liverpool children's skipping song

The Atlantic is the second largest of the earth's four great oceans and the most heavily travelled. It is 3,000 miles across and 1,700 fathoms deep, bordered by Europe and Africa to the east and flanked on its western side by the Americas. In the north, it broadens out like a champagne glass separated from the Arctic Sea by a submarine ridge system that links Baffin Island, Greenland and Scotland. In the south, it fills out like a dumper truck, merging at the capes with the tropical waters of the Indian and Pacific Oceans. Dotted within its vast desert expanse are the islands of its shelves, Newfoundland and Britain to the north and to the south the diminutive Falklands and South Sandwich. A lava belt forged from the Canaries, the Azores and the islands of Cape Verde and the Antilles decorates its midriff, while to the north looms the eerie polar volcano of Thule. Muir Eireann, a shallow, sandy stretch of water, connects Liverpool, 'the Atlantic city', with Ireland and bathes the Manx coastline. The North Channel, between Scotland and Northern Ireland, and St George's Channel, between Eire and Wales, link the skin of the Irish Sea to the vast ocean and provide a connection between England and the Celtic kingdoms.

My schoolboy geography belies the water's fury, its haunting petulance and healing touch. Nor can it express the hold the ocean exerts on the lives of its sailors and the ports from whence they hail. Liverpool Bay sucks in the brown swell of the passing Irish Sea that slaps the cast-iron shore with a force driven by a distant ocean storm. A boisterous wind born in the tumbling wastes of the North Atlantic flirts with the sea clouds, leaving them pregnant with rain. The tides answer only to the pull of a capricious moon. They climb in a slow sheet, losing their power as they unravel upwards onto the lucid tide line.

Liverpool clings to the side of this water hemisphere like a monstrous cracked limpet, while the sea's intimidating immensity keeps trying to draw it down into its deep fathoms. This former market town and aspiring spa rose out of Lancashire to control an isosceles sea triangle, yoking Georgian Britain with black Africa and brash America. People started to enter from the sea, breathe through their mouths and talk in riddles. Liverpool became known as a safe haven for wild rovers and a bolt-hole for free spirits. Sirens and coolies roamed its promenades. Restless ships travelled its inner oceans, manned by sailors with memories of welcoming headlands. Through the transport of cargo and the traffic of people, the Atlantic became the world's greatest waterway, with Liverpool a latter-day Phoenicia at its helm.

I had guessed the landlubber's Mercator projection was an equatorial distortion. The two flat, round circles showing the Old World on the right and the New World on the left were a deliberate misrepresentation. This chart split the Atlantic wide open, leading to a faithfully reproduced error and sea blindness. The enormity of the ocean was too terrifying for those beached European mapmakers and civil servants to acknowledge. Only the sailors and the humpbacks grasped its circumference and its irresistible magnetic force. I too had started to focus on these immense empty spaces.

No sooner had slave trading died and the 1812 war with the United States finished than another rich source of revenue came Liverpool's way. America was on the march, and New York was making a play to be the Eastern Seaboard's premier hub port. With the start of the construction of the Erie Canal, the Big Apple was now a centre of consumption and had a pressing need for Bradford woollens and Manchester cotton to nurture her garment trade.

A group of Manhattan Quaker entrepreneurs, drawing on the model of British mail ships, which had carried mail between Falmouth and New York since colonial times, inaugurated a regular monthly sailing schedule between New York and Liverpool. Three days late because of the Mersey's capricious tides and high western winds, the *Courier* first left Liverpool Docks bound for Long Island with a hold bulging with textiles and fleece. A day later, another packet, the *James Monroe*, headed out through the Narrows in a January snowstorm with eight passengers who had paid steerage of 40 guineas apiece for a passage to Liverpool. Two other ships, the *Amity* and the *Pacific*, were soon commissioned, and in 1818 the first regular service across the North Atlantic was in operation.

The vessels were three-masted, full-rigged ships with a conventional sail plan, each with two decks, which provided sufficient room for a large hold of heavy cargo. These vessels, buffeted along on the Gulf Stream currents, ploughed the rough seas and became the workhorses of transatlantic maritime trade. A flag depicting a round black ball on a red background flew from the top of their mainmasts and made them instantly recognisable to sailors. Red Star and Swallowtail soon joined the Black Ball Line, and within a few years these three companies had all developed a reputation for reliability and relative safety.

The American packet captains were highly respected young men who had reached the pinnacle of their nautical careers. In an age before telegrams and wireless cables, they assumed total responsibility for the welfare and safety of their passengers and crew. They were expected to receive their distinguished and affluent clients with courtesy and charm. They also needed to command authority and respect from their ragtag crew of Yankee 'packet rats', hardened able seamen who were said to be able to sail in any man's ship and enjoyed a reputation as the roughest and most unruly of sailors. Captain Arthur Clark's words reflected the prevailing attitude of most packet captains to their crew:

> The way to deal with these ingrates was to see they were kicked and beaten for all infringements of shipboard rules, and infractions of the captain's whims . . . yet for all their moral rottenness, those rascals were splendid fellows to shake and shorten sail in heavy weather on the Western Ocean.

Mann Island in Liverpool was awash with pubs run by unscrupulous landlords and frequented by crimps intent on the kidnap and abduction of unwary or drunk landsmen. Whenever the bells of St Nicholas's church chimed, Shanghai Davies would leave his lair at the Red Lion public house in Sea Brow to ply the newly arrived crew with 'Mickey Finns'. Ma Smyrden, a landlady in Pitt Street, achieved lasting infamy for bamboozling a gang of crimps into kidnapping a corpse. Navy agents and press gangs haunted the bars, buying ale for unsuspecting ratings and waiting for the opportunity to slip a shilling into the pewter tankard of their drunken prey. Some of the waterfront taverns had secret underground tunnels that allowed the sailors to flee at the first warning shout of 'Hawks abroad!' If a man did not keep his wits about him, he could leave his home on a routine errand and disappear on the high seas for years.

By the middle of the nineteenth century, steamers were eating into the packets' business, and the faster clippers were a further threat. The packets were forced to turn their attention away from the delivery of mail and towards the transportation of poor European emigrants heading for a new life in America. The Landing Stage became a place of permanent partings, with ships leaving every week full of desperate, heartbroken souls.

Once the lumpers had stowed all the cargo in the holds, the crew would be expected to clear between decks in preparation for the weary travellers and their luggage. The wild and simple Irish refugees were segregated from the small number of more affluent cabin passengers and restricted to a diet of mush made from oatmeal and water with the odd delicacy of a dry sea biscuit. These steerage passengers were banned from the quarterdeck, bundled below like bales of cotton, and in bad weather were cooped up in darkness and unable to use the communal galley for cooking or to attend to their ablutions. The occasional ham or cheese brought on board by a more affluent voyager was devoured long before the American coast came into view. Mass immigration resulted in New York's population exploding from 30,000 at the turn of the nineteenth century to 813,669 by 1860, making her far and away the most important city in the United States. Over a similar period, she became the predominant port in the country, increasing her share of America's imports from 25 per cent to 68 per cent and exports from 20 per cent to 40 per cent.

The packet ships had laid down the blueprint for ocean travel from Liverpool to New York and are still remembered with affection on the Liverpool waterfront. They were also symbolic of New York's rise to pre-eminence in the United States. One American traveller described his experience:

> It was in the last week of May, 1836, when I landed at Liverpool from the packet ship *Roscoe*, 700 tons burden, Capt. Delano, after a passage of eighteen days from New-York. The *Roscoe* was a favourite and could accommodate about 40 first-class passengers. I stopped at the Adelphi Hotel, then, and possibly now, the best inn for travellers in England. Shortly after I reached the hotel a card was put in my hands on one side of which was a miniature map of the town. On the other side I read as follows:

LANDFALL

Objects of Interest for Strangers to Visit:
1. The Royal Exchange.
2. The Town Hall.
3. St John's Market.
4. The Cemetery.
5. The Liverpool Docks.
6. The American Packet Ships.

If ever a youth felt a glow of patriotic pride I certainly did on reading at the most important seaport of the greatest maritime nation of the world, this striking acknowledgement of the superiority of our passenger ships.

The clipper was the packet's younger, more romantic and more fashionable sister, born out of the need to make longer voyages and from the American maxim that 'time is money'. The vessel became closely linked with the Eastern Seaboard town of Baltimore. America was clamouring for more cotton and wool, and there was a need to shift cargo to the Orient, Australasia, Brazil and California. Any vessel that could go along at 'a good clip' would be an asset. The first boats had light bows with hollow water lines, with their maximum depth at the aft of the vessel, which distinguished them from the more rounded packets. Flat floors with little 'dead rise', first developed in New Orleans for carrying heavy weights in the Mississippi Delta, proved to be universally successful at enhancing speed, and the Dramatic Line, which ran regularly between Liverpool and New York, was an early beneficiary. Whereas the 150 packets had all been built in New York over a 40-year period, more than 300 clippers were built in Baltimore, New York and other New England yards in less than a decade. By employing flat floors, a full clipper bow and increased water-line length, these boats were able to set record speeds of 400 miles in a day and even beat steamers across the Atlantic.

People followed the clippers' voyages in the newspapers and gambled on the races that sometimes broke out on the high seas. If the steamboats moved stiffly across the gleaming water like giant crabs, the clippers glided like regal swans. The packets and clippers were North America's first great legacy to a world hungry for international commerce. They shifted hundreds of thousands of Irish and German emigrants from the Mersey to the Eastern Seaboard and the outer reaches of the Empire, and in an age before mass communication they acted as sea swallows, disseminating innovations in art, science and culture.

In 1840, Samuel Cunard inaugurated a regular mail service from Liverpool to Halifax, Nova Scotia, with his steam packet *Britannia*. The young man had realised that the days of sail packets and clippers were numbered and that the future lay with funnels. His father, Abraham, had been a successful shipbuilder in Philadelphia before being forced to flee to Nova Scotia in 1812. His son cemented the family's allegiance to 'The Old Country' by making Liverpool his maritime base. The brass plates of White Star, Dominion, Inman and Castle later joined Cunard on the waterfront, and Liverpool rapidly grew into a great Victorian steamship port.

As part of an early agreement with the Admiralty to guarantee the safe passage of British mail to North America, the Cunard steamship company received subsidies, which helped to keep it ahead of the mounting competition. The Cunard steamers *Europa*, *Caledonia*, *Asia*, *Persia*, *Scotia*, *Umbria*, *Campania*, *Etruria*, *Lucania* and *Queen Mary* became family names, and these ships held the Blue Riband of the Atlantic for 30 years. In return for their favours, the Admiralty expected safe delivery of the mail and 11 Cunard ships were commissioned to transport British troops in the Crimean War. Speeds for eastbound transatlantic crossings rose from 10 knots – and a 10-day crossing – in 1840 to 21 knots by 1890. However, as a result of relative conservatism, Cunard eventually lost its accolade as the fastest line across the Atlantic to its two rivals, White Star and Inman.

Charles Dickens's first of several visits to Liverpool was in 1842, while on his way to Boston, when he stayed with his wife at the Adelphi, a hotel he considered to be the finest in the land. This visit would kindle a lasting fascination with the teeming streets of the town, with the vice and drunkenness he witnessed in the docks, and the misery of the Brownlow Hill workhouse providing source material for some of the main characters in *The Uncommercial Traveller*. He described his Cunard cabin on the *Britannia* paddle steamer as a small, dimly lit, poorly ventilated box, only six feet square with two narrow bunks like coffins. Perhaps because of the discomfort of this self-contained little world, he spent many hours during the 18-day voyage staring out at the changing sea:

> The Atlantic is an ocean of ghosts. I have been looking out over it when it has been grey and when it was white flecked and bright, on a day when it danced and sparkled and a day when it has been sullen and angry. Ocean and sky were all of one dull, heavy, uniform, lead

colour. There was no extent of prospect even over the dreary waste that lay around us, for the sea ran high, and the horizon encompassed us like a large black hoop.

As a result of the transatlantic passenger services and the cotton trade, Liverpool's links with America became very close. The first shots of the American Civil War were fired from a Fawcett and Preston cannon ('Fosset' gun) made in Liverpool's Duke Street. Blockade of the southern ports would lead to the desiccation of the port's cash cow and the catastrophe of the Lancashire Cotton Famine. James Bulloch, a Confederate naval lieutenant, signed a contract with Macgregor Laird for the construction of the *Alabama* and the *Florida* and then for another 30 warships. The *Alabama*, with 'Old Beeswax' at the helm and a Liverpool crew, went on to sink 68 Union ships including the entire Yankee whaling fleet. The CSS *Alabama*'s captain, Rafael Semmes, was a devout Catholic who saw the Civil War as a religious struggle. He associated Northern Puritanism with narrow-minded bigotry and Catholicism with liberty and virtue. Nine months after Robert E. Lee had finally surrendered to the Union, the Confederate ship *Shenandoah* dropped anchor in the Mersey, mid-river between the jetties and Laird's yard. Her captain, Lieutenant Commander James Waddell, lowered the Confederate flag for the last time and handed the vessel over to the Royal Navy on 6 November 1865. Waddell and his crew were arrested but immediately freed. Four days later, the Yankees raised the Stars and Stripes and tried to take CSS *Shenandoah* back to America, but a storm turned them round and the vessel never returned to the Eastern Seaboard.

Liverpool still has many buildings to remind her of the town's Confederate allegiance. The former home of Charles Kuhn Prioleau, agent for the Confederates, at 19 Abercrombie Square, has eight rebel stars embossed on its twin columns and the South Carolina cabbage palm painted on the roof of its grand hallway. Charleston House (12 Rumford Place) was named after America's major slave port in the Carolinas, and the grave of the Confederate secret agent James Bulloch can be visited at Toxteth Cemetery.

By the end of the nineteenth century, the list of Cunard Line passengers regularly contained the names of politicians, artists and celebrities, and when they arrived at Manhattan's Pier 20 they were met by a posse of 'Gangplank Willy' journalists and crowds of voyeurs, autograph hunters and hangers-on, who would jockey for position to greet the stars. For the first-class passenger, a voyage on the 'Pride of the Ocean' had become a memorable adventure never to be forgotten. Their cabins now resembled rooms in the finest modern hotels, expensively appointed and exquisitely finished in satinwood and bird's-eye maple, with passengers treated to every luxury. A lavish and varied menu was provided by live sheep, pigs, rabbits and geese carried in the holds, alongside a cow that supplied fresh milk. One traveller compared the experience to a holiday in the mansion of a hospitable friend whose home was filled with congenial company. Many lasting friendships and business contacts were forged on these trips, consolidating links between the Liverpool merchants and the New World. Each crossing also attracted a host of barflies, card sharks, ocean gazers and pimps who, with their molls, tried to trap the wealthy in orchestrated compromise.

Freight liners and tramp steamers were also increasingly needed to service the textile industry, with its new links with Egypt and India, and to bring grain, dairy products and livestock to Liverpool from Australia, Africa and South America. Notable new shipping names included Alfred, Anchor, Harrison, Brocklebank, Canadian Pacific, Elder Dempster, Furness Withy, Guion, Lamport & Holt, and Leyland.

John Bibby, a farmer from Ormskirk who founded his shipping line at the beginning of the nineteenth century, was a typical example of this new class of men whose horizons extended far beyond Liverpool. His first ship weighed anchor at Parkgate, on the Dee, but he soon moved his fast-growing operation to the Mersey. In 1840, footpads murdered him for his gold watch, but the family business continued and thrives to this day. However, as they accumulated wealth and created history, tycoons found little time for compassion or favours; Charles MacIver, who controlled Cunard during the company's period of critical growth, was reputed to have responded to a request by a captain to take his wife on board by issuing the couple with passenger tickets and relieving the man of his command. With fleets of steamers and cargoes from all over the globe, Liverpool grew into a leading maritime insurance and banking centre, with Martins Bank, the city's flagship, the only major English bank with its headquarters outside London.

Commercial relations with the Caribbean, Southern United States and India flourished, and the port's trading links extended to South America through the Pacific Steam Navigation Company. Liverpool was among the four greatest world ports, handling a third of Britain's exports and a quarter of its imports and owning one seventh of the world's registered shipping. Her shipowners, merchants and bankers were spirited and adventurous operators looking to the countries bordering the great oceans for their business. The machinations of these outward-looking Liverpool moguls, with their global contacts and secretive networks, roused suspicion and jealousy amongst rivals in Manchester and London. For example, the MacIvers, who ran Cunard from their home at Calderstones, depended on direct government contacts in Washington and Westminster to safeguard the mail-contract subsidies.

For those with a stake in the port, Liverpool had turned into a quasi-imperial cosmopolitan power, with the muscle of her industrial base in the north-west and Midlands helping to maintain her supremacy over Atlantic competitors like Bilbao, Lisbon, Cádiz, Bordeaux and Bristol. Her wealthier streets, with their tidy rows of stone-stepped houses, resembled Manhattan: her elegant Lord Street shops and high-roofed St John's Market sold a wide selection of luxury American goods and she had acquired the sobriquet of 'The New York of Europe'.

On 14 April 1912, in calm seas off the coast of Newfoundland, in an area of underwater plateaux called the Grand Banks, the four-funnelled Liverpool-registered Royal Mail ship *Titanic* was holed by an iceberg on her maiden voyage from Southampton to New York. Postcards celebrating her construction had shown the *Titanic* standing on her end, dwarfing the Pyramid of Giza and the new Woolworth skyscraper in Manhattan. As she plummeted into the freezing water, the indomitable orchestra continued to play 'Autumn' and Jacob's song 'Nearer, My God, to Thee'. Drowning to the sounds of the doleful music were 1,523 passengers and crew. Most of the 706 survivors were women and children. Many first-class male passengers gave their lives for women travelling third class. As the ship went down, a Scouse purser is reputed to have said, 'Boys, it will be sand for breakfast in the morning.'

I read now in the *Echo* that the last survivor of the *Titanic* has died. There are no ships to count from that bench where I once sat with my father at the bus terminus on the Lanny. Those stations on the Welsh and Irish coasts – Perch Rock, Great Orme's Head, Point Lynas, Skerries, Holyhead, South Stack, Caernarfon Bay, Bardsey, South Arklow, Coningbeg, Hook Point, Mine Head, Ballycottin, Roches Point, Daunt's Rock, Old Head, Kinsale, Galley Head, Fastnet – are all but closed. The Cunard Building is a helpless museum piece. Cunard had operated 12 ships to the United States and Canada, but by the time I left Liverpool the liners had all but capitulated to jet travel. Within the space of five years, the *Mauretania*, *Caronia*, *Queen Mary* and *Queen Elizabeth* were retired from service. Guests sat in the Adelphi drinking tea with nowhere to go. The Americans had very little reason to come. The escape routes were being closed off one by one. Cunard was left to concentrate on cruising and, long after common sense dictated, reluctantly moved its headquarters to New York and switched its shrinking English operation to the Solent.

I wanted to know what it would feel like to leave Liverpool for New York by sea, but it was too late. I did the next best thing and set off for Southampton. As we sailed down the Solent, I closed my eyes to the bathing huts and Luttrell's Tower and managed to convince myself the Isle of Wight was the Isle of Man. I pretended I was going through the Channel Tunnel until I could look out at the open sea. Fading belles in timeless gowns now waltz the night away with grey-haired men in tuxedos as my ship careers towards America. Wide-eyed and blinkered, I stare out on a moving grey infinity, searching for lost ghost ships. I feel the irresistible wrench of the waves and the pull of the waters. Looking over the side for that city in the sea of which my father had spoken, I peer down into the deep. It would be easy to fall in and meet its healing touch. At dinner, a cyanotic Bostonian in a tuxedo told me he had been cruising for the last ten years and had come on board to die.

On the seventh day out, I could make out dimly lit apartment blocks and the factories of the small towns. We slipped under the Verrazano-Narrows Bridge, beyond which the silvery pallor of the Statue of Liberty welcomed me to America. To starboard, a shiny sea wall of skyscrapers loomed out of the clouds. I'd arrived in a place I'd already got all locked up and where the clock was turned back. A visit to the Imagine Mosaic in Central Park and a hamburger at the Blue Jay was enough. I headed for LaGuardia to get the plane back to Speke. Epic tales and flights of fancy kept alive in a few unfashionable cafes and pubs doubling as makeshift mess-rooms and forecastles waited for me back on the Liverpool waterfront.

The Lost Lands

Tickled by her old Catholic-Liverpool comebacks,
those Things-She-Keeps-Coming-Out-With,
their doggedness and mental double-jointedness
that's Irish as the Blarney Song is long,
he wonderfully provides for her, fusses her pillows,
fetches things on trays. She has us all in tucks.
Even today a neighbour's death is glossed
'If the Good God spares me meself 'll soon be dead.'

Extract from 'Gifts of Language',
Catching up with History, by Matt Simpson

The Welsh tribes had been on the move through the north-west of England since the time of Christ, but in the eighteenth century many young rural poor started to swarm east, some arriving in the Pool on small boats from Anglesey and Caernarfon, hoping to find work in the Liverpool dock. By the end of the century, Pall Mall was nicknamed 'Little Wales' and a Welsh penny was currency in the town; one in every twelve people in Liverpool was Welsh, and in 1782, at the Pitt Street home of William Llwyd, the first Welsh-language prayer meeting occurred. These new fortune-seekers kept themselves to themselves and considered the people of Liverpool to be untamed, immoral and wickedly sly. The English, on the other hand, considered the Welsh to be frugal, mournful and two-faced, but held a grudging respect for their achievements.

By the second half of the nineteenth century, 70,000 people – a quarter of the town's population – were Welsh or had Welsh roots, and Everton, Kensington, West Derby, Wavertree and Walton, known collectively as 'Welshland', functioned almost as a town within a town, with its own local advertisements and social gatherings. Many of the new arrivals continued to speak *yr hen iaith*, 'the old language', at home, travelled considerable distances to attend Methodist chapels and bought Welsh-language newspapers. The Welsh quarrymen built many of Liverpool's docks, and men from Anglesey ran the town's largest building companies. Most of the warehousemen on the docks were Welsh, and their diligence meant that they were preferred over the Irish as porters.

The sixteen rows of red-brick terraced two-up two-down cottages that comprised the 'Welsh streets' in Toxteth, with their welcoming names like Powis, Wynnstay, Rhiwlas, Voelas and Madryn, were the first Liverpool homes for many of the new migrants. The connections between North Wales and Liverpool far exceeded any between North Wales and Cardiff. In the late nineteenth and early twentieth centuries, Liverpool hosted four National Eisteddfods, including the last one ever to be held outside the principality, in 1929 in Sefton Park. Liverpool mayors sat on a bardic chair, and there were 70 Welsh chapels and numerous choral societies in the city. A few of the Liverpool Welsh headed out to form sheep-rearing communities in Patagonia and the Falklands, but most remained to play a major role in forging Liverpool's twentieth-century persona. The Anglesey bonesetter family the Thomases and Sir Robert Jones made Liverpool a famous centre for orthopaedic surgery, and David Lloyd George's father was a schoolmaster in the city until the family moved to Manchester.

Some of the residents of Denbigh Road and Snowdon Lane remembered the Welsh myth of a lost land of prosperous gleaming towns protected by sluices and dams that, as a consequence of the people's hedonism and debauchery, was destroyed by a winter storm, leaving its few survivors to live the rest of their lives in poverty on the mainland. For some, Liverpool was the lost land; for others, it was an Atlantis under the sea in Cardigan Bay.

The Potato Famine led to the death of 700,000 Irish peasants in 1845, and over the next seven years the consequences of the Great Hunger would decimate the population of the Emerald Isle. The potato had become the staple winter crop for the cottiers, and at least a third of the eight million-strong population was dependent on the starchy tuber, first brought to the west coast of Ireland by the Spanish. In an attempt to prevent mass starvation, the Tory Prime Minister Sir Robert Peel imported Indian maize from America, known as 'Peel's Brimstone', and set up a programme of public relief works, but was forced to resign a year later, in 1846, after a split in his party over the repeal of the Corn Laws.

Lord John Russell and the new Whig administration attempted to deal with the famine with the construction of more workhouses under a naive belief that market forces would resolve the crisis. The new government also passed the Gregory Clause of the Poor Law Extension Act, which decreed that welfare aid be offered only to those who owned less than a quarter of an acre. This had the effect of forcing the starving Irish smallholders to either relinquish their homes and become destitute or hang on and risk starvation. A 'notice to appear' by an unscrupulous English landlord was usually enough to cause the poor cottager and his family to flee their home. Some landlords even paid to expatriate their tenants, giving false promises of money, food, clothing and opportunity before packing them off in the dreaded coffin ships to Quebec. The term 'coffin ship' was originally given to over-insured vessels that were worth more to their owners sunk than afloat, but it came to be associated with the disease-ridden, cramped boats used to transport the Irish across the Atlantic. Those who hung on were thrown in jail and their family cast onto the streets. Sir Charles Trevelyan, in charge of the administration of government relief, deliberately limited the amount of aid because he thought 'the judgement of God sent the calamity to teach the Irish a lesson'. This occurred at a time when England was enjoying unparalleled imperial prosperity and was still importing large numbers of calves and large amounts of bacon and ham from Ireland.

By the middle of the nineteenth century, thousands of ravenous Irish families had crossed 'the bowl of tears' for a sixpence and transformed the Liverpool waterfront into a diasporic space. Those who survived the hazardous three-day crossing arrived hardly able to walk and were met at the dock gates by a reception party of predatory crimps and runners. The Mersey was now the main artery through which these starving and half-naked paupers flowed as they fled in their thousands from a doomed and devastated homeland on their way to the New World. The welcoming effigy of St Patrick clutching a shamrock on the pub wall of retired pugilist Jack Langan provided cold comfort to these homeless country folk. The better informed headed straight to the overwhelmed soup kitchen on Fenwick Street to claim poor relief. The lucky few with money slept on the wooden floors of cold, cheerless Moorfields boarding houses, while the rest ended up huddled together without food or water in pestilential cesspits. Packed in like slaves on the middle passage, prostrate on the stone floors of dingy closed entranceways and dank, sunless, mud-floored cellars, they succumbed in their hundreds to typhus, scarlatina, typhoid and cholera. Liverpool behaved like a stepmother with a heart of stone.

A thousand new refugees arrived on the waterfront every day, and soon the streets were full of Irish 'gobdaws'. Shining shoes, carrying travellers' luggage, scouring the streets for rags and horse manure, and performing acrobatics were some of the ways the Irish learned to survive. Some were forced to beg and steal, and, at one time, gangs controlling Liverpool Irish slum children were so highly organised that they set up 'markets' in the cellars of empty warehouses where unscrupulous shopkeepers came to buy the goods pilfered from the docks. Every twentieth house in Liverpool was an alehouse, and over some was written 'This way to Hell going down to the chambers of death.'

Despite the many hardships, the Irish-born population in Liverpool doubled to 83,000 in 10 years. They tried their best to blend with the local scenery, and Gaelic was rarely heard in the port. Most settled in crummy accommodation to the north of the Prince's Landing Stage in a narrow strip of land between Vauxhall and the Scotland Road, or in the South End between the docks and a line running along Park Lane, St James Street and Park Road. The even less fortunate ended up in the country's biggest workhouse on Brownlow Hill, close to the site of today's Metropolitan Cathedral. By 1851, half the 25,000-strong population of Vauxhall was Irish-born. Many had fled Ireland to escape colonial exploitation only to be confronted with religious bigotry from a hostile Protestant workforce. One in four of their children died before their fifth birthday. Every stairwell and 'jigger' swarmed with pale-faced, filthy children, and there were hundreds of waifs running around the docks. The eldest girls in the families nursed babies, while the rest fought and swore over scraps. One woman was discovered sharing a bed with her stiff, dead husband for lack of anywhere more suitable to lay the body out.

An article written in the *Liverpool Herald* of 17 November 1855 berated the new Irish migrants for all the misfortunes of the city:

> Let a stranger in Liverpool be taken through the streets that branch off from the Vauxhall Road, Marylebone, Whitechapel and the North End of the docks, and he will witness such a scene of filth and vice, as we defy any person to parallel in any part of the world. The numberless whiskey shops crowded with half clad women, some with infants in their arms from early dawn to midnight – thousands of children in rags, with their features scarcely able to be distinguished in consequence of the cakes of dirt upon them, the stench of filth in every direction – men and women fighting, the most horrible execrations and obscenity, with oaths and curses that make the heart shudder, all these things would lead the spectator to suppose he was

in a land of savages where God was unknown and man was uncared for. And who are these wretches? Not English but Irish papists. It is remarkable and no less remarkable than true, that the lower order of Irish papists are the filthiest beings in the habitable globe, they abound in dirt and vermin and have no care for anything but self-gratification that would degrade the brute creation . . . Look at our police reports, three fourths of the crime perpetrated in this large town is by Irish papists. They are the very dregs of society, steeped to the very lips in all manner of vice, from murder to pocket picking and yet the citizens of Liverpool are taxed to maintain the band of ruffians and their families in time of national distress.

Liverpool was now a black spot on the Mersey. In the North End between Great Crosshall Street and Addison Street, 8,000 people occupied just 811 houses, giving the area a density of 658,000 persons per square mile, double the figure recorded for the most crowded parts of the East End of London. In the parish of St Simon, 6,000 people were crammed into a 15-acre plot of 21 streets and 68 courts, which the Anglican priest, the Reverend John Connors, described as 'a moral wilderness'. A leading article in *The Times* at the time railed:

Ireland is pouring into the cities, and even into the villages of this island, a fetid mass of famine, nakedness and dirt and fever. Liverpool, whose proximity to Ireland has already procured for it the unhappy distinction of being the most unhealthy town in this island, seems destined to become one mass of disease.

Eventually, the British government came to the rescue of an embattled Liverpool Corporation. A draconian law was passed that allowed local authorities to repatriate the homeless Irish forcibly. Within days, a new business had started to flourish on the quay, with 15,000 homeless people, some of whom were also sickly, being transported back across the Irish Sea and dumped on the Dublin and Cork landing stages. To avoid immediate deportation, some of the new arrivals at Clarence Dock set off with their shillelaghs and distinctive brogues for the industrial heartlands of Lancashire, Yorkshire and the Midlands, but wherever they stopped to lay their heads they were unwelcome. A prevailing misconception amongst some of Liverpool's merchants was that much of this mass immigration stemmed from the Irish love for change and adventure, and that their misfortune was a direct consequence of their dissolute lifestyle. The transportation of a new wave of human cargo out on the cheapest route to America offered a business opportunity that couldn't be passed over.

The strongest and most determined of the Irish headed out to the El Dorado of New England in the hundreds of ships that left Liverpool every year, but even those in a hurry to leave had a wait of a few days in tumbledown lodging houses close to the river. The distraught yet not quite beaten Milesians crammed into boats where they would be forced to survive for weeks on starvation rations. One unworthy vessel sailed down the Mersey jam-packed with fleeing Irish only to sink within sight of the Prince's Landing Stage. Conditions below deck were little better than those experienced a generation earlier by the African slaves. Many of the migrants lay dehydrated, malnourished and dying, bathed in their own excrement and anaesthetised with rum. Diarrhoea and vomiting were endemic and medical aid non-existent, and those who died during the journey were perfunctorily dumped overboard to minimise contagion – without even receiving the last rites. The lucky survivors arrived at 'The Island of Tears', in the mouth of the Hudson River. Anarchists, polygamists, syphilitics and paupers were summarily rejected by the Manhattan immigration authorities, and as many as one in fifty was sent packing down 'The Stairs of Separation' and onto the next boat back to the hell of Liverpool.

Liverpool had become a pioneer town devoid of tradition or ancestry, whose clarion call had brought colonists in from the sea and Britain's fringes. The long-distance rapid influx of transients, nomads and people who had arrived by sea had the effect of cramping local movement into the town from the neighbouring countryside and resulted in spatial segregation, still recognisable today in some parts of the city. The Irish had arrived with a grievance and a resolute defiance, and their massive presence led to certain Liverpool constituencies returning Sinn Fein candidates to Parliament. Pat Garton, a Liverpool councillor with Republican sympathies, allowed his skiff to be used in the daring rescue of the Irish Republican Brotherhood leader James Stephens from a Dublin jail, consolidating the links between Liverpool and Ireland in its struggle for independence.

The 'low Irish' who had left the countryside and made Liverpool their home slowly dragged themselves up by their bootstraps. Some of them worked on the construction of the Manchester Ship Canal, earning the nickname 'navvies' (abbreviated from navigation). Upward mobility was impossible for most, but within two generations some Ulstermen and Leinstermen had left the docks to become artisans and shopkeepers, and a few exceptional individuals had joined the professional classes. Dixon Scott, in his book about the Liverpool slums, highlights the linguistic apartness of the Irish as a reason for lack of progress:

> They speak a bastard brogue: a shambling degenerate speech of slip-shod vowels and muddied consonants − a cast-off clout of a tongue, more debased even than the Whitechapel Cockney, because so much less positive and acute.

These Irish were the *caput mortua*, ancestors of a wingless underclass who had failed to cross the Atlantic, leaving them stuck in the first circle of Dante's Inferno. They continued to live separately, retaining their own traditions, and hated the English 'Johnnies', who they believed must hate themselves by the way they carried on. To the English, the Irish had a past but no future and continued to be considered a problem, holding back the town's drive for prosperity.

By 1871, one in twenty-five of the town's population was of Scots ancestry. Some crofters evicted during the vicious Highland Clearances had arrived in Liverpool hoping to make a new life, and a group of skilled Glasgow dockside workers had settled in Kirkdale. Scottish churches were built in Oldham Street and Rodney Street, and many Scots dreamed of seeing the light in this frontier town, which they romantically saw as a new Jerusalem. Caledonian balls, Burns Night celebrations and St Andrew's Day dinners helped to maintain Scottish roots. The shipowners Macgregor Laird, Alexander Elder and John Dempster, at the fore of developing the West Africa trade, were all Scots, and the MacIver family, originally from the Hebrides, secured Liverpool's control of the transatlantic steamship trade with Cunard. The Scots were also to prosper in rope-making, sugar-refining and engineering, and some of these successful men brought links golfing to the area. William Duncan, a second-generation Scot born in Liverpool, was appointed the town's first medical officer of health and advocated urgent expenditure on sanitary works to cope with the dreadful health record of the city. He castigated the Irish for:

> Such an innate indifference to filth, such a low standard of comfort, and such a gregariousness, as lead them, even when not driven by necessity, into the unhealthy localities where they are found to

congregate; and which they render still more unhealthy by their recklessness and their peculiar habits.

Duncan's view reflected that of many Liverpool Scots who regarded the Irish ghettos as no-go areas because of the Fenians' debauched wickedness and unreliability.

When the Reformed Church started to splinter into smaller groups, the Welsh adopted Methodism. Their tightly knit tribal communities were attracted to charismatic preachers who affirmed the power of the spirit. This rise of Nonconformity gave the Welsh language a new authority, as in contrast to Anglicanism God was responsive only to the native tongue. John Wesley's inspirational preaching diminished the congregations of the established Church, and by the early nineteenth century a new chapel was opening every week in the valleys. Zealous and ecstatic congregations jumped, shook and howled in exaltation. Meanwhile, north of the border and in Ulster, an austere Calvinist and Knoxian Presbyterianism was tugging at the souls of the Gaels. These new branches of Protestantism had little sense of hierarchy, decorum or theatre and emphasised the Pelagian vision that each individual could positively choose to live a worthy life. Each had risen out of a vehement rejection of the established Church and a re-emphasis on traditional Gaelic values. This awestruck flock of natural-born sinners had opted for a hard, unforgiving God who demanded outward evidence of their faith and adherence to the fourth Commandment. Their darker side was never far from the surface.

Liverpool had become a Celtic enclave full of minorities, an ancillary metropolis for the Welsh and the graveyard of Ireland. It was an earthy place full of self-deprecating laughter and chutzpah. Many of the new Walter Mittys had a past they wanted to forget in a town that was cruel and where persecution prevailed, but that was still shaping itself. They were frequently ignored but usually lived to tell the tale. Identity was determined by the kind of person you were rather than the tribe or class you came from. Where you had come from was unimportant, but where you wanted to go meant a great deal. Desperation was understood, and tolerance for human frailty a given.

Paradise

When I was a youngster I sailed with th' rest
On a Liverpool packet bound out to th' west.
We anchored a day in the harbour o' Cork,
Then put out to sea for th' port o' New York.
An' it's Ho! Ro! Ho, bullies, ho!
Th' Liverpool Gir-ils have got us in tow.

Extract from 'The Liverpool Girls',
Capstan Bars, by David Bone

Conrad was particularly complimentary about Liverpool sailors, considering them to be hard cases and made of the right stuff for the high seas. They performed difficult and dangerous work, often in appalling conditions, but preserved a cruel sense of humour and refused to kowtow to rank. Some were a real handful, the grandsons of men who had worked the Guineamen, independently minded and not averse to mutiny, but without these hardened seafarers the most modern and efficient marine service the world had ever witnessed would not have been possible.

The Scousers took a perverse and fierce pride in their job and in their ability to absorb hardship, battling with their American counterparts for supremacy. In the end, the most important thing on board was how good you were at making sure your ship got back safely. Solidarity with brother tars and a 'one and all' philosophy were the universal code of the sea, united by shared peril. The redoubtable 21-year-old American packet captain and former cabin boy Samuel Samuels considered Liverpool sailors to be tough and difficult to handle. On one occasion, a gang of feared foul-mouthed Liverpool seamen who went by the name of 'The Bloody Forty' signed up for service on the *Dreadnought* deliberately to try to get the better of Samuels. Like many before them, they were eventually beaten into submission by the autocratic and pugnacious American.

The moon and its regular pull on the changing tides governed the sailors. Their day was from noon to noon, their greatest fear the blinding sea fog that blotted out the stars, casting them adrift without bearings and leaving them totally reliant on plumb lines. 'Call and response' work songs helped keep them going in storms. Particular shanties were sung for specific tasks, such as hoisting topsails, raising the anchor and turning the windlass. Many of the favourites on Liverpool ships referred to life in the home port, such as 'Maggie May', a song about the infamous harlot who walked Lime Street, and 'Blow the Man Down', which refers to the pleasures of drinking on Paradise Street. Many clipper captains believed a good 'shantyman' was worth ten sailors in gaining time on the tea runs.

Liverpool's Church of Our Lady and St Nicholas, known locally as 'the sailors' old church', was a place of peace where they could pray and leave offerings to guarantee safe return. The basement of the chapel of ease doubled up as a 'dead house', a place of passage for the drowned and drowning. The sailors sang the following lines from 'May We Hope to Find a Patron' at evensong every 6 December in reverence to the patron saint of sailors, merchants, thieves and children:

> One there is whom once our fathers
> Took their own, their Saint, to be
> Since his prayers had helped the children
> And the sailors on the sea;
> Lord, Who dost Thine angels send,
> Make Saint Nicholas our friend.
> Here the shrine in which they worshipped
> Here the Chapel by the sea;
> Nicholas, their chosen patron,
> With Our Lady of the Quay
> He, and Mary at his side,
> Magnifying, Magnified.

With the growing number of ships entering the port, a floating church and refuge was opened in 1827 on HMS *Tees*, an old sloop moored in St George's Dock. On Sundays, a retired sailor from the floating chapel would raise the bethel flag as he called the seamen to their devotions. A priest would then deliver a plain-talking sermon from the quay to a dissolute group of hung-over tars.

Herman Melville discussed the character of sailors in *Redburn*:

Consider that with the majority of them, the very fact of their being sailors, argues a certain recklessness and sensualism of character, ignorance, and depravity; consider that they are generally friendless and alone in the world; or if they have friends and relatives, they are almost constantly beyond the reach of their good influences; consider that after the rigorous discipline, hardships, dangers, and privations of a voyage, they are set adrift in a foreign port and exposed to a thousand enticements, which, under the circumstances, would be hard even for virtue itself to withstand, unless virtue went about on crutches; consider that by their very vocation they are shunned by the better classes of people, and cut off from all access to respectable and improving society; consider all this, and the reflecting mind must soon perceive that the case of sailors, as a class, is not a very promising one.

Captain Samuel Samuels of the *Dreadnought* also highlighted the difficult life of his crew in his memoirs:

Driven like slaves, taught to obey commands and whipped like circus animals, their working lives were briefer than those of men in any other following. From the fecal alleys of slums ashore they were trundled into the galleys of slums at sea.

Melville, however, also tried to draw his readers' attention to the intrinsic worthiness of sailors, calling them a 'bridge of boats across the Atlantic', the 'primum mobile of all commerce' and the 'wheels of this world'. He deplored that on land they were shunned by society and considered flotsam and jetsam washed in by the sea and worthy only of charity.

Even on board ship, the sailors were not safe. Captain Henry Rogers of the *Martha and Jane* murdered the 25-year-old Scot Andrew Rose on a return voyage from Barbados. During the journey, the weak-willed sailor was whipped, kicked black and blue, made to eat his own excrement and shackled. Rogers regularly set his dog on him, allowing it to bite off chunks of flesh from his legs, leaving maggot-ridden suppurating wounds. The sailor was so badly beaten that the crew advised him to jump ship. When Rose found the strength to sing a hymn, Rogers instructed the first mate, William Miles, to fetch him a large iron bolt, which he rammed into Rose's mouth. Rose was then strung from the mainmast for two minutes, after which his eyes were bulging and his tongue black. Rogers boasted to the crew, 'If I'd kept him there just a half minute longer, he'd have been a goner.'

Shortly afterwards, Rose staggered onto the deck, uttered the single sad word, 'Why?' and died. Rogers ordered the mutilated body to be thrown overboard.

On arrival at Liverpool, some of the crew reported Rogers, Miles and the second mate, Campbell, to the police. When the men were found guilty at St George's Hall, a jubilant crowd of sailors congregated on Lime Street. The 35-year-old Scot Rogers turned to religion while awaiting his fate, but it failed to provide salvation, and on 12 September 1857 he stood on the gallows at the top of Kirkdale Gaol looking out on Liverpool Bay as a baying mob below cheered him to his death. The murder of Andrew Rose is remembered today in a sea ballad.

HMS *Akbar* and HMS *Clarence*, moored in the estuary, were rehabilitated as floating reformatory schools to train habitual recidivists for a life on the ocean waves. The Catholic slummies were sent to the *Akbar* and the Protestants to the *Clarence*, but both institutions were equally strict. Every Sunday, the apprentices were bombarded with admonishments of hellfire and brimstone and filled with a sense of guilt. The HMS *Indefatigable* served a similar purpose for poor orphans whose fathers had been lost at sea and for the children of respectable seamen. HMS *Conway* made up the quartet of naval vessels on the river but was reserved for the training of boys from better homes who had the potential to become naval officers.

'Training schools', such as Paddy West's in Great Howard Street, catered for criminals on the run, fleeing debtors and abused boys who, despite the hardships, actually wanted to escape to sea. Paddy's crash course involved learning to furl a sail by rolling up a window blind, placing one's hands briefly on a ship's wheel, having a bucket of water thrown over one's face to simulate a storm, and walking around a bull's horn and stepping over a cod line so that graduates could later claim that they had 'rounded the Horn and crossed the line'. These raw recruits would be slowly assimilated into the world of the deep-sea sailor through a process of 'induction' and ritualistic initiation ceremonies. In return for Paddy's one day of sham instruction, they were expected to cough up their first two months' pay.

By the end of the nineteenth century, Liverpool had two main districts for visiting mariners. In the North End, Union Street and Brook Street, behind Princes Dock, were the focus, whereas the nearby older 'Sailortown' to the south still centred on Paradise Street, Hanover Street, Park Lane, Lower Frederick Street and Anson Terrace. Digs were run by seamen's wives, and the adjacent surrounding taverns, outfitters and ships stores were owned by ex-sailors. The shops sold greasy bacon, sweaty cheeses, potted herrings, hair oil and Epsom salts. Second-hand bric-a-brac stores offered up pictures of the Virgin, cracked crockery and scratched tables and chairs. Dinner for the crew consisted of boiled potatoes, beefsteaks, sausages, brawn, bread and pickle washed down with 'swipes', the lees of the beer barrels. Mealtimes either at sea or on land provided a forum for communal cursing of the captain and of the niggardly shipowner.

In *Redburn*, Melville described the street life in Sailortown:

> In the evening, especially when the sailors are gathered in great numbers, these streets present a most singular spectacle, the entire population of the vicinity being seemingly turned into them. Hand organs, fiddles and cymbals, plied by strolling musicians, mix with the songs of seamen, the babble of women and children and the whining of beggars. From the various boarding houses . . . proceeds the noise of revelry and dancing.

At any one time, there might be several thousand sailors chewing wads of tobacco and hanging around the Sailors' Home and Dispensary. The newly arrived, jovial and open-hearted five-minute millionaires, with their wads stuffed in their back pockets, were the kings of the town. The Blue Funnel and Booth sailors recently returned from Belém and Manaus often had a macaw or marmoset to sell in the Lord de Tabley pub in Park Lane. Some drifted down to the sailors' outfitters run by Jew Grossi in Paradise Street to exchange their advance notes for 75 per cent merchandise and 25 per cent cash or popped in to have their fortunes told by one of the many soothsayers. There were 600 houses of ill repute accommodating 2,000 mainly Irish harlots, including Harriet Lane, Blooming Rose, Jumping Jenny, Cast-Iron Kitty, 'The Battleship', Maggie May and Tich Maguire. These fleshpots were an irresistible magnet for the freewheeling sailor. Despite the ongoing prejudice in the town toward seamen, they were understood and seen as a source of income in the Paradise Street bars and dance halls.

The sailors were united in their hatred of soldiers and scorn for landlubbers, and many carried daggers for self-defence against the dock gangs. The American and Nordic crews, often violently drunk, had a particularly tense relationship with the locals. The Cornermen, a posse of young Irish Liverpool toughs, hung around outside public houses to goad the sailors into a fight. Local brasses lured the foolhardy to Sebastopol, where North End High Rip pimps, in their distinctive 'bucco caps' and mufflers, would roll the sailor over, leaving him battered and penniless in the narrow artery. Scuttles between rival gangs with the buckle ends of belts and daggers were common in the docklands. After a night on the tiles, the Icelandic whalers would often end up spread-eagled, stupefied and skinned naked in Lime Street. Some seamen disappeared for ever, the victims of burkers or kidnappers in murderous no-go areas like Rotten Row and Booble Alley. Charles Dickens spent a night on the beat with a superintendent and his three officers observing the traps set every night for the 'Poor Mercantile Jacks'. In the fifth chapter of *The Uncommercial Traveller*, he describes a Spanish Jack, a Loafing Jack of the stars and stripes, a Maltese Jack, and Jack the Finn – a motley crew as varied and numerous as the hostelries that never closed near the docks. The more sober sea dogs opted for the safer option of dances at Atlantic House run by the Apostleship for the Sea, attended by warm-hearted lady parishioners. The Seaman's Friend Society, with its headquarters in the Gordon Smith Institute in Paradise Street, was founded in 1820 to keep sailors away from dishonest landladies and shanghaiers, and provide them with a cheap refuge in the Sailors' Home in Canning Place. Ironically, it was surrounded by the temptations of the Great Grog Palace, penny ale cellars and singing saloons like the Sans Pareil and the Liver, stuffed with animal trophies and coffee-coloured pictures of foreign ports. 'Gomorrah', with its brothels, boozers and brawls, was an irresistible draw for those who had jumped ship, the place where any sailor torn between two beautiful women could always encounter a third.

The port had an edge. Herman Melville wrote that despite its dangers:

> Sailors love this Liverpool; and upon long voyages to distant parts of the globe, will be continually dilating upon its charms and attractions, and extolling it above all other seaports in the world. For in Liverpool they find their Paradise – not the well known street of that name – and one of them told me he would be content to lie in Princes Dock till he hove up anchor for the world to come.

The young Melville, who first arrived in Liverpool in 1839 on the *Saint Lawrence*, was impressed to see visiting black American seamen walking freely in the streets, arm in arm with white girls. In contrast to America, the only beggars here were white and mainly Irish. A common sight at the Landing Stage were the Lascars: Singhalese, Marathas, Bengalis and Siamese who worked the Malabar Coast as firemen, who dressed in elegant white linen robes and were often accompanied by a sword-wielding serang of higher caste in a cocked hat and scarlet army coat embroidered with golden lace. The East India Company had grown from simply a large trading venture to virtually ruling India with its own army. In 1858, effective rule was transferred to Queen Victoria and under the British Raj all citizens of India became British and could be made to fight under a British flag.

James McCune Smith, the son of emancipated slaves, politician and the first American-African to obtain a medical degree, had visited Liverpool seven years earlier and had been cheered by the open inter-racial discourse he observed. He attended a service at Saint George's Church and later wrote:

> There were no cold looks, no supercilious or sanctimonious frowns, none appeared to have reached that pitch of devotion in which creatures frown upon the works of their Creator – upon their fellow creatures, not for the hue of the soul, but of the skin.

Other descriptions of black integration in the riverside quarters can be found in the writings of the time such as the following piece by George Sala:

> Black Jack, very woolly headed and ivory grindered, cooking and fiddling and singing, as it seems the nature of Black Jack to cook, fiddle and sing. Where the union jack flies, Nigger Jack is well treated, English sailors do not disdain to drink with him, work with him, and sing with him. Take a wherry, however, to that American clipper, with the tall masts and the tall man for skipper, and you will hear a different tale. Beneath the star spangled banner, the allowance for Nigger Jacks decreases woefully, while that of kicks increases in an alarming proportion.

The Kru from the Liberian coast who had long bartered rice, malagueta pepper and ivory with the Liverpool sea captains were also increasingly in evidence around Pitt Street. They were recruited in West African waters to replace English casualties on the Liverpool merchant ships where they worked as 'hot seas' stokers or cooks. Others worked with the British Navy policing the Bight of Benin and on the British Niger Expedition. Five hundred of these men left of their own free will for British Guyana where they worked on the sugar estates of Demerara and on the West

Bank and East Coast of Bernice. They negotiated their own terms and, while some returned to marry in Africa, a significant number stayed and became Creole river boatmen. Some later went on to build the Panama Canal but demanded repatriation when their numbers were decimated by the appalling working conditions. Those who drifted to the Liverpool docks were respected by the dockside community for their industry and independence. The local Mary Ellens (a nickname for local girls derived from Mary Ellen Grant the 'Connaught Nigger' born of an Irish mother and West African father) regarded Liverpool-born blacks and the new Kru arrivals as 'good catches'. To live with an Elder Dempster black stoker, who drew a steady salary and was only around for three months of the year, was a far better option than to be hitched to an aggressive, drunk, unemployed Irish docker.

On his tour of the docks with the four police officers, Charles Dickens was taken to a public house where a predominantly black clientele were dancing wild sensuous quadrilles to the music of fiddle and tambourine. The superintendent informed him that black men congregated here to avoid fights in the neighbouring streets. Dickens referred to these 'simple gentle fellows' as 'Dark Jacks' and their female consorts as 'white unlovely Nans'.

In 1898, Edward Crawford of Eldon Street found a 14-year-old Guyanese-born black stowaway called James Clarke wandering around the docks and adopted him with the blessing of the local Catholic priest at Saint Augustine's Parish Church. Jim, as he was known, found work as a docker in the North End, and once he had grown up, became the renowned lifesaver of many drowning children and joyless drunks from the filthy water channel between Burlington and Athol Streets. As soon as the alert went out, Clarke would dive into the Scaldy and swim below the surface at great speed, returning sometimes with the corpse of a missing person. In his spare time, he taught children to swim in the Burroughs Gardens Pool, where one of his favourite tricks was to sit on the bottom of the pool with a bucket on his head singing songs like 'Jerusalem' and drinking lemonade. Forty years after his death from tuberculosis, the Vauxhall community fought to have him honoured, and now James Clarke Street runs between Tatlock Street and Hornby Walk.

The first Chinese sailors arrived in Liverpool on the Bibby tea ship *Duchess of Clarence* and after the Opium Wars many more left the Treaty Ports of Guangzhou and Hong Kong to join the Arabs, Jews, Greeks and Scandinavians in Cleveland Square, and Frederick and Upper Pitt Streets.

The foundation of the Ocean Steam Ship Company and the Blue Funnel Line steamship services to the Orient swelled their numbers and some of the new arrivals took rooms in boarding houses owned by the Holt Shipping Company. A Chinese Community Centre was set up to support the few hundred men who decided to cast anchor. The seamen's unions resented their presence, and the fear of cheap labour in the docks resulted in forced deportation of some Chinese sailors. Trams and omnibuses often refused to stop if they saw a Chinaman waiting at the stop. Laundries and grocery stores run from terraced homes were Chinatown's main source of contact with the rest of Liverpool. By and large they kept themselves to themselves, were self-sufficient and regarded themselves as long-term visitors rather than British citizens. Opium smoking was popular, with the drug sold legally in groceries and smoked in filthy dens in Frederick Street. Once the anti-drugs laws of 1916 were passed, a major smuggling operation began, with the poppy juice arriving on the dockside concealed in wooden logs.

I am transported back to Ship Street now, to its morbid waxwork effigies, freak shows, crash-test dummies and imaginary dance halls. I can see in my mind's eye the boarding houses full of ravenous sailors spitting downwind and splicing ropes. The high and fast tides that run through their arteries are a biting cocktail of brine and rum. From the sloping street in the Dingle, I am back cataloguing the funnel liveries and exotic names of the last rusty steamers sailing down the river. A chequered Ellerman liner, survivor of the war, glides past. The aromas of blind scouse, paddy wack, hot pot, wet nellas, and bubble and squeak drift from the cafes by the waterfront and I can still savour raspberry jellies and marzipan. I picture my father in a jaunty homburg, sipping a highball in a dive down by the docks, humming 'Tico Tico Tico' as he waited for the *Reina del Mar* to take him away to a new life. Bombed out, dead in the water, Liverpool had rescued him from the Industrial Revolution and a war that had almost engulfed him. It had provided an escape route to a paradise where he would be free to be himself.

The ships and the smell of their varied cargoes have entered the heart of the town. The Baltic Fleet and the Globe remain refuges for a few stranded penniless coves and curious young historians in search of the last remnants of Sailortown. By the gasometer, the condemned slanting terraces of old Liverpool are sprouting predatory rosebay willowherb, nettle and crocked dandelions. With the boats went the dreams of just one more trip, turning the city in on itself to let the drink do the talking. The ornamental lamp posts at the Pier Head where I once swung my life away have been chopped down. The docks lie almost empty and some have been converted for landlocked business.

There are no 'ship ahoys' to raise the spirits. Tattoos still decorate pasty flesh on Slater and Castle but there are no anchors, clippers and shellback turtles to behold. Hold and Fast became Love and Hate. Only old sailors languishing in Aigburth nursing homes have pigs and roosters on their feet.

Liverpool's meaning is now born out of small victories, dogma and childhood traumas, but she can still cut corners and break my heart. The tawdry red rock of the Regency and Victorian south side resonates with Salvador, colonial capital of Brazil. The old is dead and yet the new cannot be born. Why was she cast off and betrayed?

The town and the port have lived on – but the connection with the sea has been severed; the padlocked waterfront is silent. A hundred years ago, £250 million of cargo and contraband passed through a slum town rife with treatable epidemics. The noble ticket office on the Lanny has been demolished. The Mersey Mission to Seamen at the Pier Head has become a fitness club. The cargo ships that joined the fixed points of the Atlantic world are all but gone; the Journal of Commerce is extinct. King Edward with his cocked hat now looks out on a cheap eatery. Cromarty, Dogger, German Bight, Rockall, Faroes and Mallin are irrelevancies. The entries and back alleys are full of rubbish and the side gates smashed in. Graffiti smothers the metal blinds and the derelict walls. A wrecking ball smashes into a lonely chimney stranded in a pulverised landscape of cleared lots and dust. The sailors and their families have been erased. The place that once shifted people around the pink parts of the globe now relies on a half-hour ferry ride to bring life back to the river and tears to the eyes of the last few sailors who have returned from Pacific ports and survived the Gate of Tears.

The Paraná jacarandas seem to be growing out of the ocean, their mauve splendour driving away the blue meanies. Bougainvilleas have invaded the waterfront, spreading their lilac bracts and spikiness. Honey-scented fissured juremas are colonising the wastelands and a golden ipê lights the dismal Vauxhall sky. There are babassus, macotes, catoles, carnaubas and jussaura palms taking hold in the heavy air of Formby beach. Guavas, soursop, custard apple, mango and passion fruit orchards nourish marooned macaws and the moored ferries. Ironwood, bamboo, sapucaias, pitangas and jambos have turned Canning dock into a Tijuca rainforest. The Old Guard of

PARADISE

Vauxhall is working on this year's *samba enredo*:

> Marvellous city of the north west
> Great port on the edge of a continent
> With your richness of spirit
> Created by those sailors who long ago
> Sailed to a beautiful land
> And brought back music and dance
> And a special happiness
> We praise you, cha cha cha
> We celebrate your spirit in our drums
> And reach out to the saints and the orixás for pity . . .

The pavements of lost, levelled streets are cracking in the sun to reveal the beach below. An undercurrent of rage is running through the varicose veins of the lost lands. Effulgent humming birds have travelled through the foggy, rain-swept grey to bring spontaneity and improvisation to the tent of miracles in Saint Oswald Street. Man of War birds glide and hover over the Liver building, harassing the cormorants. The army ants swarm on the mounds and there is a cloud of large blue butterflies crossing the Mersey. These happenings have brought Old Brazil to Old Swan. They allow me to believe this is the last place on earth where beauty, magic, innocence, sensuality, elegance and the sublime still exist. They teach me that there is always a way round official barriers and that the Samba of the Fireflies is an urban myth. Sailors' ghosts still strut the waterfront of this world-class city but Liverpool now looks over its shoulder.

Shadow Line

The earliest thing I remember:
as our van dropped a gear up Brownlow Hill
I looked back at the panes of distemper
that sealed a world. We reached our overspill,
and this is where our stories overlap.
The coming of the cradle and sheet glass
Was squeezing out the ladder and the slap of leather into suds, and
    less and
less work came through the door. And anyway
you were getting too old for scaling heights.
Now, when I change a bulb or queue to pay
at fairs, or when I'm checking in for flights,
I feel our difference bit down to the quick.
There are no guidebooks to that town you knew
and this attempt to build it, brick by brick,
descends the page. I'll hold the foot for you.

                        Extract from 'Laws of Gravity' by Paul Farley

The influx of 300,000 Irish paupers in fewer than three years had overwhelmed Liverpool's housing and health resources. Most were vulnerable illiterates fearful of confinement in the fever sheds, bridewells and river hulks or of deportation back to Ireland. Forced into dingy sub-let cellars and airless courts, it was not uncommon for 20 people to sleep in a single room. Those who strayed from the ghettos found their accents marked them out for punitive action by the authorities and drew the attention of opportunist crooks. Even on the way to the New World the Irish were duped: if they had not been sold out-of-date tickets to New York, Baltimore or Boston by disreputable brokers, they were conned by swarms of swindlers and fraudsters, cheated by runners who stole their luggage and fleeced them of what little they had left. This ruthless exploitation of rural Irish innocents gained Liverpool an early notoriety for skullduggery.

By the 1850s, the working class of Liverpool were officially the unhealthiest in Britain. Infant mortality was high and the average life expectancy a mere 18 years. The town was infested with beggars, nagging at the coat sleeves of anyone who looked as if they might have money, and robbery and prostitution were rife. The putrid lanes close to the waterfront were awash with the starving and the syphilitic, scavenging scraps thrown from the boats. Some of these street people were grossly deformed and became well known to the locals by cruel names: 'Number Four' was a wretch with one leg twisted permanently over the other and was forced to propel himself on a small wheeled board; 'Serpent', whose useless limbs forced him to slither across the pavement; and 'The Seal', a woman with vestigial arms and legs, lying helpless in a bath chair.

'The people are as numerous as maggots in cheese,' wrote Nathaniel Hawthorne from his office on the Gorée. 'You behold them, disgusting, and all moving about, as when you raise a plank or log that has long lain on the ground, and find many vivacious bugs and insects beneath it.'

The prematurely wrinkled countenances and bare, dirty feet of the young women walking in the streets with baskets perched on their heads or sitting forlornly on the carriageways with their wares of fruit, crockery, oysters and combs created a lasting impression on the American.

In 1850, two years before he began his four-year stay in Liverpool, Hawthorne was introduced to Herman Melville on a hike up Monument Mountain in Massachusetts. Melville was 15 years younger, a brasher, romantic New Yorker, but both were outsiders who had experienced financial hardship in their literary careers. Melville became infatuated with Hawthorne and started an ardent correspondence, which encouraged him to complete his masterpiece *Moby Dick*. He was so impassioned that he moved his family to the Berkshires so the two men could be neighbours. Conversations must at times have strayed to Liverpool, which Melville first visited as a 19 year old. His semi-autobiographical novel *Redburn* begins with a young American arriving in Liverpool armed with a guide written by his father. As he tries to retrace his father's journey, he is filled with a sense of alienation and loss. Nothing he sees bears any resemblance to what he has read, and he despairs at the extent of the destitution and squalor he sees all around him.

Hawthorne's peregrinations were confined to the main thoroughfares and sidewalks of the town; the narrow closes and alleys of the slums were out of bounds.

Silas Hocking describes in *Her Benny* some of these backstreets to the west of Scotty Road:

> And those who have occasion to penetrate their dark and filthy recesses are generally thankful when they find themselves safe out again. In the winter those streets and courts are kept comparatively clean by the heavy rains; but in the summer the air fairly reeks with the stench of decayed fish, rotting vegetables, and every other conceivable kind of filth . . . The children that seem to swarm in this neighbourhood are nearly all of a pale, sallow complexion, and of stunted growth. Shoes and stockings and underclothing are luxuries that they never know, and one good meal a day is almost more than they dare hope for. Cuffs and kicks they reckon upon every day of their lives; and in this they are rarely disappointed . . .

The courts described by Hocking, a Methodist preacher, consisted of a cluster of five or six flimsy back-to-back shacks which ran perpendicular to the terraced streets, reached via sombre cat- and flea-infested alleyways. Some had grown out of an ordinary street house, whose lobby had been converted into a roofed-over passage leading into a yard with a filthy privy. The yard and back room were filled with a number of squats leading off the airless tunnel. Hidden away like cavities, these begrimed hovels consisted of little more than a couple of bare rooms with hard floors covered with strips of oilcloth. Outside in the communal yards, ropes of pegged-out rags and tattered underclothes criss-crossed above the starving indigents as they queued day and night at the stinking ash pits, newspapers in hand. Liverpool had 4,000 of these courts, which were home for 1 in 5 of the town's population. The hardships endured by these families coloured the outlook of their children and planted an indelible fear and insecurity in future generations.

Gerard Manley Hopkins also found the endemic vice offensive and was harrowed by the everyday problems of the poor. A Jesuit and poet, he arrived in Liverpool in 1879 to work as parish priest at St Francis Xavier's in Salisbury Street. Compared with the charming and cheery heartiness of Lancashire Catholics, he found the Liverpool Irish hard work, and observed that many of them expressed a virulent hostility towards their host town in contrast to those he had met in Glasgow. He considered many of his flock not only unreformed but unreformable. These accounts by outsiders consolidated the view of most eminent

Victorians that Liverpool was the nearest thing in England to Sodom.

The Brownlow Hill Workhouse that had stood at the top of Mount Pleasant since 1769 had grown over a hundred years to be the largest facility of its kind in the land. It resembled a town within a town with its overcrowded cobbled paths and constant stream of handcarts moving between buildings housing 5,000 inmates, who were provided with their own church and a beleaguered hospital. The hangdog, down-and-out men were dressed in regulation black Tam O'Shanters, navy pilot coats, and grey shirts with white moleskins and boots. The segregated women wore grey stripe print dresses, white starched caps and heavy boots. They dressed their suckling babies in grey calico smocks while the older children were clad in red uniforms. Everyone was put to work without pay. Breakfast consisted of bread, tea and thin porridge; lunch was a couple of jacket potatoes with an occasional helping of Scouse stew; and dinner a piece of cheese and a crust washed down with watery tea or a smuggled-in pennyworth of methylated spirits.

In spite of the hardship, many of the unfortunate rejects preferred this institutionalised existence ending with the prospective shame of a pauper's burial to the unpredictability and struggle of life outside. Not all workhouses were residential. The old Test House on Belmont Road was a governmental facility where tramps could be fumigated, get a bite to eat and a bed for the night. The next morning, after completing their ablutions and required chores, they would be given a crust of bread and a cup of tea and would leave refreshed for the next town back up the line. The Mission 'Cob' Hall was close by and a place from whence evangelicals like Gypsy Smith sallied forth to persuade foundlings to work in exchange for a cob loaf.

Life was dire for most of the population. The Reverend Acland Armstrong, Minister of the Unitarian Church in Hope Street, described the city's striking contrasts in 1885:

> I admired its public buildings, its vast docks, its stately shipping, its splendid shops, its lovely parks. It seemed to me this was a city in which one might be proud to be a citizen: a city, which must be administered and governed by men of high capacity and generous temper. But after the first glance I was appalled by one aspect of things here, which pressed on my mind more and more for several weeks, till the sin of it became at times well nigh unbearable. The contiguity of immense wealth and abysmal poverty forced itself upon

my notice. The hordes of the ragged and the wretched surged up from their native quarters and covered the noblest streets like a flood. Men and women in the cruellest grip of poverty, little children with shoeless feet, bodies pinched and faces in which the pure light of childhood had been quenched swarmed on the pavements that fronted the most brilliant shops: and the superb carriages of the rich with their freights of refined and elegant ladies, threaded their way among sections of the population so miserable and squalid that my heart ached at the sight of them. I had seen wealth. I had seen poverty. But never before had I seen the two so jammed together.

The descendants of the have-nots from those blackened, forbidding closes and courts are the people I remember as a child with their welcoming coal fires, street football and voices raised in song. Poverty is demeaning and dehumanising; it is not the squalor I miss but the cooperation born from a common identity and struggle.

Touched by the Hand of God

And I saw a new heaven and a new earth; for the first heaven and the
first earth were passed away, and there was no more sea. And I,
John, saw the holy city, new Jerusalem, coming down from God out
of heaven, prepared as a bride adorned for her husband.

St John the Divine, *Revelation* 21:1–2

Catty, Catty go to Mass,
Ridin on the divil's ass.
Proddy, Proddy on the wall,
A penny bun to feed yiz all.

Liverpool Irish Traditional rhyme

I have now taken the 1,200 steps from the Behemoth to Paddy's Wigwam
but still accept that the monarch cannot marry a Catholic. I believe in the
sacraments and an all-knowing and all-loving God, I recall little of the
Catechism but can confirm the purgatory of Sunday school and the
Harvest Festival. I believe in the resurrection and an afterlife, and have
fallen in love with Virgins and candles.

Gentle Jesus meek and mild, look upon this little child, suffer him to
come to thee and pity his simplicity . . . Hail Mary full of Grace, the Lord
is with thee, blessed art thou amongst women and blessed is the fruit of thy
womb Jesus . . .

Holy places are harder to find now, a bitter wind of non-belief is blowing
through the suburbs. Hope and love are still important here in Liverpool
but to understand the historical influence of religious sectarianism I have
had to take a choppy eight-hour ferry ride on the *Lagan King* from the
Twelve Quays Birkenhead to the Belfast Lough and the Bogside.

In 1795, the Protestant Peep O'Day Boys fought off a Catholic
onslaught at Dan Winter's Inn in Loughgall, County Armagh, in what
later came to be known as the Battle of the Diamond. This attack on the

'Ascendancy' led to a group of Loyalists setting up an organisation to protect themselves and their interests. It came to be known as The Loyal Orange Institution, in honour of the Dutch Protestant King William of Orange who had defeated the Catholic King James in the Battle of the Boyne on 12 July 1690. As many of the founder members were Freemasons, the early Orangemen adopted similar secret rituals including the mandatory Three Degrees. The 'Orange Degree' required the candidate to kneel blindfolded, swear allegiance to the Crown and take an oath that he would never marry a Catholic or a member of the Greek Orthodox Church. The sharing of a secret underpinned the ceremony, with the first clue provided in the song 'The Orange ABC':

> Q is for the Question you are asked at the door
> R is for the Road my boys some of you have trod before
> S is for the Secret you are sure there to find
> T is for Travels you will always bear in mind

The 'Marksman' or 'Purple Degree' derived from the elision of English scarlet and Scottish blue was created to exclude United Irishmen and plebeians. Finally, in 'The Royal Arch Purple' or 'the Two and a Half', an arcane reference to the tribes of Israel who refused to worship the Golden Calf, Orangemen empathise with the Old Testament Jews and regard themselves as the chosen people. Once this final stage had been completed, the candidate could claim to have 'ridden the goat', a cryptic reference to the initials of The Ark Of God written backwards.

Campaigns for political reform, the seeds of trade unionism and a challenge to the Church of England's claim to be the national church were all in the air when English and Scots soldiers who had helped to quell the 1798 rebellion started to spread the Orange movement to the mainland. The Act of Union increased the Roman Catholic electoral vote at a stroke by four million. England, a Protestant country rife with fear and loathing of Roman Catholics, would soon find itself host to thousands of destitute Irish fleeing the Great Potato Famine. The 'Roman trumpery' of rosaries, medals and adoration of the English Martyrs and Saints was considered the root of all evil. Protestant textile workers started to form civilian Orange Lodges in the Lancashire cotton-mill towns. They worried about the influential writings of the Oxford Ritualists who wanted to protect the Church of England from state intrusion, a debate that had opened up old sores relating to the true nature of the Anglican Church and resulted in several notable defectors to Roman Catholicism.

The First Grand Lodge in England was established in Manchester in 1808 following fighting between rival groups at an Orange procession. The early lodges met in local pubs and their members if challenged vehemently denied that they were anti-Catholic, stating that 'Orange men have no animosity to Papists as such but on the contrary respect every loyal man of that and of every other religious persuasion.' Most of their members, however, considered the Church of England an integral component of an ideal political system involving the English monarchy, Parliament and Constitution. The Orange Brigade soon came to be associated with ritual confrontations in the Lancashire cotton and West Riding woollen towns. Men dressed in ermine and pontifical robes carrying images of the lamb, the ark and the Bible marched to the music of 'Boyne Water' and were regularly attacked by a growing number of stone-throwing Irish Catholic immigrants.

Liverpool had a long pedigree of Nonconformism since its acclaim for the reign of William III of Orange and Mary after the Glorious Revolution. The Toxteth Puritans, originally from Bolton, had set up farms in the deer park and continued to support Protestant Succession and the Act of Settlement of 1701. They insisted on the sole inspiration of the Bible and a conviction of man's innate wickedness. When Bonnie Prince Charlie marched south in 1745, the garrison port came under threat, but the Jacobites were repulsed by the Liverpool Blues, a regiment funded by public subscription, and the Young Pretender was forced to flee back across the border. Once the uprising was over, a spike of anti-Catholic feelings encouraged a group of Liverpool seamen and carpenters to desecrate and burn down the town's only Catholic church. The jubilant Dissenters celebrated in the streets on Easter Sunday by waylaying ladies and tossing them in the air.

A collective conservative force made up of a Protestant caucus on the Liverpool council, the influential Orange Order and a cabal of Irish evangelical clergy led by an urbane talisman, the Reverend Hugh M'Neile, worked together to kindle animosity against Irish Catholics. To many Protestants embittered by poverty in Chisenhale, Smithfield and Milk Streets, the waterfront had become an unrecognisable foreign place.

Ninety thousand disinherited Irish had settled in the Exchange, Scotland and Saint Paul wards in the north, and around Great George, Toxteth and Pitt Streets on the south side. They also started to organise themselves through the secret ritualistic Ribbonism movement of Northern Ireland, and its more conciliatory official face, The Ancient Order of the Hibernians. These networks of friendship claimed 'to protect their emigrant brothers and sisters from all harm and temptation, so that they should be still known for their chastity all over the world'. In reality, they functioned as a very crude form of trade unionism, helping Catholics to corner a niche in the portside labour market. Religious organisations like the Sons of the Shamrock and the Knights of St Patrick helped the refugees to keep the faith and preserve their cultural identity. Local regional loyalties and private vendettas would eventually give way to sectarian violence. The Irish Catholics had redirected their frustrated anger away from their old English landlords to the Protestant bosses and the 13 Liverpool Orange Lodges and their 2,000 members. They had fled from poverty only to find themselves stranded in a brutal cesspit.

Membership of one of the growing network of Protestant Associations opened doors in many lines of work, and as a consequence Ulstermen had come to dominate certain shipbuilding trades. At a meeting of workers in 1840, Samuel Holme, a leading Conservative Liverpool builder, argued that to attack the Roman Catholic Church was justifiable:

> Popery is a double evil. It is a political evil, for it enslaves instead of giving liberty. It is a religious evil, for its creed is false and it withholds the scriptures from the people, for the Pope knows well that popery and the free circulation of God's holy word cannot be co-existent . . . Two antagonistic systems are struggling for ascendancy in Britain – the Church of England and the Church of Rome.

The 12th of July became known as 'Carpenter's Day' in Liverpool, acknowledging the Protestant Irish dominance of that part of the shipbuilding industry. During the 1841 parliamentary elections, the Apprentice Boys of Derry were on the streets with a flute band sporting the banners of the Royal Black Institution. Scuffles occurred between the supporters of the Tory Lords Sandon and Cresswell and the Irish who backed Palmerston. The carpenters threatened anyone sporting Whig colours and the homes of some Irish Catholics were attacked. The Tories attributed their ultimate election victory to the concerted Liberal attack on corporation schools through the Municipal Reform Act and the voters' sincere and ancient attachment to the Constitution, the House of Lords and the hereditary privileges that all Freemen of the realm enjoyed as their divine right. M'Neile had spoken out strongly against the proposed Whig secularisation of elementary schools that threatened withdrawal of the Bible, and had succeeded in currying so much public support that every Protestant child could instead be provided for in new Church of England schools. The priest of St Jude's Church also became a vociferous opponent of the Tractarian movement led by Newman and Pusey and the doctrine of the 'Invisible Church'. Despite being a pious controversialist, M'Neile's philanthropic initiatives did much good in Liverpool. One of his opponents, Edward Russell, also praised the Ulsterman's power of oratory:

> He made himself the leader of the Liverpool people, and always led with calm and majesty in the most excited times. His eloquence was grave, flowing and dignified in delivery, a perfection of elocution that only John Bright equalled in the latter half of the nineteenth century. Its fire was solemn force. M'Neile's voice was probably the finest organ ever heard in public oratory. His action was as graceful as it was impressive. He ruled an audience.

The Tory election victory and the growing tension in the streets about 'the conspiracy to return England to Rome' led to an attempt to reinstate the 12th of July walks. Carpenters from the Toxteth Orange Lodge formed a procession but were confronted by gangs of angry Irish dockers. A mob of Protestants led by a man wielding a carving knife ran down Mount Pleasant bellowing, 'We're Orangemen. We'll have no Popery. Down with the Popery Bible.' Large groups of Irish Catholics congregated on Tithebarn Street and Vauxhall Road and at dusk a serious riot broke out culminating in a concerted attack on the local bridewell. When fighting continued the following day in the South End, 400 special constables had to be sworn in.

Funerals were another opportunity to wear the sash, with large numbers of coat-trailing Orangemen strutting behind the Lodge Master's hearse through Irish Catholic ghettos. Sectarianism had become a fact of life, with the Irish generally regarded as the curse of Liverpool. They were seen to be slovenly, addicted to the demon drink and reluctant to move out and search for a decent living elsewhere. They came to be despised, the butt of cruel jokes and the recipients of national abuse. *Punch* published a piece claiming to have found the missing link between Neanderthals and *Homo sapiens* that it called the 'Irish yahoo':

It talks a sort of gibberish. It is, moreover, a climbing animal and may sometimes be seen ascending a ladder with a hod of bricks. The Irish yahoo generally confines itself within the limits of its own colony, except when it goes out of them to get its living. Sometimes, however, it sallies forth in states of excitement and attacks civilised human beings that have provoked its fury.

By the end of the nineteenth century, parts of Liverpool had become a bright and militant Orange, with the most partisan families living in Everton, Kirkdale, Edge Hill and the Dingle. Great Homer Street was the front line between Orange and Green. Most Protestants remained more concerned about the iniquities of Ritualism than Home Rule, the appalling crime levels or their own abject poverty. They were also worried about the growing Irish power base and looked to the Tories and the Reverend M'Neile's successors for help. The Protestant Association, the National Protestant League, the Churchman's Council and the Layman's League were all founded with the sole aim of destroying Anglo-Catholicism and the High Church. The carpenters found a new champion in George Wise, a rabble-rousing Evangelist from Bermondsey in London whose mentor was J.C. Ryle, the first Bishop of Liverpool. Under the patronage of one of the old Liverpool Tories, J.A. Bramley-Moore, Wise formed the British Protestant Union allegedly to fight Romanism, Ritualism and Infidelity. These issues, of little import to most of the country, had become matters of major political relevance in Liverpool, Belfast and Glasgow. The Orangemen staked out their territory with decorations on 12 July and, risking further civil disorder, insisted their walks be granted the freedom of the city. By then, Liverpool was bursting with male-only secret societies. They swore oaths, made rules, devised passwords and slunk into the night to seek out the enemy. Wise launched a Protestant Crusade against Roman Catholicism and wherever he and his Fifedrum band went they were met by fierce resistance from angry Catholics singing 'Faith of Our Fathers', 'The Boys of Wexford' and 'God Save Ireland'. It was not long before this flabby little man had become a Protestant folk hero, aided and abetted by the founder of the Protestant Truth Society John Kensit and the Wycliffe Preachers.

At the start of the twentieth century, Liverpool's Orange Lodge had 17,000 members. Most were skilled workmen who celebrated the anniversary of the siege of Londonderry and King William's birthday in public houses and with high-profile banquets in the city centre. The building of the Cathedral Church of Christ on St James Mount began in 1904, keeping Protestantism in the ascendancy. The docks and warehouses became a battleground for jobs and to be an Orangeman guaranteed patronage. Men of humble origins now had the opportunity to gain the kind of authority and respect held by mill owners in Lancashire. Without a strong sense of class community in Liverpool, the Protestantism and anti-Catholic Irish resentment filled the gap. Despite fines and court restrictions, George Wise continued to inflame Catholics with a series of meetings in Islington Square and Saint Domingo's Pit, on one occasion targeting Catholic priests who, he alleged:

> Waste their lives with harlots, they rob the poor to feed their own children; they are incarnate devils. The Saint ought to know what they are, I don't. Your Mass is gambled away. They live upon you and you know it. No man likes whiskey more than them. The monks in monasteries were living lives of devils. The Monks and Nuns live together in impunity.

As divisions deepened, Wise was imprisoned and used the experience for political ends, stirring the fires of unrest. In 1903, he won the Kirkdale seat at the municipal elections but was forced to give it up shortly after, following his appointment as pastor of the Protestant Reformer's Church on Netherfield Road. There, his Bible classes attracted more than a thousand people who heard him warn of the evils of alcohol and the virtues of an abstemious life. His church had a thriving Sunday school, the largest cycling club in town and provided a network of support for needy Protestants. All the while, acts of civil disobedience related to sectarianism continued to damage the city. Houses were marked to denote the religion of the occupants and religious cleansing continued on Netherfield and Scotland Roads. Newspaper advertisements for jobs would baldly state: 'No Roman Catholics or Jews need apply.' Catholics were derogatorily referred to as 'left footers' or 'coggers' and were said to have close-set eyes, whereas Protestants could be recognised by their use of fancy words. The bitter Transport Strike of 1911 aggravated the situation further. A last-ditch attempt at conciliation between the factions came to nothing and the Tories continued to play the Protestant card for political advantage.

Fighting was expected on Saint Patrick's Night, with 'No Popery' and 1690 graffiti seen on walls in Protestant strongholds. Gangs of youths threatened children on their way home, demanding, 'I or O?' – I standing for Irish and therefore Catholic, and O for Orange. If the answer offended the assailant's sensitivities, the unfortunate young victim arrived home with a bloody nose and torn clothes. The community was now segregated by a distrust that not even the First World War and the death of Wise in 1917 could break.

In the trenches of Normandy, Catholics and Protestants had no choice but to fight on the same side, but despite this unity the differences between them returned once they were back in Liverpool. Marriages between Catholics and Protestants invariably led to unhappiness, with the Catholic clergy going to extraordinary lengths to safeguard the souls of the unfortunate progeny. A hundred years of Orangeism had produced a vibrant Protestant working-class culture with its songs and a network of benefit clubs and burial societies. Netherfield Road continued to be a Protestant enclave, with Great Homer Street the front line for the Church of England community. On 12 July, the police would mass behind their barriers on 'Greaty' (Great Homer Street) as the bands marched down from Everton Valley. The parades were led by a pair of men carrying a colourful banner acclaiming the victory of the Boyne, stretched between two brass-tipped oak poles from which spilled silk cords to be clutched by following Orangemen. The white-gloved drum major would throw his silver-crested baton high in the air to signal the bass drummers to join the Fifes and kettle drums. The band took more than an hour to pass down Bostock Street, where it was greeted by the cheers of the Protestants and the jeers and catcalls from the Catholics. Behind the band came the Netherfield Road dry-land sailors, the Liverpool Scottish Regiment heralded by a skirl of bagpipes, veterans from the British Legion sporting the sash, women dressed in white and then the Apprentice Boys. Behind them were the nurses, the St Helens Miners and the Warrington brewers, the Knotty Ash Orange Lodge and the boy scouts; the march of a thousand rehearsed feet. At last the replica of King William III and the children dressed as William and Mary would appear, ringed by sword-bearing Scots and flanked by mounted policemen.

Pat O'Mara in his *Autobiography of a Liverpool Irish Slummy* describes the day a gang of his friends ventured up to Netherfield Road to watch:

> A crowd of our enemies (the Orangemen) with bands and banners carrying inscriptions that made our blood boil surged round us. Orange everywhere and not a bit of green! I had never known there were so many enthusiastic Protestants. I had always been brought up

to believe that Protestantism was a dying cult and its adherents cowards and easily frightened but this mob up here led by the magnificent white horse bearing a little boy dressed as a perfect duplicate of King William did not look frightened at all.

Neither side of the religious divide ever condemned this century-long mayhem and in the end football probably did more for unification in the city than either the Church or the city's politicians. Liverpool's two professional clubs both sprouted from Saint Domingo's Football Club, founded in 1878 as a recreational arm for the newly built Methodist church in Everton. It started to attract support from all over the city and moved to a new ground when it changed its name to Everton Football Club. In 1892, a rent dispute blew up, forcing some of the discontented club officials to move across Stanley Park, taking the name of Everton FC with them. This left John Houlding, a local businessman and Orange Unionist politician, and John McKenna, an Irish Freemason, with a football ground but no team. In their very first game against new rivals Everton, the newly named Liverpool FC fielded nine Irish Glaswegian 'Macs' from both sides of the religious divide who looked 'as likely a lot of raw-boned Scottish laddies as ever skipped over the thistles'. In the early years, all the board members of both clubs were staunchly conservative with a Scottish Methodist work ethic, and they maintained close links with one another. Every Saturday afternoon, the children of men who had sought refuge in Liverpool arrived in their droves to cheer on their team and their adopted city by the sea. Migrants looking for a new identity who had torn free from their roots to forge a different life in a strange place joined them in what became an unbreakable union of solidarity.

Now whenever I walk up Breck Road, I feel the divine passion of Christ's love and am overcome by a recurring vision where I am a little sunbeam wearing a crimson school cap and shining sandals and holding my mother's hand. Mother you are always there, full of pride at my small successes, with your infinite patience and healing hands, left alone now in those foreign parts with your sharpening memories. Your flat is full of echoes, talc, crucifixes, Paracletes, yesterdays, lavender water and recordings of young people's voices. Be careful, look after yourself, make sure you eat well, send me a letter when you arrive, and never lose that capacity for excitement on your birthday.

Gelton

When the Stranger says: 'What is the meaning of this city?
Do you huddle close together because you love each other?'
What will you answer? 'We all dwell together
To make money from each other'? Or 'This is a community'?
And the Stranger will depart and return to the desert.
O my soul, be prepared for the coming of the Stranger,
Be prepared for him who knows how to ask questions.

T.S. Eliot, choruses from *The Rock*

In spite of her Irish and Welsh underbelly, Victorian Liverpool had a very English feel. Her loyal Tory leaders rejected any notions of isolationism and emphasised Queen and Country in their public speeches. Much of the city's mercantile infrastructure and architecture was modelled on London, some districts received names like Islington, Kensington, Vauxhall and Whitechapel, and many leading merchants had second homes in the capital. More than any other English town, Victorian Liverpool had profited from recurrent cycles of boom and bust. The Western 'Emporium of Albion' and 'Second Metropolis' was better suited to venture capital and speculation rather than the mucky unimaginative world of manufacture and was proud of her place as a New World city.

Toryism in Liverpool was underpinned by a landlord mentality and sectarianism. Ship owning, commodity broking and marine insurance were now all part of her enterprise, and the 64th share divisions allowed the town's rich shopkeepers and manufacturers to dabble in the stocks of the smaller shipping companies. These commercial partnerships had also created economic and social networks that underpinned local politics. Sam Holme, a respected local master builder, helped to develop a populist identity based on Protestantism, protectionism and a one-nation philosophy. His support came mainly from the English riverside craftsmen and skilled Scots and Welsh labourers who resided in the inner suburbs. These Freemen, who worked as shipwrights, coopers, chandlers and carpenters, supported the Tories to a man and many were Orange Lodge members.

Another important chain of influence was the Irish Brigade, promoted through the eloquent sectarian speeches of the Reverend Hugh M'Neile, who invoked a libertarian struggle for a free press, an open Bible and independence of mind. To M'Neile, nobody was absolute or infallible and he viewed unlimited Irish migration as a major threat to the British way of life. Holme, on the other hand, realised the value of 'marginal privilege' and the pressing need for a cheap, willing labour force to carry out menial, low-paid jobs. Despite his vulgar background and exclusion from polite Liverpool society, Holme also embraced Roscoe's Florentine vision and pressed for the implementation of British engineering skills to rectify the tattered fabric and sanitation crisis, which had bedevilled his home town for the last 80 years.

Although Liverpool's old families had by now largely withdrawn from a direct role in local politics, they continued to provide large amounts of financial backing and as a consequence expected a big say in the Tory caucus. The new elite looked upon the city's poor as a separate society and almost as a different race. At dinner parties in the grand mansions of Aigburth, the ne'er-do-well rabble were often a matter of indignant outrage. The polyglot nature of many of the city's wards was considered an obstruction to civic progress and the city's elders did not find the town's nickname of 'The Marseilles of England' flattering. Although poverty was distressing and hopeless, it did not engender sympathy or serious concern. Discussion frequently centred on the inherent fecklessness of the Irish and the need for strict discipline in the workplace. In London, the poor were perceived as a serious threat to civil order after the dock strike and were referred to in the press as 'the people of the abyss' and 'the volcanic masses'. Through the Working Men's Conservative Association, the Tories reached into the Protestant-controlled port, while the Liberals used electoral pacts with the Irish Nationalists to gain an inside track to the Irish Catholic dockers in the South docks. This kept the ruling class well informed of any pockets of unrest on the waterfront and defused any concerns the Corporation leaders might have had of similar revolts in Liverpool. A caste system as intricate and complex as that in Bombay was now evident in this hungry town.

Liverpool gentlemen were considered to be adventurous and spirited if somewhat idle compared with the indefatigable endeavour of Manchester men. Many elegant big houses had gone up on the south side of the city and retirement mansions were built over the water in Caldy. The new halls and granges of Otterspool and Mossley Hill had adjoining dwellings for servants and usually a lodge cottage to guard the perimeter of the estate. The wealthy took the New Brighton and Seaforth waters and enjoyed the horse racing on Crosby sands. In letters to the press, they also expressed concern that Stephenson's Rocket, the victor of the Rainhill trials, would bring jumped-up riff-raff with ideas above their station from that grubby blue-collar place to the east. Manchester meanwhile continued to look upon Liverpool as a cancer where no one did a decent day's work. In 1825, the following ditty celebrating proposals to build the ship canal to Parkgate was sung to rapturous applause in the Theatre Royal:

> Alas then for poor Liverpool, she'd surely go to pot, Sir,
> For want of trade her folks would starve, her Custom House would
> rot, Sir.
> I'm wrong they'd not exactly starve or want, for it is true, Sir,
> They might come down to Manchester, and we could find them
> work to do, Sir.

Many of the new breed of successful entrepreneurs and parvenus who had amassed large bounties were not Liverpool-born. Some were adventurers from the European mainland who saw in Liverpool an exciting frontier town of limitless opportunity. Others had moved there from other parts of the North of England or come down from Scotland with a highly developed Calvinistic work ethic, sense of duty and social responsibility.

One such example was Henry Tate, born in 1819 at Terrace Mount in Chorley, the 11th child of a Geordie Unitarian Minister of the Dissenters chapel. His mother, Agnes Booth, born just the other side of the Pennines in Gildersome, could trace her Northern roots back to the twelfth century. Tate's father William opened a private school where he taught Chorley's poor children and his young son copperplate writing. On his 13th birthday, Henry was apprenticed to his elder brother Caleb in the grocery trade. The young man had inherited his father's industry, open-mindedness, altruism and curiosity, and so great was his drive and application that by the age of 20 he had risen to become a master grocer with his own shop in Old Haymarket, Liverpool. In 1847, he opened a second shop in Old Hall Street and quickly acquired a further property in nearby James Street. His next move was to expand across the Mersey and buy premises in Birkenhead, while taking control of the family's country shop in Ormskirk.

His sixth grocery store opened shortly afterwards in Fox Street and he then bought a wholesale base in Moor Street from where he could supply all his retail outlets through the James Street headquarters.

By the age of 36, he was a successful and respected Liverpool retailer but his restless mind now drove him on to new commercial challenges. Instead of focusing on the expansion of his grocery chain throughout the north-west, he found himself drawn to the lucrative but highly competitive sugar-refining business. The tropical addictions of rum and tobacco acquired by the old families had kindled the slave trade, but it was the lethal over-consumption of molasses by the English working classes that established the sugarocracies of the Industrial Revolution. The slave crop had become linked with power and a romantic sense of exotic danger. Secret metaphors of sex and pleasure were linked with the brute physical labour of Barbados as sugar blackened the teeth of the poor of Liverpool and Manchester.

Tate's entry into sugar in 1859 was stealthy but well conceived. The refineries of Birkett, Fairie, Sankey, Crosfield, Heap, Jager, Leitch, MacFie and Wright were already established and competition was tough. First, Tate bought a partnership in John Wright and Company in Manesty Lane (east of Paradise Street) and over the next two years learned his new trade. With the support and encouragement of his Scottish wife Jane, he decided to gamble all his profits on the favoured child of Liverpool capitalism, disposed of all his grocery stores and bought a small refinery in Earle Street.

The traditional method of sugar baking involved running the molten sticky brown liquor through bag filters and then through charcoal cisterns. The rapid degradation of the charcoal meant boiling water had to be flushed through the cisterns and charcoal periodically burned in the pipes to revitalise the filters and stop the sugar turning brown. In 1815, the introduction of animal charcoal (burnt bones) as a decolourising and refining medium improved the liquor, and around the same time a new type of pan, which operated in a partial vacuum at lower temperatures, helped to prevent caramelisation. Centrifugation was then used to remove the supernatant blended syrups and leave the prized dried yellow crystalline sugar in the vacuum pans.

Inside the boiling houses, a foul black crust covered the walls, with stalactites of sugar crystals hanging from the ceiling. Here, the new sugar men, many of them of Irish descent, worked long hours stripped to their waists in an oppressive heat, risking heatstroke and dehydration, or the chance of being boiled alive in a molasses vat. Several hundred boilers and bakers who understood 'the art and mystery of the trade' were lured from Hanover and Hamburg by good wages and liberal rations of beer. On any day, half a dozen men could be seen crawling like frogs over the moulds to stir the glutinous liquor with their bare hands. Small explosions were commonplace and the nauseating, clammy sweetness of sugar pervaded the neighbourhood.

The early years were hard for Henry Tate, and by the mid nineteenth century competition from Belgian, French and Dutch refiners, and the levy system that favoured European sugar-beet production, had started to drive some of the Liverpool refiners out of business. Tate realised modernisation was essential to success and approached John Wright and Company in Greenock to bring the efficient new Scottish centrifugation methods south of the border. By 1869, things had looked up, he had severed his partnership with John Wright and opened a large factory in Love Lane where he melted 400 tons of cane from Mauritius, Peru and the West Indies in the first year.

As he was preparing to install the Greenock machinery in his new refinery, he learned about the new lime-and-carbonic-acid French purification method invented by Boivin and Loiseau. Without compunction, he cancelled his Scottish order and purchased the new French process. This shrewd decision allowed him to increase production to 90 tons a week at Earle Street and within two years Love Lane had an output of 1,319 tons a week. He then negotiated a patent with the German Eugen Langen that would prove to be the most important business decision in his life. This new process allowed him to be the first in England to produce small dice-sized sugar cubes instead of the unpopular, wasteful loaves. Personal sacrifices still had to be made and a temporary cash shortfall left him with no alternative but to take his beloved daughter Isolina out of boarding school, but by 1874 the Love Lane refinery had become the successful hub of the Tate sugar baronetcy, employing 642 workers. The demand for refined sugar remained high and Tate next decided to build a second huge refinery in a deserted dockyard at Silvertown on the north bank of the River Thames.

Henry Tate never forgot the less fortunate or the social inequities of his youth. He remained humble despite his enormous wealth and engineered his many benefactions to do the greatest good for the largest number. He deplored slavery and invested in people with the aim of opening new cultural and humanitarian doors for all. While Liverpool had provided the workforce for many men to make mercantile fortunes, Tate's entrepreneurialism was in many ways more typical of the Manchester tycoons. When he eventually left Liverpool and moved south to Park Hill in Streatham, he was welcomed as a notable member of Britain's new industrial middle class.

The gift to the nation for which he will be most remembered is the National Gallery of British Art at Millbank on the Thames, downstream from Silvertown. The original exhibition included 65 paintings from his own collection. In Liverpool, he provided University College with a library block and built and furbished the Hahnemann Homeopathic Hospital. Tate took little part in public life and hated oratory, although he did sit briefly as a Liberal on Liverpool city council. At 77, he finally retired and shortly before his death reluctantly acceded to Lord Salisbury's importunities that he accept a baronetcy. Philippe Chalmin's account of the Tate & Lyle Company explains the success of Henry Tate as a Victorian industrialist:

> As a businessman, he possessed the essential gift of tenacity, an ability
> to take risks (and above all a knack for analysing situations rapidly),
> a talent for surrounding himself with the most competent men. He
> does not strike us as having been a 'leader' nor as having been
> endowed with any particular charisma or imagination . . . He was not
> known to harbour clear-cut political opinions and was never seen to
> take sides, even on sugar problems. A personality that is difficult to
> grasp therefore, but one which remains very original among the great
> figures of Victorian capitalism.

Another notable Liverpool opportunist was Joseph Williamson, who had moved from a small village near Barnsley first to Warrington and then on to Liverpool where he had risen to become a rich tobacco magnate. After the death of his wife, he began an extraordinary project on an old sandstone quarry, which would later earn him the nickname of 'the Mole of Edge Hill'. Over a 30-year period Williamson set 1,000 men to work to build a capacious subterranean banqueting hall and a vast labyrinth of brick-lined underground passages in an area to the east of where the Metropolitan Cathedral now stands. The men worked underground for hours on end in candlelight and were paid on the basis of how many children they had rather than on the number of red-and-blue wheelbarrows of rock they shifted in a day. Some of the more superficial arched underground structures on the sloping ground dropping down to Smithdown Lane served as gardens for the houses above, and a sweet shop was constructed above another. One gang of men unknowingly found themselves burrowing away below the line being built for the Liverpool and Manchester Railway. Williamson's vermiform tunnels were his sacred catacombs and perhaps his entry to heaven.

New millionaires like Tate and Williamson were magnanimous philanthropists who followed the example of the old families committed to the tradition of *noblesse oblige* good works, laid down in England by the aristocracy and the landed gentry. Monies were raised for public parks through the Steamship Owners and other trade associations. University College was opened in a disused lunatic asylum in the slums and became a seat of learning. Although most of these aspiring patricians had been resident in the town for a relatively short time, their public-spiritedness and commitment to civic duty gave them a cachet.

This new generation of self-made men had an outspoken contempt for scholars and thinkers, whom they derided as effete wastrels. Preoccupied with building fortunes, they made Liverpool a place to make money, not a place to live in; a cluttered port lacking beauty and elegance, overburdened with columns and pilasters.

Nathaniel Hawthorne arrived in Liverpool on the Cunard steamer *Niagara* in 1853 to take up his appointment as US Consul General. Hawthorne was a cautious, cultivated outsider described by one of his literary friends as a 'dark angel'. He considered most of the town's executives to be philistines, lacking in education and without cultural aspiration:

> As to the company they had the roughness that seems to be the characteristic of all Englishmen so far as I have yet seen them: elderly John Bulls. And there is hardly a less beautiful object than the elderly John Bull with his large body, protruding paunch, short legs and mottled, double-chinned, irregular-featured aspect. They are men of the world, at home in society, easy in their manners, but without refinement: nor are they especially what one thinks under the appellation of gentleman.

Hawthorne included the Stanleys in this description but excluded the Rathbones. The Stanleys were equally despised by much of the Liverpool gentry because of 'their arrogant and unsocial habits'. Hawthorne claimed that he had been told that the present Lord Derby had been expelled from Rugby School for stealing a five-pound note. The view in London was that Liverpool gentlemen were always tainted by their dialect and the vices of the common folk. R.A. McFie, one of Henry Tate's sugar rivals, was described in *Liverpool's Legion of Honour* in 1893 as:

> Sugar refiner, millionaire, social magnate, Presbyterian busybody, member of the Imperial Legislature was . . . not quite the giant intellect he would have the world believe. Clever in a sense he undoubtedly was, for during many years he managed a refinery so enormous that I scarcely dare to say how many hundreds of workmen there earned their living, and a business so widespread that its operations extended all over Europe. But apart from the influence this secured, he was merely a sensible gentleman and a great bore. Fond of speaking as he was, even the most patient listeners fled in terror from his orations.

The children of the rich were sent away to England's most exclusive public schools, where competitive ball games were being encouraged on the premise of 'a healthy body, healthy mind'. These forms of recreation had their roots in raucous melees staged in country villages, but had been restructured for the sons of gentlemen on playing fields and imbued with the ethos of fair play. At Harrow School and Eton College, a kicking game referred to as Socker appeared, which in a short time would rise to become the national sport. Through the long arm of the British Empire, this new game spread to all corners of the globe and came to be known as Association Football. By the turn of the nineteenth century, the game had also become the opiate of the working man. Liverpool was acknowledged as a football city to such an extent that Lord Birkenhead commented that any attempt to ban the game there would lead to misery, depression, sloth, indiscipline and even civil disorder. An article in *The Field* magazine hinted at impending professionalism, stating: 'In the North of England the game is often played in a very different spirit and at times the desire to win leads to great unpleasantness . . .'

Liverpool remained in Tory hands throughout the nineteenth century, resisting any return to Liberalism and fiercely defending the vested interests of Protestants. The Irish had their family and the Pope, the Jews their traditions and the blacks their music, but they were all considered visitors with no permanent share in the city. Optimism was so great that one local writer prophesied the port's quays would stretch all the way to Manchester, surrounded by elegant squares, vibrant mills and bustling offices. From the marble-ledged gallery of the Exchange, one looked down on a buzzing swarm of cotton merchants negotiating prices for the Lancashire mills, and the brokers moving purposefully between the easels and slates covered with telegrams giving notices of London stocks and the latest sailing times.

Peter Ellis's skyscraper Oriel Chambers had been standing for more than 20 years before the Windy City across the water joined the bandwagon. George Stephenson's Liverpool and Manchester Railway was the first passenger and freight railway service in the world and consolidated the north-west's already burgeoning self-belief. Merseyside was throbbing with energy and vitality and at times it seemed as if Liverpool was on her way to becoming the wealthiest city in the world. Unfortunately, despite this growing affluence and the investment of wealth in art and culture, Roscoe's Medici dream remained unfulfilled, and in 1875 the Nonconformist liberal Philip Rathbone bemoaned the continuing failure of the city to recognise the importance of art to municipal life:

> It is for us, with our vast population, our enormous wealth (as a town), but without either politics or philosophy that the world will care to preserve, to decide whether we will take advantage of our almost unequalled opportunities for the cultivation of Art, or whether we shall be content to rot away, as Carthage, Antioch and Tyre have rotted away, leaving not a trace to show where a population of more than half a million souls once lived, loved, felt and thought. Surely the home of Roscoe is worthy of a better fate?

As the Victorian era finally ended, the old guard had all but been absorbed by public companies and corporations, leaving their legacy only in the names of docks, streets and public buildings and a persisting rhetoric, which proclaimed Liverpool as an important world force. The rich had stopped attending church, their daughters attended London balls rather than the Wellington Rooms, and many of the big houses were sold off as one by one their owners started to desert the town where they had made their money. The general view amongst the wealthy was that public-spiritedness and charity would never solve the city's social inequalities, and local and central governmental taxation seemed the right way forward.

Despite these social changes, the city's star continued to rise, her brash New World architecture reinforcing her feeling of imperial superiority. Queen Victoria had been elevated to an Empress and the business of Liverpool continued to be business. From what in truth was a putrid sewer, there flowed a sea of pure gold. Liverpool was the fulcrum for Britain's mercantile enterprise. Elder Dempster and Company that had started life as the African Steamship Company had built up a flourishing freight and passenger business with the Gold Coast (Ghana) and Nigeria, while the Blue Funnel Line run by Alfred Holt had formed a vertically integrated group of companies in the Far East. Holt, from rural Lincolnshire, ruefully commented that in Liverpool, 'mankind is like a lot of hungry pigs fighting over a trough of milk.' The 'Second City of the Empire' had been granted governmental city, university and diocesan status and its prosperous waterfront had adapted to the challenges of protectionism, the hazards of mercantile speculation and the threat of the Manchester Ship Canal.

It was no mean city.

The Royal Liver Building had gone up by the Mersey waterfront in 1911, inspiring a legend that if the copper Liver Birds ever left their roosts on its clock towers, Liverpool would cease to exist. While the Mother of Liverpool bird scans the water for the arrival of sailors, her male partner has his back turned on his mate to look towards the pubs and football stadiums.

Bald eagles perched on each corner of the Cunard Palace, where film stars and actors deposited their luggage before their 3,000-mile crossing to America. The Third Grace completing this now world-renowned Liverpool waterfront was the affluent Port of Liverpool Building, Edwardian home of the Mersey Docks and Harbour Board. The port was handling more than a third of Britain's exports and a quarter of its imports. In 1886, Wavertree hosted the International Exhibition of Navigation, Commerce and Industry, an honour that reflected the town's position as one of very few global commercial centres. In 1905, The Olympia, with its regal balconies, Indian panelling and proscenium stage modelled on the Kirov Ballet Theatre, opened on West Derby Road. The enthralled audience waited nervously for the lions and elephants to be hoisted up into the auditorium and strained their necks to admire the aerial courage of The Flying Hendersons.

Liverpool is an unidentifiable red-brick Victorian certainty but it is also a community where I am trying to construct continuity from jumbled fragments and make ties with the ocean and the world outside. I am trapped by the town's mad avarice but am not ready to submit to the sea's pull for that last risky voyage to America or Africa.

The town, with its crowded arcades and haunted buildings, still holds me firm like a close family, and today a few lengths in Woolton baths is enough to close off my ears and carry me away in quietness.

Dock Road

Though there is a harbour into which
it is best never to find the way,
a sea-route it is best
never to follow,
fate and chance meetings will always
undo reason.
Extract from 'Ghost Ship' by Brian Patten

In the seventeenth century, a handful of small sailboats which travelled from Liverpool to the Isle of Man, Drogheda and Ravenglass were moored in the estuary's deep natural harbour, three miles from the sea. They keeled over at low tide or were left high on the flat shoreline. A bottleneck in the estuary forced the water to run faster, creating a deep channel in the narrows: when the sea came in, it buffeted the stranded vessels with 'a wild raging beast of a river' and the tumultuous swell created by the ebb of seven knots. Boats were forced to anchor in the Pool, in the lee of the Castle, or worse out in the river, where the unloading of cargo was carried out piecemeal by a precarious convoy of rowing boats.

A bridge was then built over the tidal inlet and a small harbour and quay were constructed between the old Paradise Street and what is now the entrance of the Mersey Tunnel. As the number and size of the boats increased, the need for a mole and a longer quay on the flat riverbank became a matter of urgency. Rubbish and ballast dumped in the Pool created additional hazards for the increasing number of ships.

Liverpool had become a free and independent busy little port and on 3 November 1708 her council sanctioned the building of a dock at the Pool's mouth. Under the direction of Thomas Steer, dredging and buoying of Rock Channel began and the first wet dock controlled by floodgates was completed in 1715. Its large basin at the east end of the town channelled the Mersey into a south-facing opening so that the craft entering from the river were protected from the rise and fall of the tide. Ships were now sheltered from north-westerly gales by the growing shadow of the town and the surrounding Welsh hills. 'They have made a great wet dock, for laying up their ships, and which they greatly wanted,' wrote Daniel Defoe in 1725:

> for though the Mersey is a noble harbour, and is able to ride a thousand sail of ships at once, yet those ships that are to be laid up or lie by the walls all winter, or longer, as sometimes may be the case; must ride there, as in an open road, or (as the seamen call it) be haled ashore; neither of which would be practicable in a town of so much trade. And in the time of the late great storm they suffered very much on that account.

Over the next 50 years, the docks of Canning, Salthouse, George, Duke, King's and Coburg were constructed and stretched out from the Old Dock. In 1826, Steer's Dock was filled in to build the Custom House and 20 years later the town's engineer Jesse Hartley, a rough diamond with grand ideas from Pontefract in Yorkshire, constructed the granite Albert Dock with its inventive connecting passages, hydraulically powered Pump House and what became the world's first enclosed dock system. Before high water, the dock gates would be thrown open and the dock master would bawl his commands to his minions as a queue of vessels jockeyed with one another in order to be the first to dock.

The 150-mile Leeds to Liverpool Canal connected Stanley Dock to the River Aire for barges transporting coal and wool across the Pennines. Then the Liverpool and Manchester Railway linked the port to 'Cottonopolis' in what would become an enduring love–hate relationship. Stretched along the northern shoreline was an uninterrupted seven-and-a-quarter-mile plateau of granite and sandstone wet docks, fronted by warehouses filled with hardware, railway parts, casks of ale, muslin-wrapped cheese, pottery, iron bars and reels of wire. With heavy gates, monotonous walls and stone piers, these towns within towns represented the new Liverpool: the Ganges and the St Lawrence were the Mersey's tributaries and almost half of Britain's imports were being handled in the 'Port of a Thousand Ships'.

The port's interconnecting alleys and streets filtered down towards the docklands to keep cargoes on the move. Goods were shifted from the waterfront to the bustling storehouses and factories, and it was from there that one could savour the town's intoxicating opulence. Liverpool had become a maritime giant, close to the pinnacle of the food chain and sensitive to vicissitudes in the world's economic temperature.

From the river basin, the docks were entered through a water gate flanked by pier heads. At low tide, the moored vessels would be 20 feet higher than those queuing on the river. The waterfront became a rainforest of masts: a sombre Scottish brig, a sturdy emigrant barque with its flock of Welsh shepherds bound for New Holland, and a teak country ship stashed with Egyptian cotton could be observed, all neatly docked side by side. Small black salt droghers with red sloop sails worked the passenger ships; tidy, broad-hulled, flat-bottomed galliots ferried cargo between the Pool and Rotterdam. A symphony of brigantines, colliers, steamboats and schooners ploughed up and down the river. The Princes Dock, berth for the New York packets, was immured by a narrow jetty of masonry and a barricade of walls. Tiers of hillside dwellings, their chimneys rising like minarets and church spires, topped a girdle of masts.

From John Atkinson Grimshaw's detailed landscape paintings of gas-lit puddles and shadowy moonlit booms, I learned to appreciate the endless comings and goings of the port and the romance of those silent sailing ships. The Leeds railwayman clerk's beautiful nocturnes helped me to divine Ship Street in all its Victorian glory.

The rowdy Dock Road and surrounding lanes pulsated with the ring of prosperity: the banter of carters mingled with the shouts of coach-drivers and the shrill cries of flower girls. Teams of sweating Flemish draught horses rose sparks as they lugged heavily laden wagons over the stone setts. Wheeled platforms piled high with bales of raw cotton, sacks of sugar, tobacco and grain, kegs of rum and baulks of timber were forever being pulled in barrows, wagons and four-wheeled drags between dock and the cyclopean ramparts of the warehouses. A brown double layer of horse dung marked the route from Bootle to Garston.

The French historian Hippolyte Taine visited the Mersey docks in 1863 and marvelled at their enormity, scope and ingenuity:

> Over six miles of its length canals open into it, carrying shipping into the basins, which are lined with stone and put one in mind of rectangular, aquatic streets multiplied and ramified into a whole town. Here ships are loaded, unloaded and repaired. Their crowded masts appear like a leafless, winter-bound forest extending as far as the eye can see and barring the whole horizon to the north – The spectacle of the Liverpool docks is, I think, one of the greatest in the whole world.

Liverpool Corporation had been building new docks since the early eighteenth century and by the beginning of the nineteenth its dock committee had started to transform into a semi-independent trust. After a period of sustained and unrelenting pressure from the Lancashire and Cheshire merchants, the London ship owners and Parliament, it was forced to replace the Dock Trustees with the Mersey Dock and Harbour Board, an institution which over the next hundred years was destined to become as much part of the fabric of the waterfront as the ships, sailors and dockers. It was argued that however well the docks were run, Liverpool could not be allowed to exploit its position as a major seaport by overtaxing one of England's most vibrant regional economies. The new board took over immediate responsibility for the upkeep of the lower Mersey and Birkenhead docks, the Creetown quarries in Scotland and more than a hundred miles of rail track. Large sections of the dock estate were hurriedly reconstructed in anticipation of changes in maritime trade. The Board capitalised on 'The Great Victorian Boom' and the growth of steam shipping, and its standing was so great by the turn of the century that it was able to move its vast battalions of clerks from the Old Custom House to an impressive new domed cathedral of commerce on the banks of the Mersey. The Dock Office, now known as the Port of Liverpool Building, was the first of the Three Graces, with its Baroque octagonal hall and galleries adorned with Portland stone, Danzig oak and Calacata marble. Inscribed under the lowest tiers of its arches are the words from Psalm 107: 'They that go down to the sea in ships, that do business in great waters; these see the works of the LORD and his wonders in the deep.'

The Liverpool and Birkenhead docks were now the largest port system in the world run by a single organisation and it was widely acknowledged that Liverpool had led the way in creating a successful cohesive system for port management.

As the twentieth century dawned, the dock estate comprised 40 wet docks, 1,600 acres and 35 miles of riverfront. The skyline was as monumental as the Pyramids or the Great Wall of China. Hartley's granite and lime lagoons were 35 ft deep, 40 ft high and 10 ft thick. The town's steamships were shifting one sixth of the whole of the world's cargo. The seaport had become the world's greatest cotton market and Stanley Dock boasted a 14-storey tobacco warehouse.

Liverpool was one of four global centres for trading in grain, and its futures contracts always most closely represented world figures. Multitudes of officious, hurrying men prepared invoices, weighed and measured packages and lugged merchandise to a soundtrack of shanties, dock-masters' barking and the whinny of workhorses. Bales, boxes, cases and crates were ever on the move from iron quayside sheds to waiting trucks. The Birkenhead cannon boomed across the water and the dredgers with clanking hoppers sifted the Mersey silt. The Mersey Docks and Harbour Board was in control of a system that had no rival. Using Scottish granite from the Board's own quarries, large sections of the network had been reconstructed to adapt to the rapid changes occurring in maritime commerce. The great wet and graving docks now included the Albert, Alexandra, Brocklebank, Brunswick, Canada, Clarence, Gladstone, Herculaneum, Hornby, Huskisson, Langton, Princes, Sandon, Stanley, Trafalgar, Victoria, Wapping, Waterloo, as well as the Morpeth, Egerton, Wallasey, Alfred, Great Float, Victoria and Bidston docks across the water. The electric Liverpool Overhead Railway, which opened in 1886 and ran from Herculaneum dock in the south to Alexandra dock in the north and carried thousands of dockers to work each day, replaced the horse-driven trams. The seven-mile journey now took just half an hour. As the port grew, it had begun to wall itself off from the town.

A crowd of men inextricably linked with port life met each new merchant vessel. The master stevedore was the first on board to discuss the unloading of the cargo, with the riggers waiting to unbutton the hatches and top derricks. The Customs officials were too soon at work, beavering for contraband, while the Port Health Officials secured assurances that there were no contagious sailors aboard. A tailor's runner with his tape measure and an insurance broker with bargain deals hovered around hoping to waylay the departing officers. Various union representatives barred the sailors' escape until they had coughed up their subs. For those confined to ship, bumboats ferried in badly needed comestibles and provisions. A few linked industrial exploits including a match works, tannery and dye factory appeared in the suburbs: at its peak, the port provided a service industry for up to 60,000 such people. This was an age, however, when to be away from sea, or away from war, was almost a disgrace. All that was left for the land-locked scalers, warehousemen, chandlers and riggers was to decide whether a hospital ward or a threadbare bedroom was the best place to die.

Despite this growing prosperity and the effectiveness of the dock estate, wages for the workers had dropped by 10 per cent and there was growing indignation in the ranks. Thousands of Liverpudlians were famished, frozen and ill, forced to queue for farthing bowls of soup at the Clarion van with its slogan 'Socialism: a system of government that will make poverty impossible.'

Ben Tillett and Tom Mann formed a Strike Committee made up of a loose trade union of 30 allied bodies called the National Transport Workers Federation and marched on the eastern plateau of Saint George's Hall. Tillett was born in Bristol and had worked as a sailor before moving to London to work on the docks. In conflict with many of his comrades, he was a strong supporter of Britain's involvement in the Great War and was acutely aware of the working man's scepticism of socialism. He grumbled that if Labour could elect a king 'he would be a feminist, a temperance crank, a Nonconformist charlatan . . . an anti-sport, anti-jollity advocate, a teetotaller, as well as a general wet blanket.' He also detested the class distinctions in the docks between shipmen and porters and the patronising skilled and unskilled categories. Mann, in contrast, was a colliery clerk's son from Coventry who had trained as an engineer. He was introduced to socialism by his foreman and started to educate himself through the writings of William Morris and John Ruskin. In 1886, he read Karl Marx's *The Communist Manifesto* and became a Marxist determined to destroy capitalism through militant politics. His religious beliefs were as strong as his politics and he organised support from Anglican organisations like The Salvation Army during strikes. The Seafarers' Unions demanded a minimum working wage, an end to the demeaning medical examinations, and a conciliation board. The Shipworker's Federation flatly refused their demands. The dispute escalated when the crew of the White Star liner *The Baltic* demanded a pay increase of one pound a month and declined to sign articles for their next voyage. Five hundred sailors were soon refusing to work and the Liverpool Dock Strike was underway.

Tom Mann arrived in Canning Place to support the men under a banner of 'War declared: Strike for Liberty.' The fragmentation on the waterfront was put to one side and both the Catholic dockers and Protestant carters refused to unload *The Pointer*, which was now manned by blacklegs. The Federation was reluctantly forced to agree to recognise the legality of the syndicate but most of the dockers rejected the settlement and the government began to prepare for military intervention. For three months, nothing moved in the city and piles of rotting food littered the baking summer streets. As a national crisis loomed, Mann, in a series of last-ditch meetings, managed to persuade the resentful men to accept their gains and return to work. No sooner had they gone back than the porters from the Lancashire and Yorkshire Railway came out, demanding more pay as a wave of unrest spread through the city's workforce.

A young girl called Elizabeth Bamber had accompanied her mother to Tom Mann's mass protests. It had opened her eyes to the growing political struggles of her hometown, and later, under her married name of Bessie Braddock, she would become a redoubtable rebellious fighter for the workers. Much later, after she was elected as a Labour MP, she recalled her childhood: 'I remember the faces of the unemployed when the soup ran out. I remember blank hopeless stares, day after day, week after week, all through the hard winter of 1906–7.'

Mann and Tillett then led a further large demonstration of 100,000 workers on St George's Plateau but the strikers were confronted by armed troops from the Warwickshire Regiment and massed ranks of policemen. Fist fights broke out, the police baton charged the malnourished strikers, leaving broken glass, wooden planks, iron nuts and stones in their wake. Resistance continued behind barricades north of Lime Street, an attempt to storm the police station then occurred and some workers attacked the Black Marias. Two protesters were shot on 'Bloody Sunday', tramcars were wrecked and property looted. The Riot Act was read but did nothing to stop the numerous further confrontations between police and public. The ship owners dug in and locked out 20,000 dockers. Lord Derby informed the Home Secretary, Winston Churchill, that it was the Lord Mayor of Liverpool's opinion that a full-scale revolution was taking place. The events were reported in the press as a 'Nightmare for Civilisation' and the work of 'The Crimson Flag of Anarchy'.

The naval cruiser HMS *Antrim* was anchored in the Mersey with its guns trained on the town, and 260 troops from the South Yorkshire Regiment were sent to Everton where they were met by a hail of bottles and slates. After the funerals of the two dead men, one a Catholic docker and the other a Protestant carter, a General Strike was called. The rank and file, under the leadership of Tom Mann, took control of much of the city and organised massive peaceful picketing. Two hundred thousand workers now supported the strike. After desperate last-ditch arbitration and mediation together with a great deal of special pleading, the Liberal government managed to get the trades union leaders to try to persuade the obdurate workers to go back. A year later, the Conservative Prime Minister Neville Chamberlain described Liverpool as a 'bastion of the working class' and a 'hotbed of militancy'.

Just as things had started to calm down, the police went on strike because a constable's pay had fallen below that of the lowly dock rat. The army and a cohort of hurriedly conscripted reinforcements were forced to guard the streets from looters on London Road. When the strike was over, the Watch Committee refused to reinstate any officer who had gone out on strike. Winston Churchill reflected the prevailing view of the 1911 riots when he later stated in Parliament: 'You need not attach great importance to the rioting last night. It took place in an area where disorder is a chronic feature.'

The preponderance of foreign sailors living on the waterfront had not led to a homogeneous society and the South End became increasingly divided from the rest of the waterfront on racial grounds. Ethnic and social hierarchies emerged within individual streets and the cosmopolitan mosaic did not lead to tolerance or inclusiveness. A new school of Liverpool-Irish writers that included James Hanley, James Phelan and George Garrett started to explore the dislocation and alienation that came from a life at sea. Thousands of white soldiers returned from the Normandy trenches in 1919 to find themselves unemployed. Resentment against foreigners mounted and led to racial tension with waves of violence. Mobs of angry veterans attacked 'palm boat' sailors in the streets and a few foreign sailors were stabbed on their way home. A pogrom began in the Mill Street area led by groups of soldiers, sailors and rebellious youths, many of whom resented the black man's success with 'their women'. The Elder Dempster and David Lewis Hostels for black ratings were ransacked and buildings in Parliament Street, Chester Street and Stanhope Street were set alight. Toxteth Park was reported in the local press to be 'in a wild state of excitement with thousands of people filling the thoroughfares'. Seventy men who sought refuge in the Ethiopian Hall were transferred in Black Marias to the Cheapside bridewell for their own protection. A lynch mob of servicemen stoned Charles Wooten, a young Trinidadian seaman living in Upper Pitt Street, before the police intercepted them. The mob tore the terrified man away from the officers and threw him to his death into the waters of Queen's Dock with heartless cries of 'Let him drown' echoing round the quayside.

The authorities took 700 endangered black people to the bridewell for their own safety. They were, according to Liverpool's Lord Mayor, 'an irritation that needed to be removed'. At the height of the rioting, the *Liverpool Courier* poured flames on the situation with an editorial entitled 'Black and White', demanding swift police action against the black scoundrels:

One of the chief reasons of popular anger behind the present disturbances lies in the fact that the average negro is nearer the animal than is the average white man, and there are women in Liverpool who have no self respect . . . The white man regards the negro as part child, part animal and part savage . . . It is quite true that many of the blacks in Liverpool are of a low type that they insult and threaten respectable women in the street, and that they are invariably unpleasant and provocative.

The besieged blacks retaliated, with razor attacks on whites by West Indians and the ransacking of the Scandinavian Home in Great George Square by African seamen. Many of the local police blamed the mayhem on outsiders, affirming that people in Liverpool got on well with the black community. A number of black labourers were sacked at Tate & Lyle when whites refused to work with them. The trades unions insisted that whites be reinstated first, with even Scandinavian seamen being given preference over the locals from Pitt Street. 'The Homes for Heroes' propaganda had been slow to materialise for black veterans, with a colour bar now in place in many waterfront businesses. The 'Aliens Order' was used unfairly to deport 'troublemakers' who were unable to provide documentary evidence of British citizenship despite having fought with courage and distinction for their country. Black English servicemen were even denied the chance to join in London's victory celebrations.

By the end of the Great War, the hidden population of 'Dark Town' had risen to 5,000 and those lucky enough to find work in the sugar refineries had moved their families inland to the Granby, Arundel, Abercrombie and Smithdown wards. The Colonial Office introduced a repatriation scheme in which two pounds would be offered to cover outstanding debts and five pounds given as a resettlement grant to any black British subjects who wished to return to the colonies. The Elder Dempster Line, which had grown out of Laird's African Steamship Company, repatriated 100 black sailors to West Africa in 1919. Elder Dempster maintained its hostel for African sailors in Upper Stanhope Street until 1925, with its deckhands retained at twelve shillings and denied any chance of British citizenship.

Liverpool was officially wedded to the sea in front of a large crowd on a platform on the Pier Head. Sir Archibald Savidge related how the city had always earned her living from the ocean and had overcome the fast tides to become a port of worldwide importance; he then threw a heavy gold-covered bronze ring into the water. The Lady Mayor asked the citizens of Liverpool to pray silence to the memory of those of every land who lay sleeping in the deep and praised the sacrifice of the city's seamen before she dropped a wreath of laurel into the Mersey. This was the only Venetian tradition to enter the history of Liverpool.

At the opening of Gladstone Dock in 1927 – 'the greatest dock the world had ever known' – the Lord Mayor reminded the city that Liverpool was not just a terminus for cruise liners but that its lifeblood flowed out of the docks. The city was still laying down new tidemarks. Twenty thousand men were employed in casual labour in the port. 'Mammoth', the world's largest floating crane, had arrived as a conciliatory post-war gift from Germany, and Bryant and May had built a new match factory near Garston Docks, supplied by a steady flow of top-heavy Baltic timber ships.

Argon flashes, choking fumes and the sound of the hammering of red-hot rivets were the signatures of Grayson's shipyard, with smoke from outbound freighters hanging low on the horizon. Lever Brothers took copra off the Bank Line ships and palm oil from the monkey boats, and with the help of St Helens alkali turned it into soap. Rank and Spiller ground the Canadian grain for Crawford's biscuits. Heaps milled basmati rice arriving from Burma and India, and Evans Medical synthesised concoctions, pills and tinctures from the herbs, spices and seeds arriving from the Orient. The world's finest timbers were stacked up in sheds within the dockland archipelago, waiting to be transformed by master carpenters and cabinetmakers into quality furniture.

The National Dock Board required battalions of clerks and administrators to oversee the dredger crews, rail men from the Dockers Umbrella, pier masters, and controllers of the water hydraulic lines and pump houses. Armies of boilermakers, shipwrights, iron moulders and blacksmiths all essential for the maintenance and smooth running of the lock gates and busy cranes also came under its administrative wings. Its marbled and mahogany offices had become the pacemaker for Liverpool's heartbeat. The other side of the Dock Road was full of bustling private warehouses, retailers, processing factories, flourmills, gasometers and railway tracks.

Working conditions in the docks remained arduous and employment in the port was still considered the 'last refuge of the unfortunate'; the dock rat was 'the Lazarus of the working class'. It was claimed a docker required the mechanical resource of an engineer combined with the agility and cunning of a ring-tailed lemur. Liverpool's overdependence on its port was acknowledged in government circles and some token initiatives were made to give it a broader-based economy. British Insulated and Helsby Cables (known locally as 'The Automatic'), which produced telephone-exchange equipment in Edge Lane, was one firm that took advantage, and a number of munitions factories also sprouted up.

Each ship owner handled their own porterage in a deliberate ploy designed to fragment the workforce and reduce the risk of strikes. Here, an element of sectarian geography remained, with a Catholic north controlling the liners and a Protestant south shifting cargo for independent firms. The men were expected to work on piece rates, fast and with no regard to their own safety. A few shippers had their regulars who were well rewarded and treated kindly but casual engagement was the norm. The ritual remained unchanged for decades: the men would arrive outside the dock at the crack of dawn and be herded into one of eleven pens where they would fight and climb over one another to get the bowler-hatted foreman to 'take their book'. As the foreman walked the line he would bark, 'Face up,' and start to tap the selected men on the shoulder or growl, 'You and you,' as useless shouts of, 'Hey la', remember your old school mates!' and, 'I've got four kids at home, give us a job!' echoed round the bleak waterfront. Familiar faces the 'putter-on' already trusted were invariably picked (as his job was on the line too and he couldn't afford to take risks with strangers), leaving young men and new arrivals little chance of regular work, even when they carried the statutory 'button and tally'. When the port was busy, these 'blue eyes' got four days' work a week, but even for them work was sporadic, arduous and dangerous. The unfortunate rejects would head for a greasy spoon like Frank's Café or the British Workman's Public House opposite Huskisson Dock, to wait over mugs of cocoa, coffee and tea for the afternoon stand later in the day. After a second rebuttal, they'd drift home grey-faced to greet their wives with, 'There's nottun down for ya, girl.'

Dockers worked in gangs, with each man delegated a specific role. The 'holdsmen' stowed or unloaded the cargo while the 'winchmen' operated the derricks, with the 'man at the rail' (usually the oldest man) acting as coordinator. A constant stream of traffic ran down the Dock Road, with runners' traps, battered vans, cabs, lorries and dock trains ferrying the world's commodities to their resting point. Inside the docks the cries of the weighers, checkers and markers were almost drowned out by the rattle of winches and the groaning of cranes.

Men who came in without social status were forced to develop other qualities to gain the respect of their colleagues. Some learned to fight, others to sing or play an instrument and some became comedians and clowns. Dark humour was a form of self-defence and laughter the only affordable pleasure. A banter called 'dockology' emerged. New arrivals that couldn't 'take the mick' or 'have the skit taken out of them' were frozen out. No man on the docks had just one name; surnames were abbreviated or lengthened and nicknames that recalled a funny incident, a memorable fight, or a relationship were common. 'Stanley Matthews' was the docker who joined others to lift a cargo with the words 'I'll take this corner.' 'Wedding Cake' was any man who had been married more than once, and 'The Drunken Caterpillar' for the man seen crawling out of The Cabbage pub every night. Any foreman who kept saying, 'Cut it out lads,' became 'The Surgeon'. 'Van Gogh' was forever putting his men in the picture, while 'The Sheriff' always wanted to know about the hold-up.

To outsiders, the city's docks were grim places inevitably surrounded by slums with, as J.B. Priestley wrote:

> Trams whining down long sad roads; a few stinking little shops; pubs with their red blinds down and an accumulation of greasy papers under their windows; black pools and mud and slippery cobblestones; high blank walls; a suspicious policeman or two.

Tom Mann, the former leader of the Dock Strike, was now right behind the Republican cause in the 1936–9 Spanish Civil War. Although he was not allowed to fight on grounds of his advanced age, a unit of the International Brigade fought with gallantry under the name 'The Tom Mann Centuria'. Mann was not alone; there were many like-minded men fighting for a decent living and better working conditions in the Liverpool docks. Some had read widely and become committed to their side in the class struggle. The 'Coke' (The Cocoa Room) on the Dock Road with its wet nellers (slabs of fruit cake) and mugs of soup became a forum for revolutionary talk.

The strikes and lockouts united the dockers when in 1947 the National Dock Labour Scheme introduced a register that began 'decasualisation'. The 'welt', a practice allowing dockers to share a job, was controversial but widespread. One man went to work while another stayed home, giving both three idle days and qualifying them for state benefit under the Unemployment Insurance Act. The same year, a group of Liverpool seamen delayed the *Queen Mary* in New York Harbour in protest against the proposed rationalisation of work practices designed to enforce rigid terrestrial-based time measures. By 1954, Liverpool was riddled with squabbles related to casualism and working practices. Her 25,000 dockers equated their own trade union leaders with the Mafia when they branded their action as a 'strike of Teddy boy dissidents'.

Left-wing Labour MP Eric Heffer recalled the post-war dock cafes as political seminaries, where hundreds of flat-capped men attended meetings on the Dock Road with hooks over their shoulders to debate trade-union issues.

Nearby, the Russian icebreaker *Lenin* was being overhauled in a graving dock where boilermakers had a working practice, won during the Depression, of an agreed ratio of helpers to craftsmen. *Lenin*'s increasingly impatient Russian captain complained to the management that the job was overmanned and his Liverpool workforce lazy. The brusque reply was: 'We can do nothing about that la'. There are too many communists here.'

Perhaps a more accurate term would have been 'natural seafaring democrats with a strong sense of loyalty and fellowship'. No wonder Gorky had called the Odessa waterfront his university. On the day Nye Bevan died, Heffer was passing a ship on the waterfront when a docker shouted down, 'Bad day, Eric, it's like your brother dying.'

Despite improvements and a resentful acknowledgement of the dockers' rights by the employers, 'The Evil' of casual piece-work continued to lurk below the surface and the labour force shrank. The hated 'flat hat' dock police snooped around to reduce petty thieving. The Liverpool dockers had by then developed a deep-seated distrust for the apparatchiks at Transport House. Coats were hung on a bust of Ernest Bevan, the pre-war General Secretary of the TGWU, in the union office, and stewards were treated with contempt. Bitterness and anger frequently spilled over into blind rage. These men became their own worst enemies. While some were complacent, others were idle, and many simply burnt out from years of hard manual labour. But they all hated the bosses and they stuck together. The fear of standing in line, like the slaves their forefathers had transported to America, was imprinted in their psyche. Muscle and brawn were all they had ever had to sell. Having been treated like beasts of burden for generations, their sense of worthlessness was very hard to eradicate.

Liverpool Slummy

Ghost-like I paced round the haunts of my childhood,
Earth seem'd a desert I was bound to traverse,
Seeking to find the old familiar faces
> Extract from 'The Old Familiar Faces'
> by Charles Lamb

The twentieth century brought no relief for the underclass; poverty brutalised the soul and gave rise to a callous, hard-wired inhumanity. The Liverpudlian's sense of humour acquired a sardonic cutting edge, which not infrequently turned cruel. Most poor whites hated 'blammos' (blacks), yids (Jews) and the pork-butcher 'krauts' (Germans). The sight of 'Farder Bunloaf' knocking on the door of the slums and tenements, collecting money for poor black babies in Africa, was greeted with disdain. Some unemployed men turned to rag tattering, where they travelled the streets exchanging old clothes for goldfish, balloons and even chickens; others sold blocks of salt cut with a handsaw; and a few cruised the streets on bikes with buckets of ice cream.

Cigarettes all week and the pub on a Saturday night were the women's only relief from the drudgery of endless washing, cooking, doing the dishes, ironing and cleaning the home. They had learned not to depend too much on their men even when the unopened pay packet was reliably laid on the table. In hard times, they fed their families' empty stomachs through Co-op credit notes, 'tick' from the grocers and by pawning their husband's suit. Some were on permanent call to earn an extra copper or two in the docks by cleaning an incoming ship. Washing behind children's ears to avoid 'potatoes taking root' was a maternal obsession. Worms and lice were everyday threats and every school had a 'nit nurse', dispatching any shamed child to the disinfection centre. Chicken pox, whooping cough and diphtheria were killers and keeping things spotlessly clean was essential to save lives. Every street had its own woman to wash and lay out the dead, drape sheets around the windows and prepare the flowers. When the corpse was fit for view, friends would come and stand round the coffin to pray and show their last respects. The arrival of the horse-drawn hearse was a time for the whole street to come out and say goodbye.

More than 200 children lived on a few small streets around Great Homer Street where they spent most of their waking hours kicking bundles of paper tied up with string, skipping or playing 'shop', marbles and hopscotch. Some had cropped hair and were dressed in 'police clothes', charity outfits of brown corduroy suits, shirt and tie and steel-rimmed clogs. Back then, whistling in the house was bad luck, and if you didn't have 'a show' before your 14th birthday you were considered terminal.

Sectarianism remained a dark and pernicious influence in the lives of Liverpool's working class. Dockers and warehousemen affiliated to the Orange Lodges had managed to move from casualism to regular employment but old uncertainties and the fear of unemployment were never far away. Support for the Labour Movement was growing and three weeks before King Edward VII came to lay the foundation stone of the new cathedral in July 1904, two Socialists – the Protestant stonemason Fred Bower and the Catholic docker Jim Larkin – secreted a message between two courses of brick. In addition to copies of *The Clarion* and the *Labour Leader*, they left a note for future Socialists 'from the wage slaves employed on the erection of this cathedral':

> This message, written on trust-produced paper with trust-produced ink, is to tell ye how we of today are at the mercy of trusts. Building fabrics, clothing, food, fuel, transport, are all in the hands of money-mad, soul-destroying trusts. We can only sell our labour power as wage slaves on their terms. The money trusts today own us. In your own day, you will, thanks to the efforts of past and present agitators for economic freedom, own trusts. Yours will indeed, compared to ours, be a happier existence. See to it, therefore, that ye, too, work for the betterment of all, and so justify your existence by leaving the world the better for your having lived in it. Thus and thus only shall come about the Kingdom of God, or Good, on Earth. Hail comrades and farewell.

Across the city, there was potential support for Labour at by-election time. Edge Hill was now the home to large numbers of skilled Welsh builders who went to chapel every Sunday and despised any form of militant evangelism. Everton also had a vibrant Welsh Calvinist community as well as a fair sprinkling of skilled Catholic workers and to this day their descendants can be found in the Liverpool phone directory, with 59 columns of people named Jones and 36 columns of people named Williams. Saint Anne's ward had some poor Jewish immigrants working in furnishing and the rag trade. Many of the migrants had come with heavy hearts, a feeling of alienation and a frustrated desire to return home. These disparate tribes became linked by a remembrance of things past, a sense of place and an undying belief in the future. Nostalgia made them dangerously sentimental and fuelled a preoccupation with the preternatural. Nothing was taken for granted and everything was plotted in the stars.

With no Irish Nationalist candidates standing and a high membership of craft unions, these wards were now potential Labour seats. At the Kirkdale by-election, where Labour made a concerted effort to gain power from the Tories, the Protestant Standard warned the electorate that socialism would mean 'absolute infidelities, the grossest immoralities and rivers of blood'. Ramsay MacDonald, who had paid a supportive visit to the constituency, ruefully commented that 'Liverpool is rotten and we had better recognise it.' The Liberals won the 1906 General Election, but the Labour Representation Party had achieved modest gains. Lenin would later remark that the shadow of revolution hung over Britain.

After the General Transport Strike and the First World War, economic decline set in with a vengeance and kindled an epidemic of incontinent sentimentality on the city's streets. Traditional commercial practices and lifestyles were lionised, and the qualities of toughness and resilience that had underpinned the city's glory years were invoked as her salvation. One in nine men each with an average of seven children was unemployed.

For many of the unemployed poor, criminality seemed the only way out. The 'friendly' corner shop often cheated people, raising prices, encouraging debt and using defective scales to underweigh food. The public houses adopted a policy of apartheid, relegating the local rabble to the threadbare tap room and reserving the back room snugs for the well-heeled topers. Scotland Road was considered so rough that policemen were forced to patrol in groups. Liverpool was a cruel city where poverty kindled bigotry and bitterness. Fights didn't end with a loose tooth or a black eye but with people being kicked to death or thrown through a shop window. Women could throw a left hook as well as any man and it was not uncommon for a policeman to wake up in hospital on a Sunday morning with a black eye after an altercation with a Liverpool Lou. Local disputes were settled by 'straighteners', fist fights on waste ground watched by crowds of baying men.

Liverpool's nightlife was brash and violent but it could never be accused of half-heartedness. The Grafton opened in 1924 as a purpose-built venue for a thousand flappers. The swing music of Joe Loss, Duke Ellington and Victor Sylvester led to a host of jitterbug romances. If you couldn't afford The Grafton or The Hippodrome picture house, then there was always an open Irish house party to fall back on. Ale was bought in demijohns from the pub at the end of the street and quaffed to the rowdy strains of 'Nelly Dean'. Pigs' feet, cockles and watercress were favourite snacks sold on every street corner. Singing and jigging made scrubbing floors with pumice the next day tolerable.

Irish Nationalism started to decline as a force in Liverpool after partition, and in 1923 the first Labour Party MP was elected at the Edge Hill by-election. A year later, Elizabeth Bamber, a strong-minded girl with socialism running through her blood, married Jack Braddock and joined the Communist Party. She would later attribute her decision to join and later leave the party to an innate rebelliousness. In 1930, Bessie Braddock, as she was now known, was returned as a councillor for the Saint Anne's ward. Two years after she had been elected to the council, the unemployed third of the city were on the streets protesting against the means test. The National Unemployed Worker's Movement marched on the home of Alderman Baker, Tory Chairman of the Public Assistance Committee, and then laid siege to a police station, parading the blood-stained shirt of Paddy Devlin, who had died following a rooftop chase with police.

After the Second World War, Bessie Braddock was elected to Westminster as the Labour MP for Liverpool Exchange. In her maiden speech she described the Liverpool slums as 'bug-ridden, lice-ridden, rat-ridden, lousy hellholes'. Throughout her 25 uninterrupted years in Parliament, she remained a vociferous backbencher, making life uncomfortable for whichever political party was in power and fighting the iniquities of poverty and social injustice. By most of the right honourable members, she was regarded as a vulgar figure with no right to be in the House. She was hated by the Welsh for supporting the flooding of the Trywern valley and for her combative comment that the protesters 'wouldn't do that in front of the Kop!'

'Battling Bessie' eventually earned a grudging respect from many of her Tory adversaries for her sincerity and single-minded crusades to help the disadvantaged, tackle youth crime and improve maternity care and child welfare.

The post-war international recession with mass unemployment impeded Liverpool council's plans to rebuild the heavily bombed town centre. This led to a mounting disenchantment with the government and a growing resentment towards the capital. Many had believed the democratic principles of the Co-operative Society would one day lead to a better world. Every Liverpool family knew their Co-op member number as well as they knew their own address, and some would not have survived if it had not been for the quarterly 'divis' of one shilling and sevenpence in the pound and the support lifeline the Co-op provided. A privy in the backyard – however spotlessly whitewashed – and two bedrooms for a family with six children did not seem an adequate reward for putting your life on the line for King and Country. Nazi Germany had seen Liverpool as a strategic nexus for the Western Approaches and the Atlantic, and crippling it would have paved the way for an invasion. All they had to do was aim for the lights of Dublin and follow a straight line east. The Luftwaffe's main onslaught on the city finally came in the summer of 1941 with 79 bombing raids over a 6-week period. Streets burned under a scarlet, smoke-ridden sky as 10,000 homes were razed to the ground and 20 times as many were damaged. The Sailor's Church was gutted and the Gorée Piazza and Corn Exchange reduced to rubble. The Custom House was destroyed, the docks pounded and Lord Street was devastated. Every bombing raid on London was reported on the wireless but Liverpool was considered so vital to the war effort that a blanket of secrecy was thrown over the city's devastation. This may have been justified on grounds of national security but it had the psychological effect of making Liverpudlians feel they were of secondary significance to the nation.

Remarkably, despite the downturn in her fortunes, Liverpool continued to cling to carpet-bagging Toryism long after Manchester, Sheffield and Leeds had become Labour strongholds and 20 years after London's socialist conversion. In 1955, Labour finally gained control of Liverpool council but it was not long before a Liberal revival began. Catholic parishes central to the new Labour movement after Irish Independence were now beginning to be dismantled by the urban clearances. These wards had always operated on a horse-trading approach of nods, winks and family favours and eventually this became the modus operandi of the city party itself. Within another ten years party organisation in the Labour Catholic wards had degenerated to little more than the sitting councillor and a small bunch of ageing acolytes. The city was very slow to set itself straight and was now being torn apart by Tammany politics and frustrated anger. The 1963 Scotland ward by-election was an opportunity for the Tories to remind voters that Romanism was the foe of civil and religious freedom and that if they lost these inestimable privileges for a mess of Socialist pottage they would be unworthy of the heritage won for them by the grand Protestant sires.

As Merseybeat enraptured the rest of England, the dockers, their families and their communities were being decanted into the new towns, terrifying Martian terrains of jerry-built boxes full of rising damp. Arterial roads and utilitarian tower blocks were carving the last remaining communities asunder. Long-suffering wives saved up for a divorce that never happened. Liverpool was still large of spirit but had become an anxious place with a rapidly falling population.

The sea was in the city's blood but the commercial tides had left the shrinking port. A few disconsolate men could still be seen scrubbing the decks of freighters but everyone on the waterfront knew their way of life was dying. The aphorism 'There used to be wooden ships and iron sailors; now there are iron ships and wooden men' summed up the mood of angry desperation. Ships move while ports stand still. These displaced alienated water boys were on the back foot, bruised but not yet beaten by their city's declining circumstances. The old dock estate had been unable to adapt to bulk carriers and containers, and Albert, King's and Brunswick were now abandoned and derelict. Hamburg and Rotterdam were now the modern Mercantile Jacks' chocolate ports. The modernist dream of no-frills architecture would leave a permanent eyesore in the town centre. While cronyism staggered on in the city's rotten wards, Liverpool was ripe for takeover. Revolution inspired by the power of music was close at hand. A new tolerance of ideas and individualism was on the verge of being born.

Dead Scouse

Water is fountainous is gymnast is flash.
Water is mountainous is scallywag is splash
Water is mysterious is playhouse is dream.
Water is serious is stargazy is steam.
Inscription around the fountain
in Williamson Square,
by Roger McGough

Brought east at seven, I was forced to bite my tongue and swallow my pride. Some words were lost forever; I downplayed difference and slowly modified my accent to fit in. Landlocked dirty Leeds on the other side of those lonely moors inspired fear in me the way a cruel face frightens a stranger. I cried uncontrollably for days. I had been cruelly uprooted to live within a stone's throw of Towton, a village where 10,000 brothers had been butchered in a blizzard under the Tudors and Plantagenets. The Armpit of the North was the old enemy and at my new school it was not long before indoctrination began.

'Hear all, see all, say nowt. Eat all, drink all, pay nowt. And if thee ever do owt for nowt, do it for thee sen.' 'On Ilkla Moor Baht 'at' ('On Ilkley Moor Without a Hat') – a dirge essentially about cannibalism dressed up as an ode to thriftiness was the anthem of God's own county.

I was encouraged to call a spade a spade, be bluff and outspoken and to say it as it is. I was also taught to peel an orange without removing it from my pocket.

Yorkshire born, Yorkshire bred, thick in the arm and thick in the head.

A starched photograph of a proud young father and his five-year-old son, looking out at the remains of the Empire from the Pier Head sustained me. It reminded me of that tribe of quick-witted tolerant people who despite the fault lines enjoyed laughter and parties. It freed me from a deep, vacant stare, which gave nothing in return. The first time I left the house a surly man shouted at me, 'What's tha looking at lad?' My galoshes had become pumps and no one in Yorkshire knew that rag and bone men, midden men and knife grinders were galoshermen. Soft sandstone had been replaced by millstone grit, stone houses and a cold easterly wind.

In Gledhow, there were no reassuring neatly shorn privet hedges fencing in cluttered back-to-back terraces, no cocky watchmen to turn a blind eye and no washhouse where I could glean forbidden secrets. I found it hard to retain silliness in this no-nonsense, rhubarb-loving suburb but I never stopped dreaming. The ocean was no longer at my back and it was impossible to savour the pleasure of wet gaberdine. This was lah-di-dah, gloom-filled Leeds. I tried to swim back down the Ship Canal to a place that had ceased to exist. I faced backwards, turned inwards and had no choice but to live in the past. Compelled to inhabit an alien world of surly, plain-speaking people, I felt every bit a foreigner as Tony Dibb.

To Loiners and Tykes, Liverpool was a rough-and-tumble gangland you had to brave to get a passport on the wrong side of the backbone of Old England: a rundown dump and a cheap seat that no longer mattered. Those deceptions I traced on misty Leeds windows now control everything, intrude on future plans and define me. Anywhere else has begun to inspire self-loathing and anger. For me, Liverpool was always a mythical point of departure, a launching pad for heroic voyages. Atlantic City remained a world apart, the capital of itself stranded on a peninsula between the river and the Pool, a weather-beaten place of contradictions divided by a hundred different persuasions, always on the up, and a port which never stopped believing. It was tough and sentimental, independent and insecure, good for a laugh and touchy, cosmopolitan and parochial, a self-righteous end-of-the-line haven. And I couldn't get it out of my head.

The emergence of Received Pronunciation, an outward sign of belonging to the professional middle class, went hand in hand with the rise of an Imperial Civil Service. Before the Empire, eminent Victorians had felt no pressure to lose their demotic vernacular. Lord Stanley, educated at Rugby and Cambridge, spoke a Red Rose patois and his Whig opponent William Gladstone, raised in Liverpool, had a Lancashire burr that survived Eton. William Roscoe's accent was described as that of a barbarian, wholly incongruous with his erudition. The earliest reference to the dialects of Liverpool are to be found in A.J. Ellis's *On Early English Pronunciation* in 1889, although he went on to say that Liverpool and Birkenhead had 'no dialect proper' and 'Dicky Sam' struggled to establish a recognised voice of his own. In the twentieth century, a new breed of righteous post-Education Act preparatory schoolmasters embarked on an official mission to eradicate regional accents and enforce the Oxford English of the Home Counties. While Public School Pronunciation was taking root amongst the ruling and professional classes, a loaded Irish-influenced brogue was evolving in the Liverpool docks. This accent, with its unusual rising inflexions, would remain locked away in the port for 70 years.

In the '50s, comedians like Ted Ray and Arthur Askey played it safe by using a more approachable, watered-down North Country voice. At this time, most of Liverpool's comics didn't boast about their origins in case it jeopardised their London careers. A notable exception was Deryck Guyler's legendary character Frisby Dyke, named after the town's leading draper, in the popular radio show *It's that Man Again*, which also starred another Liverpool comic, Tommy Handley. Apart from the acclaim of the wireless comedians and the popularity of music-hall artists Robb Wilton and Norman Evans, Liverpool struggled to identify cultural heroes. Much Liverpool humour remained unfathomable and incomprehensible even in Leeds let alone south of Birmingham.

In 1962, the Beatles broke and what had become an almost-forgotten backwater was suddenly awash with cameramen and journalists. Pop music had become a defining force in British culture and a cherished export. Cilla Black, Ken Dodd and Jimmy Tarbuck sold the Liverpool accent to the growing industry of radio and television. Now everyone wanted to be from Liverpool even if they didn't fancy living there. London might have the Talk of the Town but Liverpool was the Town of the Talk. If you could prove you were Scouse, girls would throw themselves at you. Overnight it had become a magic, chic place on the coast where poor people took a taxi to travel two blocks.

At the beginning of his career with The Scaffold, Roger McGough's agent sent him to a voice trainer in Golders Green. He was not unfamiliar with this process, as he had already received remedial therapy to try to stop him running his words together. The results, however, were unexpected. 'We went down to London to learn how to become luvvies and by the end of a fortnight we still had our own accents and our teacher was speaking broad Scouse.'

Willy Russell recalled a school trip to the Isle of Man. When a local man enquired of the excited children, 'Where do you lot come from?' 300 voices proudly proclaimed without hesitation: 'Liverpewl!'

Scouse cool was short lived. As the extent of the city's economic blight became common knowledge, the nation's attitude started to change again.

DEAD SCOUSE

In Thatcher's Britain of the 1980s, Liverpool was publicly derided. To be born in the city was considered something to be profoundly ashamed of. Any connection with the rotten port had become a severe handicap to finding a job. Liverpool was a shifty place full of whining shirkers and synonymous with working-class delinquency. The sceptical, upturned intonation of the vernacular was anathema. Liverpool writer Beryl Bainbridge declared in 1999 that 'uneducated regional accents', particularly Scouse, should be 'wiped out'. Paradoxically, Americans found the Liverpool sound genteel and classy.

The embattled alienation of Planet Liverpool was emphasised every time a Scouser opened his mouth. The harsh, nasal, guttural sound of the Mersey had acquired a subversive political charge while a Scottish or Irish lilt had now become trendy. The adenoidal twang was instantly recognisable and in sharp contrast to bucolic Lancashire mill talk. The joke goes that a man from Burnley visiting Liverpool was engaged in conversation in a dockside pub by a couple of Scousers who wanted to know what he was doing there. The Lancastrian answered, 'Ah'm gwin to a porrteh' (I'm going to a party), to which one of the Scousers replied, 'Arr-ey I don go t'them I go to paaaaaahties me.'

Scouse is sharp, fast, colourful and chatty, always on the edge rising out of the sea fog. You can feel the city's grievous and enterprising past in its intonations. There is guilt, belligerence, a resoluteness not to be taken for a ride and a hunger to be first in line ingrained in every syllable. The name derives from a North Atlantic sea sailor's stew called Labskaus made with red cabbage pickled in vinegar, potatoes laced with onions, boiled carrots and cuts of cheap beef and mutton. If potatoes were in short supply, ship's biscuits were added, and sometimes canned bully beef replaced the braised steak and neck chops. Blind Scouse is the poorer or vegetarian version, with celery sometimes added to the obligatory potatoes and onions. The similarity of Scouse to Lancashire hotpot and Irish stew may have helped the Liverpool sailors to make the Baltic dish their own. A hundred years ago, steaming plates of reheated stew were available on Saturday nights for a penny a plate at the Scouseboat, a huge street cauldron at the junction of Wellington Street and Scotland Road. In those days, the real culinary delicacy for the humble workman was not Scouse but salted codfish, known in the Park Lane area by the Portuguese word *bacalhao*.

It was the influx of the Irish that laid the foundations for the idiom but it is also easy to discern the singsong conciliatory influence of the Welsh and even the sound of the Potteries. There is also the slightest residual hint of Tim Bobbin's rural Lancashire dialect. Scouse is fast and exclusive, resonating with the world's great ports. In its vowels, you can discern the fraternity and tragedies of friends and the memory of streets. Its phonological peculiarities stem in part from velarisation, the raising of the back of the tongue towards the soft palate that sounds to outsiders like catarrh. At the end of each sentence, there is that rising inflection that to the English gives even formal exchanges a built-in air of Ulster mongrel belligerence and resentment.

Gaelic does not have a 'th' sound and in Scouse 'th' is replaced by something a bit like a 'd'; 'dzee do dough don't dee dough' became a national catchphrase to wind up Scousers. Borrowing from the Irish, 'three and a third' becomes 'tree and a turd'. 'The' can also sound like 'thuh' before a consonant. An interesting sound is the subtle 's' that is tucked inside the 't', as in 'tsable' or 'tsasht' (tart). The 'ck' in words like back is uttered with explosive conviction. Cool is 'kewl', fair is 'fur', care is 'cur'and bath has the flat, short northern 'a' vowel. The 'y'ending on words is uttered as 'ee' and a diphthong is added to mid-word vowels, with Mary being pronounced 'Mairy' or 'Maairy' or 'Mury' and curtains as 'cairtains' or 'ceertans'. Scouse substitutes a letter 'r' for 'w' and 't' so 'what a lot of laughs' is elided to 'warra lorra laffss' or 'Wossamarra?' for 'What's the matter?'. 'Ing' is replaced by 'n' in the seminal 'nutt'n' for 'nothing'. Occasionally 't' at the end of a word is replaced with a 'ch' so that 'up front' becomes 'up frontch', and the lazy glottal stop is prevalent in words such as 'buh' for 'but'.

The dank, corrosive air also contributes to the distinctive congested inflexions, which along with a bad chest are God's gift to those born close to the river mouth. 'You' does not exist and as in Dublin and New York more than one is 'yews'. When a Liverpool teacher says, 'Stand up, Hughes!', the whole class get to their feet.

Conversation is the food of life but in contrast to the charming lilting blarney of Cork and Galway, Scouse often has a cutting and cruel edge. In every sentence, you can feel the anger, the flippancy, the guilt, the guardedness. In *Writing Home*, Leeds-born Alan Bennett, reflects the national antipathy:

> I have come to dislike Liverpool. Robert Ross said that Dorsetshire rustics, after Hardy, had the insolence of the artist's model and so it is with Liverpudlians. They have figured in too many plays and have a cockiness that comes from being told too often that they and their city

are special. The accent doesn't help. There is a rising inflection in it, particularly at the end of the sentence, that gives even the most formal exchange a built-in air of grievance. They all have the chat, and it laces every casual encounter, everybody wanting to do you their little verbal dance. One such is going on at hotel reception tonight as I wait for my key. 'You don't know me,' says a drunken young man to the receptionist, 'but I'm a penniless millionaire.' You don't know me but I'm a fifty-one-year-old playwright anxious to get to my bed.

Every Scouser, Bennett complains, considers himself a comedian fitted out with smart answers.

Within Liverpool, there are different accents and sounds stemming from the segregated ghettos of the new settlers in the nineteenth century, but a love for colourful language binds them all together. South Liverpool has a lilting, singsong ring; across the water in Birkenhead they whine, while the staccato Bootle sound is raucous like a hungry kittiwake, harsh heavy metal. The Catholics say 'airly' for early while Protestants say 'urrly'. There is even a posh Scouse where the 'u' in 'sugar' is made to sound like 'bugger'. Consonants are delivered with explosive nasal force and at the end of a word with a fricative alveolar scrape so 'back' becomes like the Welsh 'bach' or a harsher threatening Scots 'loch', and 'book' is pronounced like 'puke'. 'Clare with the fair hair' becomes 'Clur wid de fur ur' or 'Cleer with the feer eer'. A classic training name for those keen to learn Scouse is that of the Polish goalkeeping hero Jerzy Dudek chanted as 'Jeerzy Doodech' at Anfield and Istanbul. Irish whimsy, Scots sharpness, Welsh melodrama and English irony served up in a voice which links the Red Rose with the Irish Sea and the Welsh mountains are the raw ingredients of this distinctive lobscouse.

Academic studies confirm that socio-linguistically, Scouse along with the other urban working-class accents of Cockney, Brummy and Geordie remains bottom of the league, synonymous with lack of culture and social inferiority. In spite of its increasing denigration and ridicule, Scouse has stood firm and has largely resisted pollution by the rootless and fast-spreading Estuary English, Jafaican 'da voice of da yoof' and the influence of the Australian TV soaps. The accent has even successfully spread west into the poorer parts of the Wirral and North Wales and travelled out to the new overspill towns of Kirkby, Skelmersdale, Winsford and Speke. Changes occur with each new generation, with the Cockney 'v' replacing 'th' in 'brother' and 'f' for 'th' in 'think' creeping in. 'Innit?' has also moved north for 'isn't it?' Rhyming slang is quite rare in Scouse, although 'loop de loop' for 'soup' can still be heard.

Liverpudlians share the Irish love for novelty in speech and delight in Spoonerisms, doggerel and neologisms. They also love to pun and create a demotic vocabulary of fantastic rotten English or 'cacology'. They are never at a loss for a word or a piece of ready repartee and can talk the hind leg off a donkey. The sea brought new words like 'banana' and 'tornado' and the Lascar's gift of 'head serang' for 'boss'. Some phrases like 'When Donnelly docked', meaning 'long ago', provide a link with a lost local history. The popular pastime of word bending beloved of John Lennon and the word salads and tropes of the Beatles in 'A Hard Day's Night' and 'Happiness is a Warm Gun' can be traced back to Gaelic tradition. Lennon had a great love for Edward Lear, Lewis Carroll and the zany fun of the Goons. At a time when the inoffensive mopheads generated sweetness and light, Lennon's descriptions of low-lifes, his sick parodies and scathing satires of the media and the establishment reflected his darker side. His chaotic output of malapropisms, verbal near-misses (Merseypropisms) and gibberish in *A Spaniard in the Works* reflected the Liverpool-Irish subversion of upper-class English. To many Liverpool-Irish, the English language remained the voice of their historic oppressor. When asked why he disrespected standard English, Lennon replied, 'I change words because I haven't a clue what a lorra words mean half the time.' His 'Ladies and Genital men' became a lasting classic. Although he always maintained he wrote only for fun, the critics greeted his work with solemnity, acclaiming him a rebellious folk poet, destined to become a cult among the Camden literati. An extract from 'Partly Dave', a story in *In His Own Write*, illustrates Lennon's irreverence:

> Partly Dave was a raving salesman with the gift of the gob, which always unnerved Mary. 'I seem to have forgotten my bus fare, Cobber,' said Dave not realising it. 'Geroff the bus then,' said Basuboo in a voice that bode not boot, not realising the coloured problem himself really. 'O.K.,' said partly Dave, humbly not wishing to offend. 'But would you like your daughter to marry one?' a voice seem to say as Dave lept off the bus like a burning spastic.

Unique Scouse expressions which have not spread outside the city boundaries include 'eck-eck' for 'hello' or 'watch out', and 'ay ey' for 'I say there'. 'Fab', 'gear', 'grotty', 'sarny' and 'made-up' have all entered

English usage, as have 'fit' (attractive) and 'sound' (good guy). However, 'Cum 'ed' meaning 'come on let's get going' and 'it's last' meaning 'it's terrible', remain local.

In the pub, Vat 69, a brand of whisky, is referred to as 'Dee Pope's phone'. 'Black 'n' Tan' is a mixture of Guinness and pale ale, 'a droppa dee crater' is whisky and 'jungle juice' is rum. 'Kaylied' and 'lushed as the landlord's cat' are terms for drunkenness and a 'Paddy Kelly' is a dock policeman. A 'jowler' is a rather wider back alley than a jigger, 'abnab' is a sandwich and a 'sticky lice' is liquorice. The doctor's surgery also provides many funny examples of Scouse: 'He got conclusion of the brain and she's had her overtures removed'; 'Paradised all down one side'; 'Comes outta hospittle tomorrow, he's had a post-mortem. Luckier than our George who was took to the symmetry to be created'; 'It'll be all about infernal combustion'; 'E's a creepin Jesus'.

Many Liverpool jokes depend on word play, such as: 'Why did the chicken cross the road lightly?' The answer: 'Because he couldn't walk hardly.'

One hears funny things everywhere one goes in Liverpool but parental advice is a constant source of humour. 'Don't come running to me if you break your leg' and 'If you get you's killed I'll bloody murder yer.' Some expressions are abstruse and imaginative: 'Got a gob on it like a farmer's arse on a winter's day' and 'shove it where the sun don't shine'. In a letter, Gerard Manley Hopkins described a visit to a church bazaar in St Helens where a man tried to persuade the priest to go out riding with him, assuring him that if he agreed it would make Hopkins's 'lip curl like a bee's knee in a gale of wind'.

The long-suffering populace ruefully comment that you need to be a comedian to live in Liverpool. The dialect, with its colourful turn of phrase, reflects the typical personality: a desire to be independent and to live life to the full, and a determination not to be taken for a ride. The Scouser is always quick with a deadpan riposte to any put-down or pretension. Through comedy, the Scouser defends England against the evils of vanity and intellectual self-deception.

If you are not Liverpool's answer to Brad Pitt or Angelina Jolie, you'll get told with expressions like, 'You've got a face that only a boxer's glove could love' or 'Our dog would love to bury you in the garden.' The love of language, the dark humour and light heart, the tension between fanatic localism and a roving eye to the distant horizon bind its folk as one. Liverpool's way with words extinguishes any attempts by the capital to instil conformity and reinforces her exceptionalism.

Many thousands of elderly Liverpudlians learned a peculiar gibberish that is still used in some parts of the city and by South Liverpool hoods and tarts. Several distinct versions of obscure origin exist, some of which may come from Romany. Thus 'window' is 'indoway' and 'money' is 'oneymay'. The vulgar form takes regular words, breaks them up and inserts meaningless syllables. When spoken fast with the accent of Liverpool 8 it is a secret unintelligible code: 'He's a de-g-ad ti-gite bastard an hes fri-g-hitened of judies so I don't nay go yasy getbur he's got da mer-goney so wa gait and see.'

Liverpool backslang has been considered a dialect of pig Latin so that words beginning with a consonant move the leading consonant to the end of the word and add 'ay' or 'ah', so ball becomes 'all-bay', star 'ar-stay' and truck 'ruck-tah'. Words beginning with vowels on the other hand have 'way' added to the end of the word so of becomes 'of-way'. A conversation might go:

'Otsway orfay innerday?' ('What's for dinner?')

With the reply 'Yuk! Oldcay eatmay omfray undaysay.' ('Meat from Sunday.')

Other variations were butcher's back slang with 'yllis dlo woc' for 'silly old cow' and car mechanic's slang with 'it's an old knocker' coming out as 'itsay na-ay dolay ockernay'.

Matt Simpson, son of a Bootle docker, has written that his poems are explorations of lasting memories that randomly break through into consciousness. His books of poetry can be read as a set of implied narratives, with each poem feeding into the next and creating clusters of significance. In 'My Grandmother's African Grey', he imbues the bird with the ability to imitate the speech of both his working-class grandmother and her much posher Aunt Bella who had been a stewardess on a liner. This allowed him to reconcile the linguistic schizophrenia of dual voices and to give the poem integrity. T.S. Eliot's *The Love Song of J. Alfred Prufrock* acts as the matrix for a light-hearted parody in which he illustrates the inherently poetic nature of Scouse with its lavish use of simile and metaphor.

> Less juss shin off me an yooze
> Seein as ow its as soddin borin as
> someone avin der appendicks out.
> Less juss bugger off down ere

DEAD SCOUSE

Where thee ardlee is no one
Where the moanin minnies toss n turn
in the doss ouses or Yatzis Wine Loge
Where thee spew der rings up
An piss on the floor down streets
That go fuckin on-n-on like some beady-eyed
bastid big-ears luckin fer a barney
an tryin t catch yer out not knowin sumpin
But don't gerrin a tizzy doin yer ed in
juss fuck off down there anyroad
Ders diss posh do wid lah-di-dah judies
janglin about ow thee once-t knew John Lenin.

Everyone in Liverpool behaves as if they've been on the telly, much to the annoyance of the rest of the country. They justify their gift of the gab with their Irish heritage and because they feel no one listens to them even when they shout from the rooftops. A dignified silence in response to a put-down is not part of a Scouser's mindset. This proud city has always had a big mouth.

Jericho

Everything to keep me from sleeping
A lot of sailor boys they were leaving
And everybody there was jumping
To hear the sailor boys in Alcora singing
Brown skin girl stay home and mind baby
Brown skin girl stay home and mind baby I'm going away in a
    sailing boat
And if I don't come back
Stay home and mind baby

Extract from 'Brown Skin Girl' by Norman Span

J.B. Priestley arrived in Liverpool on a murky winter day between the wars to find it 'imposing and dignified like a city in a rather gloomy Victorian novel'. He went on to describe it as a 'heart of darkness where the sun never seems to rise properly'. His intention was to visit a school in the 'queerest parish in England' as part of his research for his book *English Journey*:

> All the races of mankind were there wonderfully mixed. Imagine an infant class of half-castes, quadroons, octaroons, with all the latitudes and longitudes confused in them . . . We could see them down there, like a miniature League of Nations assembly gone mad . . . Although they had mostly been begotten, born and reared in the most pitifully sordid circumstances, nearly all of them were unusually attractive in appearance, like most people of oddly mixed blood . . . Looking at them you did not think of the riff-raff of the stokeholds and slatterns of the slums who had served as their parents: they seemed like the charming exotic fruits, which indeed they were, of some profound anthropological experiment.

An exotic tapestry enveloped the bustling docks and crowded taverns at the seaward end of Upper Parliament Street where the gullet of the Mersey joined the jaws of the land. Orchidaceous Sierra Leonean princes and thin-faced Somalis in their flowing romantic robes wandered through the shabby gentility of the hidden triangle. The streets were alive with beautiful, lithe-limbed mulatto children running, skipping, hopping and dancing. In summer, there was usually one or two cricket matches in full swing, with an improvised wicket chalked on a wall. Elderly Jamaicans in Panama hats sat in doorways smoking Indian hemp and playing dominoes. Yams, plantains and sweet potatoes brought in on the 'monkey boats' were the staple diet for the African palate and could be bought late into the night. The children's mothers would dress up in coloured frocks and hats for Sunday church. A gumbo of foreign smells enriched the crazy-paving area and turned the 'stockaded or enclosed place', mentioned in the Domesday Book, into England's first global village. Many areas of inner-city England and even the old northern mill towns now feel the same but in the late 1950s Liverpool 8 was out on its own, a parallel community segregated from the rest of the city.

The ninth-generation 'black judies' from the cultural heirloom of Pitt Street welcomed the suave American GIs on their arrival at Lime Street Station and the city's dance halls swung to the music of The Platters and The Ink Spots. Their charm, film-star looks, and gifts of contraband nylons and cigarettes proved irresistible and many a transatlantic love match began on the back row of the Rialto. Some of the Liverpool-born black girls had the same slave names as their exotic escorts and shared the same Charleston genes but they had remained much more in tune with the West Coast of Africa than their dates. It would be ten more years before the American Civil Rights movement and the Black Panthers would awake American blacks to their roots and give the black GIs more understanding of the origin of the names of the Liverpool clubs like the Ibo, the Yoruba, The Crew Club and the Sierra Leone. Their black brothers in Liverpool's Harlem complained that the flash Yanks in their Cadillacs and Pontiacs were stealing their women. The truth was that they largely ignored their own and favoured the white Irish girls who more closely resembled their mothers.

The call from the mother country for a Caribbean workforce had brought the patriotic SS *Empire Windrush* generation to Liverpool. In 1948, the *Orbita* brought 180 West Indian workers to Liverpool and 3 months later a further 40 arrived on the *Reina del Pacifico*. These hopeful citizens of the Commonwealth were dismayed and demoralised by the colour bar they experienced in dance halls, hotels and factories. The Pitt Street dynasties also resented the new arrivals, deriding them as 'Uncle Toms' pandering to the white bosses and 'scurrying around like frightened little animals'. The *Liverpool Daily Post* ran scaremongering stories about black stowaways arriving on boats and clamoured for their immediate repatriation. Injustice was rife and grievances were denied or diffused. One man was told that he was not eligible for the fire brigade because if there was billowing smoke he might not be visible to colleagues. Another was told his fuzzy hair would represent a fire hazard. The government talked about the importance of integration but what they really wanted was assimilation, the need for the new immigrants to ape the customs and behaviour of the indigenous white population. There was a lot of talk about racial harmony but the new arrivals found it hard to get their foot on the ladder. The old guard meanwhile held onto their dreams of returning to Africa and hid away from the rest of Liverpool in the Nigerian and the Federation. The new arrivals sought solace in lunatic juice, a ginger beer punch, and weed, and in the calypsos of Lord Beginner and the Andrews Sisters.

The 'coon hunters' of Notting Hill with their KBW (Keep Britain White) graffiti had stayed away but Liverpool-born blacks knew instinctively it would be unwise to leave Toxteth and venture into town. The Boundary Hotel on Lodge Lane was the Berlin Wall for 'blammos' and 'shines'. If they walked a further hundred yards down Wavertree Road, they would be stopped and told to go back by the police. If they were foolhardy enough to venture even further afield towards the site of King John's Hunting Lodge, they would be greeted with sneering chants of 'nigger, nigger, nigger' or risk attack from one of the many gangs of 'Teds'. The Teddy Boys with their greasy swept-back hair, sideburns and 'duck's arses', dressed in long Edwardian drapes and velvet-collared jackets, were in the vanguard of white teenage rebellion and helped to enhance Liverpool's long-standing reputation for wickedness.

Liverpool 8 remained a poor but happy multiracial community, which at night became a renegade Left Bank stomping ground for artists, beatniks and epicureans. It was a vibrant cosmopolitan mosaic, a district of decaying Georgian terraced houses with halal butchers, a GP's surgery, a pet shop run by an ex-boxer with a passion for goldfish and an old-fashioned English greengrocer nestling side by side in Lodge Lane. Stalls on Lodge Lane sold plantain, soursop, custard apples, red peppers, ginger and bush meat. A code of respectability remained in the close-packed straight streets of by-law housing. Wherever you went, the brooding presence of the Gothic cathedral loomed, casting its lowering shadow on the decadent streets below. There were enough pews in the square mile around Princes Avenue to accommodate the entire population if they had chosen to attend. Laconic Irishmen propped up the bar at the Croxteth with a pint of Guinness for company, waiting for their horse to come in. Brasses hung off lamp posts, waylaying the dour and usually drunk Icelandic and Norse whalers. Mr Singh ran the confectioner's. Jamaicans in pork pie hats sat outside their houses talking of Spanish Town and puffing on reefers. Since the early 1950s, cannabis had been smuggled through the Liverpool docks in large quantities by African and West Indian seamen and brokered in Warwick Street, Park Road and Crown Street. One police officer claimed that smoking a reefer was the equivalent of drinking half a bottle of rum and was a cause of sexual mania.

In the summer of 1960, The Silver Beatles' only regular engagement was at the New Cabaret Artistes Club in Upper Parliament Street, a dive owned by Allan Williams and managed by a Trinidadian known as Lord Woodbine (born Harold Phillips). The lads were paid ten shillings each to play 'Moonglow' and the Harry Lime theme while Janice, a big-busted Manchester stripper, took her kit off in front of a motley crew of sailors, guilty businessmen and a few members of the dirty raincoat brigade. Phillips, who had arrived in England on HMS *Windrush*, was a Liverpool 8 scallywag who as well as managing the club turned his hand to building, decorating and playing in a steel band. 'Woody' had earned his title by way of his lofty demeanour and habit of always having a cigarette stuck on his lower lip. The Silver Beatles also played The New Colony, where a handful of merchant seamen smooched on the pocket dance floor with seasoned 'pros' while Woodbine patrolled the bar with his cutlass at the ready. Woody introduced the band to black stateside music, taught John Lennon and Paul McCartney guitar riffs and encouraged them unsuccessfully to get a drummer. His influence on the Beatles may not have been as great as he later claimed but there is no doubt that the seeds of many of their tunes drifted in on the Atlantic tides.

Allan Williams also owned a coffee bar in Slater Street called The Jacaranda, which was frequented by the Liverpool College of Arts set, the Mersey Poets and the author Beryl Bainbridge. One night, he arrived expecting to hear the familiar calypso beat of the Royal Caribbean Band, only to be informed that the group had been lured away to Hamburg. A few weeks later a member of the band contacted Williams urging him to bring over other Liverpool acts to the lively night scene, which had grown up around the Reeperbahn in St Pauli. Hamburg would prove to be the critical break for the Beatles and Allan Williams would later go down as the man who gave them away.

While the Beatles were in Hamburg, Joe and Edmund Ankrah, the Liverpool-born black sons of a church minister who had been brought up on the doo-wop sounds of Johnny Otis, the Del Vikings and the Miracles, formed a harmony group called the Shades. Their first appearance was at Stanley House on Upper Parly and soon after this they changed their name to the Chants. A new sexy black man's music that had grown out of the Civil Rights Movement in America and the urban drift to Chicago and Detroit had arrived in Liverpool 8. Paul McCartney met Joe Ankrah at the Tower Ballroom, New Brighton. When the Beatles came back from Hamburg in 1962, they agreed to back the Chants at the Cavern despite their new manager Brian Epstein's objections.

The Cavern Club in Mathew Street was a converted subterranean warehouse and former air-raid shelter with a low, barrel-vaulted, damp ceiling. A doorman barred the unassuming entrance and its cracked blackened walls were daubed with CND graffiti. To the untutored eye the venue was as unwelcoming as a night out in the Black Hole of Calcutta. At the bottom of its wooden stairs, several hundred children of the revolution were crammed between the arched walls, undulating in darkness to the muffled raw drumbeat and distinctive steely guitar twang of Gerry and the Pacemakers, the Merseybeats and the Mojos. At lunchtimes, for an entrance fee of one shilling and three pence, you could get to see the Beatles and have a bowl of soup. The Beatles would soon conquer America but a jaundiced view prevailed in Liverpool 8 that the moptops were the greatest example of the London-run white music industry ripping off black music.

The new late-night coffee bars in town, the Masque, The Basement and Streates, were attracting a new art-school crowd, which wanted more than jazz, skiffle, and rock and roll. There would be more than a hundred local bands ready to rumble every Saturday, some doing two or three different gigs in one night. Drum kits and amplifiers were main-street cargo. Musicians came and went, clubs and studios were forever burning down, boarding up and reopening but the vibe never faded and the Cavern went on to become a legendary garage. Within two short years The Mersey Sound was rocking the block and posters of The Big Three, King Size Taylor and the Dominoes, Faron and the Flamingoes, and the Remo Four were plastered all over the city. The Iron Door, the Mardi Gras, the Blue Angel and that 'Best of Cellars' the Cavern Club were packed to the rafters. There were a thousand faces and the rest were all relatives. Mediocre performances were not greeted with polite applause. National recognition for 'one of ours' was accepted but never acclaimed. No one was above anyone else and the entertainment was expected to be better than what you could get in your own front room. As the music grew, the shrinking singing city briefly dreamed on

Toxteth was now Liverpool's Haight Ashbury, a nucleus for the beat counter-culture and a charged quarter primed for fervent self-expression. It had the appearance of a newly retired gentleman with years of sterling service behind him but a period of useful life ahead. The tree-lined streets were wide and handsome and banked by fading Victorian houses. Adrian Henri, born across the water in Tranmere, was the conductor of theatrical 'knees-ups' with a soft spot for the particular. He was typecast as a visual pop artist and is now perhaps best remembered for his James Ensor-inspired painting *The Entry of Christ into Liverpool*. Amongst the Liverpool cognoscenti he was also known for his frequent allusion to panties, his lust for A level schoolgirls and his preoccupation with the monstrous anti-hero of Jarry's plays, Père Ubu. For Henri, Liverpool 8 was the Wild West, a cartoon setting where everything was possible and all was art. A journey on public transport was a magical mystery tour. One of his 'happenings' involved marking the boundaries of Liverpool 8 with a line of white flowers. His disdain for the Establishment is reflected in his poem 'Adrian Henri's Last Will and Testament': 'I leave my paintings to the Nation with the stipulation that they must be exhibited in Public Houses, Chip Shops, Coffee Bars, and the Cellar Clubs throughout the country.'

His verse describes Liverpool in witty collages as a mythical and humdrum place. One of my favourite couplets is:

> Prostitutes in the snow in Canning Street like strange erotic
>   snowmen
> And Marcel Proust in the Kardomah eating Madeleine butties
>   dipped in tea.

Africa simmered deep under the skin of the dreamless natives in Liverpool 8. At the Lucky Bar in the late '70s, one could still dance the night away to 'Going Down to Rio' by Mike Naismith or listen to working girls discussing business in back slang. The Somali Centre Club served fantastic yellow curries upstairs while downstairs it played cutting-edge blue beat and served beer in bottles; even the Lodge Lane Kwik Save played hip soul. The Niger and the Ghanaian were other late-night watering holes, which adopted a policy that you either had to be from the same country as the owners or white to get in. Every night was a carnival, a bohemian orgy catering for each new tide of frustrated seamen and a few local cognoscenti. Most of the shebeens were nothing more than whitewashed, dimly lit basements but the groping opportunities for mashers in the midnight hour were unbeatable. Liverpool was a 'chocolate port' and a twilight zone with Granby ward at its centre.

Toccy had a dozen different faces and a myriad of shebeens: the basement Alahram where Jamaican bluebeat, ska and Yemeni folk songs went into the mix; the Gladray strip joint which cost a shilling to get in and was always full of people in uniforms; the Olympus, a retreat for sad Greek gamblers who had lost everything; and Polish Joes and the Tudor (Dutch Eddie's). The Lucky Bar was little more than a dimly lit, musty ship's cabin with lifebelts, bullfighting posters and Yoruba masks adorning its bare walls, but at night it became an irresistible magnet for the sexually frustrated. Its girls ranged from hardened painted madams to bright-eyed, flirty 'smoked Irish' teenagers dressed for the kill. The men were mostly rough and ready sailors on temporary release from the drudgery of their ocean jails. By midnight the saturnalia would be in full swing and continue till the early hours. The following afternoon, as the smell of beer and engine oil blew up Princes Avenue from the river, the local brass would relax in the Lucky reading the *Journal of Commerce* to determine which ships were due in port.

There were no black people in my year at medical school – and not many women either. The counter-culture had passed me by and Jung's 'nigger' nightmare still obsessed Liverpool. The city was not ready to go black or acknowledge its own shadow. Africa was still a blank anima in the shape of a bleeding heart. Liverpool's blacks were squirrelled away from view in a run-down neighbourhood now officially known as Liverpool L8 2TU.

Spion Kop

I'm starting from the teddy-choirboy
who taught us what painting the town red meant
in a city where you simply had to know
who'd done what on any given Saturday
at Anfield or away—
where lives would be one long might-have-been
if the referee was blind or a linesman biased;
and even though you'll never walk alone
I could almost taste it in a smoky sky
welling up like burst blood-vessels round the gates,
full time blown, as down we went
with the rivers of red between brick terrace houses.

Extract from 'The Red Dusk' by Peter Robinson

One sultry Saturday afternoon something changed on the ant highways. The production line faltered and fewer comrades gnawed on the grimy pear drop which had fallen accidentally from my mouth into the gutter. The farm workers began to neglect their cows in the lupin meadow and the kitchen-raiding parties now stayed close to the nest. Pills of regurgitated soil piled up in the gap between the flags and today there was no time to bury the dead. As we listened for the first roar from Knowsley Road that would tell us Saints had scored, the full-bodied virgin princesses began to emerge from their chambers flanked by soldiers. The carnival parade was underway and was about to break the monotony of a simmering summer spent flicking half matchboxes on the paving stones of Speakman Road. Each black beauty searched for a high point and then rose up to meet the cloud of drones spiralling up with the sunbeams, samba strains and sugar clocks to darken the sky. By teatime, the ground was littered with fairy wings and dead brothers from a hundred Denton's Green nests whose life's work had consisted of a single ejaculation. As the fallen princesses scuttled for shelter in the cracks, I put one in a matchbox and subconsciously acknowledged the importance of absolute sovereignty and the need to belong and conform in my own life. The next day, the ants were back to normal business on the pavements. Old soldiers ventured into battle to save their young and those with full stomachs fed hungry workmates.

Ten years later, I was still collecting ants on gritty Almscliffe Crag when carnival broke out on the steep bank of the Spion Kop in faraway Anfield. Inspired by the music of The Silver Beatles, a surging sea of anarchists from the docks had finally found their voices. Straight from their hearts there gushed a spontaneous plainsong, with which they serenaded their port and their football club:

> Can I tell you a story of a poor boy who was sent far away from his
>   home,
> To fight for his king and his country and also the old folks back
>   home.
> Now they put him in a Highland division,
> Sent him off to a far foreign land,
> Where the flies flew around in their thousands,
> There was nothing to see but the sand.
> Now the battle it started next morning,
> Under the Libyan sun,
> I remember the Poor Scouser Tommy who was shot by an old Nazi
>   gun.
> As he lay on the battlefield dying, dying, dying with the blood
>   gushing out of his head,
> As he lay on the battlefield dying, dying, and dying these are the last
>   words he said:
> 'Oh I am a Liverpudlian and I come from the Spion Kop,
> I love to sing, I love to shout,
> I get thrown out quite a lot.
> We support the team that's dressed in red,
> And it's a team that you all know,
> It's a team that we call LIVERPOOL,
> And to glory we will go.'

The pride and shame of a whole city fermented every other Saturday afternoon on the high-sloped terrace named Spion Kop after a Boer War battle site. Diehards got married on its towering bank and in their wills asked for their ashes to be placed by the hallowed stancheon. The voices

LIVERPOOL ADVERTISER,
And Mercantile Chronicle.

THURSDAY MAY 4, 1780.   [Price THREE PENCE.]

Mafter was to have been married on his return home, was an eye witnefs. They were carried by the violence of the ftorm into Boulogne, where they are kept in prifon, but only through mock formality it is fuppofed, and the boy is kept at the Commiffary's houfe there.—The veffel and cargo, which confifted of lead and falt, were fold for 5,000 livres.

Extract of a letter from Plymouth, April 25.
"Arrived the Britannia, a Cartel from Morlaix, ft, failed from that port two French privateers, one 32, the other of 22 guns; and that the week fore two fhips with provifions from Waterford r London, and a brigantine, were carried into at port by the Dunquerkoife privateer."
A letter from Jerfey brings advice, that two ench privateers, belonging to St. Maloe's, were ft loft in the late blowing weather, between that and and the coaft of France, and moft of the ws were drowned.

FOR SALE,
JUST IMPORTED,
A Quantity of exceeding fine old *Cogniac*
BRANDY, xi
And a few Hogfheads of choice CLARET
Apply to WILLIAM SKELHORNE, James's-ftreet.

RUN AWAY,
On the 18th of APRIL laft, from PRESCOT,
A BLACK MAN SLAVE,
Named GEORGE GERMAIN FONEY,
Aged twenty years, about five feet feven, rather handfome; had on a green coat, red waiftcoat and blue breeches, with a plain pair of filver fhoe buckles; he fpeaks Englifh pretty well.
Any perfon who will bring the black to his maf-ter, Captain Thomas Ralph, at the Talbot Inn, in Liverpool, or inform the mafter where the black is, fhall be handfomely rewarded.

NOTICE to CREDITORS.
WHEREAS JOHN SALT, of the town of Frodfham, in the county of Chefter, Inn-holder, hath lately affigned over his effects to John Barnes, of Helfbey, in the faid county of Chefter, gentleman, and Francis Clayton, of the city of Chefter, wine-merchant, in Truft for the equal benefit of all his creditors who fhall execute the faid affignment on or before the 24th day of June next enfuing.
NOTICE IS HEREBY GIVEN, That fuch of the creditors as have not already executed the faid affignment, may execute the fame, by applying at Mr. Wilbraham's office, in Chefter, and at the fame time deliver in their refpective ac-counts. And all perfons indebted to the faid John Salt, are requefted to pay their refpective debts to the faid Mr. Barnes, at Frodfham, or to the faid Mr. Clayton or Mr. Wilbraham, in Chefter, on or before the faid twenty-fourth day of June next. or

The front page of *Williamson's Mercantile Chronicle*, 4 May 1780, showing an advertisement asking for information about a runaway black slave called George Germain Foney. (Liverpool Public Records Office)

A panorama of the Liverpool waterfront, 1860. (National Museums Liverpool)

The author (far left) holding his sword with the Speakman Road Gang, St Helens, 1953. (From the author's collection)

Speakman Road, St Helens, 2005. (From the author's collection)

The Queen's and Coburg docks, 1895. (Liverpool Public Libraries)

Castle Street, looking in the direction of the town hall, 1905. (Liverpool Public Libraries)

SS *Servia* and RMS *Saxonia* at the Liverpool Landing Stage, 1902. (Liverpool Public Libraries)

The Earl and Countess of Derby receiving guests at Knowsley Hall, 1907.
(Liverpool Public Libraries)

Residents of Lionel Street,
part of 'Little Italy', off
Scotland Road, 1931.
(*Liverpool Daily Post*,
Trinity Mirror Group)

An aerial view of the
Liverpool waterfront
showing the Three Graces,
the ferry and the docks, 1933.
(The Press Association)

Liverpool dockers, 1962. (Henri Cartier-Bresson, Magnum)

Liverpool 8, 1966.
(Philip Jones Griffiths, Magnum)

Liverpool Labour MP Bessie
Braddock aims a punch at
'Mr Moonlight', the crooner
Frankie Vaughan, 1960. The
pair shared a love of boxing and
would often attend matches
together. (*Liverpool Daily Post*,
Trinity Mirror Group)

Liverpool winger Alan A'Court
crashes against the Kop wall
during an FA Cup tie between
Liverpool and Southampton,
1962. (Trinity Mirror Group)

A steeplejack lays the steelwork for the roof of the Metropolitan Cathedral of Christ the King, circa 1964. (*Liverpool Daily Post*, Trinity Mirror group)

Rushworth's Music Shop in Whitechapel, 1964. (Getty Images)

Barbados cane cutters, 1934. (Getty Images)

The Tate & Lyle refinery, Love Lane, Vauxhall, shortly before its demolition, 1984. (Dave Sinclair)

'The Messiah', Liverpool Football Club manager Bill Shankly receiving the acclaim of the Spion Kop, Anfield, 1973. (Press Association)

A match in the Scotland Road Junior League, Flinders Street, off Vauxhall Road, circa 1978. (Scottie Press)

Granby Street graffiti, Liverpool 8, 1984. (Dave Sinclair)

Local residents watching the Caribbean Carnival, Granby Street, Liverpool, 1988. (Dave Sinclair)

St George's Anglican Church, Everton, 1988. (Dave Sinclair)

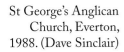

In the wake of the Toxteth Riots, 1981. (Press Association)

The gate leading into the Breeze Hill reservoir on the James Bulger walk, 1993. (Dave Sinclair)

An Orange Lodge march near St George's Hall, Liverpool, 1996. (Dave Sinclair)

The Tobacco Warehouse and Stanley Dock, 2008. (Mark McNulty)

Girls inside Cream, circa 1995. (Mark McNulty)

of the Kop choir had almost become the fifth Beatle and their triumphant, whimsical songs proclaimed the superiority and solidarity of the city and its place in global popular culture. It was a rogue branch of the entertainment business and the pacemaker for Anfield's bleeding heart. To wackers, it was also a novel form of group therapy, an opportunity to laugh at oneself, become a pop idol for two hours and unite against a common enemy. The Kop's magic conjured up an unshakeable communal faith that transformed a lippy docker's pain and suffering into grace. It craved the unexpected, the maverick genius, the heroes and villains but it was the dependable triers in the team that stole its heart. In full voice, it invoked the vagaries of life and the sentiments of the dispossessed. It emphasised life, not death, joy over sadness, strength as opposed to helplessness. It removed everyday social barriers and provided men with a stage to express communal friendship and happiness. The Redmen hijacked symbols of subversive patriotism but transformed them for their own tribal purposes. They were all on the same trip, trying to escape from the everyday fear of being touched. The Kopites insisted Liverpool FC reflected their own credo, with no place for Manchester United's fancy flickers or galacticos. One rogue sailor could sink a ship and at Liverpool Football Club everyone was in it together. In the back-to-backs around the ground, the football widows dreamed of romantic sailors and coral beaches as they looked out across the lines of houses to the scarlet roof of the Kemlyn Road stand.

The leader of the choir was Bill Shankly, a charismatic, pig-headed Scot who idolised James Cagney. After his managerial appointment at Anfield, he told the press: 'I'm going to a place where they live, eat, sleep and drink football – and that's my place.' 'Shanks' considered himself invincible and his team unbeatable. After Liverpool were defeated by Arsenal in the Cup, a huge crowd turned up to welcome the team home. 'The Messiah' mounted the steps of St George's Hall, spread his arms out and told them, 'Yesterday we lost the Cup but you the people have won everything. I've always drummed it into my players that they are playing for you, the greatest fans on earth. If they didn't believe it they will now.'

During home games, Shanks would sometimes climb over the hoarding onto the Kop to discuss tactics with his adoring flock. His defiant words often brought tears to the eyes of unemployed dockers. In 1973, after Liverpool had drawn with Leicester to clinch the League title, a young fan threw a scarf onto the pitch. As a policeman kicked it away, Shankly picked it up, handed it back to the crowd and turned to the policeman, telling him, 'Don't do that again. That scarf is the boy's life.' Shankly's philosophy stemmed from the community spirit of the tenements and his definition of family extended far beyond blood relations. He embraced the passion, pride and impudent humour of the Liverpool people. He ate, drank and slept football just as they did.

In one interview, he stated that his job was to make the people who went to Anfield each week happy and that nothing else in his life mattered. To Shanks, Liverpool FC was the best team in the world, Liverpool reserves their nearest challengers and all 22 players the product of his passion. Although he was often ruthless, inflexible and dictatorial, demanding absolute loyalty from his boot room and his team, the Kop adored him. On occasions, he was forced to resort to emotional blackmail to get his way with the club's directors, and treated injured players like traitors and cowards, but by the time he threw in the towel he had transformed a mediocre club into the best team in Europe.

Gerry and the Pacemakers' song 'You'll Never Walk Alone' was at number one when President Kennedy was assassinated. Within a few weeks, this Rodgers and Hammerstein tune from the musical *Carousel* had been adopted as the Redmen's *samba enredo*. It became a rallying cry that restored belief and hope. The Kop was the control tower of the football ground and a barometer for the city's fortunes, and whenever this new anthem broke out on the terrace it served as a sharp reminder to the opposition that Liverpool had a twelfth man. The fans invented new lyrics like 'We all live in a red and white Kop' to the tune of 'Yellow Submarine', which 40 years later was modified to 'We all dream of a team of Carraghers.' New songs were penned in the Albert, The Park Hotel, The Breck, The Sandon, The Oakfield and The Arkles public houses, with music sheets printed and distributed outside the ground on match days. Up to 150 different chants were counted at one game and every week the nation's armchair supporters were treated to an unsolicited concert of quick-witted and often obscene refrains. This fervid intonation spread from the Kop's belly like a peristaltic wave across the pitch to the Anfield Road end. Many of the signature tunes expressed confidence and superiority; some were panegyrics while others were biting, lewd insults directed at the opposition and the referee. The policeman who patrolled the perimeter was also a regular victim of cruel chants:

Who's that twat in the big black hat?
Copper, Copper
Who's that twat in the big black hat?
Copper is his name!

When Liverpool scored at the Annie Road End, the Kop would chime up with 'Who scored the goal, who scored the goal, eee-aye-addio, who scored the goal?' The Anfield Road crowd would reply with, 'Hunt scored the goal; Hunt scored the goal, eee-aye-addio, Hunt scored the goal.' The Kop responded, 'With his head or with his foot? With his head or with his foot?' This would go on and on. When Gary Sprake, the Leeds United goalkeeper, threw the ball into his own net, the Kop piped up with Des O'Connor's 'Careless Hands'. One cold winter afternoon when not much was happening on the pitch, a pigeon landed close to the goal and waddled towards the back of the net. When it finally crossed the white line, the Kop erupted as if it was the greatest goal it had ever witnessed.

The dockers were still penned in but here they could vent their rage without fear of reproach and there was no more disturbing sound than their snarling, angry roar drilled into the backs of their opponents. Shankly ruefully commented in a press conference: 'When there's a corner at the Kop end, they frighten the ball.' One day, the big Everton centre-forward Fred Pickering went down seriously injured and had to be carried off. A vicious refrain came from behind the goal of 'Dead Fred, Dead Fred, ah ha ha ha.'

In 1966, Liverpool was still living the dream. New tunes were in the air and the Beatles were bigger than Jesus. The people still believed they were living in the 'Village at the Centre of the World' and that the city was the head of Lancashire's body. After Everton won the Cup and Shankly's Liverpool FC were on the march, the city council had a vision to turn Liverpool into England's Brasília, where its citizens would find visual pleasures, colour and recreation in a post-modernist metropolis. The trams and Overhead Railway had already gone and now it was the turn of the slums. Chimneys tumbled and wrecking balls rammed into the flanks of the back-to-backs. Social engineering dictated that the residents of whole streets must be lured into new 18-storey blocks that took them far from their birthplace and neighbours. Walkways in the sky, a suburban Merseyrail and packed buses carried workers to the port and the factories. The pinnacle of this civic makeover was the St John's Beacon, a repellant poor man's Post Office Tower with a revolving restaurant at the top. The corporation ignored the fact that Langton and Sandon docks were bare, the Cavern had been turned into an electrical substation and Swinging London was a world away.

Football had always aroused burning passions. For the men working in harsh conditions, be it in the docks, the shipyards, the warehouses or out at sea, the game was a heavenly respite. The Kop rocked and rolled, applauded visiting goalkeepers and could even extend its generosity to 'Dirty Leeds'. After a dogged 0–0 draw at Anfield, which left Liverpool runners-up to their rivals, the Kop chanted, 'Champions, Champions,' in praise of the hated men in white. The unemotional United manager Don Revie had tears in his eyes and he would later send a telegram to Anfield Road thanking the Kop for their generosity. I was now going to Elland Road, still trying to fit in across the Pennines, but it was Shankly who influenced my thinking about life and football, and I could never fall in love with 'The Peacocks'.

In 1971, the Kop Choir finally became real pop stars with a field recording on 'Fearless', a track on Pink Floyd's *Meddle* album. Meanwhile, the city's own popular musicians ignored the glory game. A picture of Albert Stubbins on the front of the *Sergeant Pepper* album was as far as it went.

After his resignation in 1974, Bill Shankly stood alone on the Kop as the Redmen deferentially roared, 'Shankly is our King, Shankly is our King.' Little did they realise that their saviour was slowly dying from a broken heart. Despite his affirmation to the press that he was only retiring from football not from life, the truth was he had nowhere left to go.

Piercing the ramparts on Walton Breck Road through the wooden confessionals guarded by the heavy metal turnstiles and the shadowy priests, I now ascend for the last time the worn steps. At the summit, I look down on Dante's Divine Comedy: the grinning polo-necked Teds, edentulous Elvis Costellos and the bowler-hatted insurance men. Rising above the raucous murmuration I hear the anger of someone's grandmother letting rip at the referee from the safety of a crash barrier. A grey steam brightened by tobacco incense and flavoured with foul breath swirls up from the stormy sea of crushed bodies before sinking down once more into the fermenting cauldron of sweat, beer and onions. The caged roar reaches the river as the stinging late rain teems down on a thallium sea and the topmast of Brunel's Great Eastern iron ship. Above me are two lads crawling across the Kop's steel roof, holding firm and cheering on their team.

A Toxteth GP once told me that as he listened to the umpteenth sad tale of tower-block isolation, unemployment, a failed marriage and unfulfilled dreams, he had often wished he could write out the following prescription:

Mr George Aspinall. Occupation: warehouseman.
Prescribe: The Spion Kop, 1962.

prn. Free admission Saturday afternoon 3–5 p.m.
Take once a fortnight for a heavy heart.

Shanks had resurrected a sleeping giant and created an ethos that would make his successor Bob Paisley one of the most successful managers in the English game. He had also instilled belief and loyalty in a people who had begun to lose their sense of purpose.

For several years after Shankly had gone, the Kopites gorged on the success of his legacy and travelled to places they had never dreamed of. Adrian Henri described one of these sorties in his essay 'The Glory that was Rome':

> Shortly before leaving Rome, we were sitting at a pavement café. A pretty young Italian woman with two children was standing at a bus stop nearby. A Liverpool supporter, obviously still celebrating, lurched over to her and started gesturing. Oh no, we thought, trouble. He went inside and returned a few minutes later with two enormous ice creams, which he handed solemnly to the children. On the flight home after the champagne had been emptied, we were about to come in to land at Speke Airport. A well-dressed middle-aged man in front of us called the hostess over: 'Hey, love, can you get the pilot to do a victory roll?'

Halewood

The white seagulls dip for scraps above
Long Lane's central reservation; brittle leaves
are ousted by heaped shreds of paper
and, at a football pitch's edge,
I'd watch a while the Sunday League game,
clouds and my father's parish in its hollow;
now across those pieces
of a swallowed industrial village. I know
I shan't reach a destination –
for avenues proliferate
taunting each approach, crossroads appear,
beyond a cutting and a railway station
distances congeal, it's late
and front doors shut

Extract from 'Faith in the City'
by Peter Robinson

After the Second World War, Liverpool managed to attract more than 50 companies to provide factory jobs for 27,000 unemployed port workers: Dunlop, GEC, Napier, Kodak, Massey Ferguson, Lucas and others. This had only a marginal effect on the city's spiralling economic decline and Merseyside continued to sink into a deep, damaging recession. After the British government had refused to allow Ford to further expand its Dagenham plant, the motor company was pressured into building a new £40-million, 346-acre plant on potato fields to the east of Widnes in the Knowsley village of Halewood. The prospect of 9,000 stable, well-paid jobs in motor manufacturing brought fresh hope to the unemployed masses.

Liverpool was increasingly associated with strike-happy subversives, militancy and Bolshevism, a perception that did not hold up to objective scrutiny. Nevertheless, Liverpool workers had gained a reputation within trades union circles for being formidably well organised, particularly in their demands for local autonomy. The town's long history of civil disobedience and lack of a manufacturing pedigree were further disincentives for big business.

In an attempt to circumvent some of these potential problems, Ford tried to poach docile, semi-skilled 'greenhorns' from Dunlop and other Liverpool factories in order to improve its chances of competitive productivity. Everything began smoothly and Halewood was soon turning out gleaming lime-green Anglias from sheets of steel. The men fed metal into state-of-the-art presses, which with a single bite of their vicious jaws would transform the scrap into panels. The components were then slung up on hooks, which moved slowly round the plant on a revolving chain. Welders in protective clothing fired rows of sparking spot welds into the seams of the panels using guns suspended from springs. The plant resembled a perpetual-motion machine of gigantic, automated, floodlit boxes on a never-ending line. The noise was deafening.

Many of the new factory workers found the monotony of the shop floor difficult to endure. Absenteeism and staff turnover were astronomically high and some of the men even asked for their cards at the end of their very first shift. Those who stayed felt like automatons and survived only by blanking out their minds to everything around them. Despite the management's reluctance to hire unemployed dockers, the waterfront welt system of job sharing was soon in place and special merit payments had been introduced to keep the workers happy. Ford had made the cardinal mistake of employing cockney managers, who were regarded with innate suspicion by the locals. In 1967, four years after the plant had opened, the shop stewards began to rebel against the 'ball-and-chain system' brought in by 'foreigners' from the East End of London. In his book *Working for Ford*, Huw Beynon quotes the view of one Liverpool shop steward:

> They thought they could treat us like dirt, them. We were just dirty Scousers who'd crawled in off the docks out of the cold. We'd never even seen a car plant before and these sods had been inside one since they were knee high. We took a hammering . . . they were robbing us blind up here. They were getting away with murder. Doing things they wouldn't have dreamed of in Dagenham.

In what became a war of attrition, the Liverpool shop stewards fought for modern operational procedures, ratification of deals by the rank and file and for shop-floor representation on the National Joint Negotiating Committee. In their meetings with the supervisors, they considered management was ignoring their views and adopting a colonial and patronising mentality in response to their real concerns. Beynon contrasts the cockiness of the Liverpool shop stewards with the home-knit resignation prevalent at the new Swansea sister plant whose labour-force heritage lay in the pits rather than the docks:

> The stewards were young men. They wore sharp clothes: suits with box jackets. They thought of themselves as smart modern men; and this they were. They walked with a slight swagger, entirely alert and to the point of things. They walked, talked and looked as they were. They knew what their bit of the world was about and they were prepared to take on anybody who challenged it.

A 'go-slow' reinforced deep-seated national prejudices about Liverpool, and Halewood was soon embroiled in a self-destructive series of unofficial wildcat strikes, which brought the production of the new Ford Escort to a halt. The workers walked off the line in response to 'speed-ups' and the female sewing machinists came out in protest against unequal pay. Workers who had escaped the insecurity of casual labour and the fear of permanent unemployment were now putting well-paid jobs at risk for something that amounted to more than just money. An entrenched resistance to exploitation led to a dogged determination by the Halewood workers to fight for perceived justice. Many of these altercations were of national importance and not restricted to Liverpool, but because of the press fascination with anything related to the city in the 1960s, a disproportionate amount of adverse coverage was given to her industrial relations.

Throughout the 1970s, national strikes seemed to last longer in Liverpool than anywhere else, with Scousers continuing to shout defiance long after everyone else had gone back to work. During the 'Winter of Discontent' in 1978, 15,000 Ford workers turned down a pay rise within the government's 5 per cent guidelines and in a short time 57,000 plant workers were out on strike. Things were to get worse for the city, with the Liverpool cemetery workers leaving the dead unburied in an empty factory in Speke. The Medical Officer of Health contemplated the possibility of sea burials if there was no rapid resolution to the dispute. After two weeks, the men went back with a fat 14 per cent pay rise. Merseyside militancy hit the headlines again and the tag of 'Lazy Scousers' was now on every tabloid journalist's lips. These fights for more money led to bad publicity for the city and put a blight on any last hope of regeneration as England's dwindling manufacturing base continued to move south and east.

Liverpool's reputation as a Marxist stronghold was given further credence by the Nob Hill rent strike. In 1972, a small number of displaced 'wackers' living in the overspill Tower Hill estate in Kirkby defied the government's House Finance Act. The rebels, under the leadership of International Socialist Tony Boyle and Communist Party maverick Maurice Lee, refused to pay their rents or rates for a year and ripped up the council's court summons. With the help of a battalion of angry young mothers armed with prams, they also managed to force the chairman of the local Birds Eye factory to reinstate 24 men who had stayed off work to support the rent strike. The tenants blocked the main roads around Tower Hill, causing traffic chaos on the West Lancashire motorway network. Some ended up in prison when the mass industrial action against the Edward Heath government the agitators had hoped for failed to transpire and their actions left many of their supporters in debt for years.

Solidarność and the bloodless revolution passed Liverpool by, an irrelevant spiritual resistance that had long ago been won. As I stand here beside the small memorials and plaques to the victims of totalitarianism, I start to think again of Joseph Conrad and his stories of life at sea. At Halewood, a parallel revolution had occurred in support of egalitarianism and meritocracy, a fight for respect, a concordat that every man, regardless of his rank or class, was as good and important as the next, a natural democracy which grew from life at sea.

On the horizon is the weather-beaten Nowo Port. I can see the beaks of the bulbous cranes and feel the weight of the leaden sky. There is a harsh Baltic wind and a lashing rain, which feels like Liverpool on my skin. Tumbledown tenements where hungry dogs roam in packs border the perimeters of the shipyard, mothers push their babies through cheerless roads with smashed windows and men huddle in bars drinking vodka before confession. As two well-to-do Polish beneficiaries enter the Roads to Freedom Exhibition, the hooter drones and a shrinking workforce starts to check out. I watch muttering fathers and helmeted sons covered in oil and grime with rucksacks containing leftovers trickle through the gates. Most are in cheap hoods, jeans and trainers, and seem relieved the working day is over. A few look grim and almost beaten, as if their peaceful struggle had solved nothing. Down the road, the Old Town fills with German tourists chasing their roots, Spaniards hunting amber and a new breed of entrepreneurs liberated by Wałęsa's blind courage and the words of Pope John Paul II. I see no real changes for these hollow men trapped on gantries and locked away in portside blocks. The new rapacious, corrupt world of modern Poland may force them to rise again; for now, most have pinned their hopes on getting out to a new world of opportunity that leads their children to Liverpool and the Enterprise City. If it hadn't been for Salford, the Soviet Union might never have existed and it was the Beatles, not the Pope, that raised the Iron Curtain. Marxism was untenable if you owned your own house and your own car, and especially if your wife was of a different political persuasion. The ports of Gdansk and Liverpool, labouring under different political systems for so long, stood firm on common ground but Poland had moved forward faster than Liverpool.

Cacotopia

I remember graffiti: KILLER CELTIC on a wall in Netherley,
TAXI WHORE on the footbridge at Belle Vale Shopping
Precinct, LES GROOVES DOGS BOTTIES on the railway at
Childwall . . .
I remember walking for miles on hot days down long straight
industrial roads out towards the chemical works at Widnes . . .
I remember my first night in London. It was a shared room in a
hostel in Knightsbridge, and somebody had carved I stumbled
into town into the headboard.

> Extracts from 'I Ran All the Way Home' by Paul Farley

By the 1970s, Liverpool was decaying. Hitler's bombs had destroyed large swathes of the city and the older buildings that had survived were being torn down as part of the city council's well-intentioned but thoughtless slum-clearance programme. It tore the working-class communities apart. Many 'slummies' were uprooted against their will to soulless new towns on the fringes of the port. Kirkby had mutated from a hamlet of 3,000 Lancashire farmers to a sprawling rustic theme park catering for 52,000 people displaced from the inner city. These outcasts, with their broods of children, were shoved out to the peripheries to work for Birds Eye and Kraft, lived on groves and brows but no longer knew who they were. Like snails, they carried an inner-city shell on their backs as they searched for nurture amongst the fenced-off saplings. Within a single generation, dreams had turned to nightmares and Kirkby had spawned squads of unemployed Scouse bootboys, who in order to lay anchor defended their manors in Northwood, Westvale, Tower Hill and Southdene. Some of the resulting turf wars were so serious they required the intervention of mounted police. It took almost ten years for the first main shopping and leisure facilities to be put in place and the tram line into town ended in Fazakerley. Appalling neglect had been allowed to fester and take root, and the vandals took pleasure in desecrating the unpopular tower blocks and uprooting the hated trees.

Much of Liverpool continued to live on the breadline but its dysfunctional underbelly was now no longer to be found in the shrinking, tightly knit, back-to-back rookeries around Scotland Road, or in the decaying Victoriana of Liverpool 8. Totalitarian emotional oppression was at its worst in these new Lego-brick Skinner boxes of the overspills, the amorphous, ill-designed social housing of schemes like Cantril Farm (Cannibal Farm to the locals), semi-detached Croxteth, Edge Hill, Norris Green's Boot Estate, Halewood, the Netherley Estate, The Bluebell Huyton and the Everton Brow prison block sinks built to accommodate redundant port-side tenement refugees. By the '80s, twice as many inner-city people had been uprooted to these 'New Jerusalems' as were left in town. The Scotty Road and North End dockers who had settled 20 years earlier into their swanky properties, ordering their visitors to take their shoes off on crossing the threshold, had long ago had their hopes dashed by a generation of unemployment and the rapid dilapidation of their new homes as a result of the council's inertia and lack of money.

These spaces were now the badlands for racists, wife beaters, child abusers and heart-dead muggers; subhuman swamps of lost souls where the few trees were shadowy and forbidding. In some of the most desolate areas, houses less than five years old were already boarded up awaiting demolition, and others had been incinerated in the new powder wars. Empty properties had their windows shattered and their roofs smashed within days of the occupants' desertion. Old cookers lay on the sickly grass next to walkways littered with shards of glass. Even bumblebees feared to land. Speke, the land of shell suits and the frozen burger, was cancerous. These were places of terrifying dereliction where all living things seemed to have died. Croxteth had so many junkies that it was renamed 'Smack Heights'. For many young people brought up in Kensington and Anfield, a cataclysmic descent into a netherworld of drug abuse and self-destruction was the final common pathway. Some came out of jail on methadone but most were soon back selling their bodies, burgling their neighbours or stealing from their family. The lucky ones remained banged up in Walton or Strangeways.

Many good, honest families still made ends meet but they had had to learn to keep themselves to themselves. Their children were wanted and loved but insurmountable obstacles confronted them every day. Some had never been inside a bank and relied on loan sharks and handouts to survive. The days when burglars were battered and old people respected were almost gone. Christmas trees were chained up in the windows. The locked-up churches became embattled centres for resistance against despair. It was much rarer for people to pop next door to borrow some sugar and mind everyone's business. Neighbourhood Watch, satellite dishes and burglar alarms had replaced neighbourliness, turning the terraces into a lonely planet of iron grilles. While the odd shuttered shop still sold basic comestibles, many more were boarded up and permanently closed for business. Health centres had walled battlements as heavily fortified as the neighbouring crack dens and skunk factories. This was a submerged redline area. Some of the old two-up two-downs had their windows filled in with metal sheets bearing the crest of the City of Liverpool. Benefits were stripped to make those on the dole get on their bikes and fight for work. People saved for their bus fare not their holidays and died a lingering death while still dreaming of a lottery win. Hard-faced young women dragged their broods to TJ Hughes to comb the rails for a cheap top or a pair of seconds. There was no Avon lady here, only a sad trade in laxatives for weight loss and Imac hair remover. Dull-eyed, cropped and hooded child-men patrolled the alleys looking to prey on the old and infirm. These teenage 'Soljas' possessed a callousness and lack of remorse, which stemmed from penal immunity and a 'Scarface' dream. They sniffed glue, smoked dope, laughed and kicked balls in society's face. Grasses, poofs, students and blacks were on the hate list for the gangs of self-appointed *Clockwork Orange* vigilantes. There was a loss of confidence and respect and a destructive, damaging anger.

Walton was now officially classified as an inner-city urban-priority area by Liverpool city council. Some of its impoverished, enslaved residents were in need of psychiatric treatment, but cutbacks in the National Health Service pushed back into the glacial dampness people who found life outside impossibly difficult. Most settled into a restricted life of chaotic squalor: the alcoholic surrounded himself with empty bottles and plastic packets of rotting fast food, the depressed young mother was in Accident and Emergency with slashed wrists, while the terrified, forgotten old man kept ringing the police to remove the phantoms on his stairs. An occasional headliner ran amok and killed a stranger. In these social experiments hidden from the few Japanese tourists, 60 per cent of the people of working age had no job or were prematurely retired, disabled or on government schemes. A third generation of unemployed men walked the streets, living off income support and theft. A few smack pioneers of Narcotics Anonymous stayed on the side of the angels but for most, old habits died hard. Overdoses had become a modern morality tale and the fallouts with whom the few winners shared needles went on dying from suicide, cancer, AIDS, endocarditis and hepatitis C. Countless victims of heroin still arrived in casualty, blue, sweating and vomiting. There were many fractured lives and a fair few who could no longer handle the pain of living, even on methadone. Most of these broken-down losers were the grandchildren of laid-off dockers, ship builders with no orders, redundant car workers and the ever-dispensable warehousemen. The spectral streets had become the terrain of the emotionally damaged and the mentally disturbed.

By the end of the week, food often ran out in Everton but now there were no friends to turn to. Candles and cigarettes replaced heat and light, and the water was cut off. Scousers had stopped looking out to sea and the Mersey seemed to be flowing by as fast as it could to escape this dying city. The Walton insomniacs queued up at supermarkets to try to get early-morning bargains. Strays as young as four could be seen wandering the streets at night, some of whom had already lost all their teeth to gum disease or gone deaf from middle-ear infections. Others ended up in hospital with the forgotten Victorian killers of tuberculosis, pneumonia and meningitis. Some were registered 'at risk', attended special schools, and many were habitual truants. Without structure and surrounded by mayhem and catastrophe, these children fell hopelessly behind and would eventually become unemployable. After years of 'sagging off', they left failing schools at 15 without hope or ambition, to enrol as full-time gang members.

Bright university students did not return home after graduation. The city's remaining rump of skilled workers plied their trade in Germany and Holland, returning like the sailors of old with sweets, five-pound notes and a few toys. The unskilled and unemployable also headed out to the Haydock Roundabout and the motorways to hitch a ride to the seaside.

The Independent once ran a headline: 'Scouse Equals Louse in Genteel Bournemouth'. The piece stated that 'Liverpudlian' had entered the resort's vocabulary as a derogatory word for all that is bad in people. Scousers were the ringleaders in a rising Boscombe bed-sit drugs and prostitution trade that threatened to destroy the seaside town's reputation as the Riviera of the South Coast and had led to the first UK town-centre CCTV surveillance. An exiled Scouser replied in the correspondence section that there was white racism in Bournemouth, with people from Liverpool doing all the most menial tasks in the resort. They were blamed for everything that went wrong and the local football league passed a new rule that there must be a maximum limit of five Scousers per team. Ironically, Bournemouth, officially the happiest town in England, was also now the home of the Liverpool Victoria Friendly Society.

The 8

well
dere woz Toxteth
an dere woz Moss Side
an a lat a addah places
whey di police ad to hide
well dare woz Brixtan
an dere woz Chapeltoun
an a lat a addah place dat woz burnt to di groun
it is noh mistri
wi mekkin histri
it is noh mistri
wi winnin victri.

Extract from *Making History*
by Linton Kwesi Johnson

After being badly bombed in the Blitz, Pitt Street was demolished in an early slum clearance, and Granby Street, a broad thoroughfare of shops and two-storey brick buildings, became the new focus for Liverpool's black community. Although black people made up an estimated 8 per cent of Liverpool's population, they were still largely hidden away in Toxteth. A group of Granby blacks picketed the town centre, complaining that they had to be twice as good as their white counterparts to even be considered for a job. There were apocryphal tales of young black men who had tried to move out of Liverpool 8 only to be forced back to the ghetto. London may have been full of black bus drivers but Liverpool didn't have a single one. Everton Football Club held out against signing black football players and there were very few blacks working at Halewood. Between 1974 and 1981, unemployment rose in Liverpool by 120 per cent but in Granby ward it went up by 350 per cent. The employers defended themselves by saying they never received any job applications from Liverpool 8, but the truth was that they had closed ranks against blacks from 'Jungle Town' with chips on their shoulders.

Forty years earlier, in 1930, the Liverpool University social science graduate Muriel Fletcher had produced her influential *Report on an Investigation into the Colour Problem in Liverpool and other Ports* for the Liverpool Association for the Welfare of Half-Caste Children. Fletcher asserted that when freed from their rigid tribal discipline, African seamen tended to seek out short-term sexual relationships. Based on her analysis of 91 families, she considered most of the marriages to be loveless and concluded that the 'hybrid' children had little prospect of becoming employable citizens. Her paper was distributed to the police, philanthropic organisations, the National Union of Seamen and Parliamentarians, and the conclusions disseminated through newspapers and radio. It had the full backing of the prominent eugenicist Rachel Fleming and was supported by other influential racists. Those in the black community who had participated with Fletcher felt betrayed and hurt. In the end, she was stabbed and forced to leave her job as a social worker in Liverpool but the damage caused by her report would leave a painful scar on Pitt Street. Many of the racial stereotypes which passed into common currency and the assertion that there was a serious problem in Liverpool 8 could be traced back to Muriel Fletcher's ill-conceived project. Black people became the butt of jokes, the subject of scurrilous articles and were even portrayed in children's comics as evil simpletons. 'Half-castes' were backward, inferior and incompetent, and needed to be secreted away from the respectable society of white Liverpool.

P.M. Roxby, chairman of the Liverpool Association for the Welfare of Half-Caste Children and a lecturer in geography at the University of Liverpool, believed that the most effective prevention of mixed-marriage children would be the total exclusion of black labourers on ships entering the port. The stereotype of the Liverpool Chinaman as a sexual deviant, gambler and opium dealer was temporarily forgotten with the emergence of 'the black peril', allowing Roxby to contrast the 'real social menace of the negro' with the virtuous character of the Oriental. The Shanghai and Hong Kong sailors who had married Liverpool Irish girls were now put on a pedestal as perfect husbands and in his foreword to the Fletcher Report, Roxby observed that the Chinese men lavished their spouses with luxuries and spared them from drudgery to ensure they would be rewarded with sexual favours. In contrast to Liverpool's 'half-castes', their children were invariably bright and industrious, well cared for and – more importantly for the racists – their colouring and features were less distinctive than 'Anglo-Negroids'.

THE 8

By 1974, the mood was changing as Liverpool 8 cheered its homeboy John Conteh to the world light-heavyweight boxing championship. Granby youth felt it had a right to be in Liverpool and was starting to fight back. This new generation of Liverpool-born black youths were listening to 'Ghetto Child' by the Detroit Spinners, 'Young, Gifted and Black' and 'Say it Loud I'm Black and I'm Proud'. Their grandfathers had travelled the world on slave ships and now they were caged up in a few square miles around Granby Street. Locally inspired radical groups like L8 Action Group and Liverpool Black Sisters, which had sprouted from the Stanley House Community Centre and the African Church Mission, led a call for the introduction of Black Studies on the school curriculum and made demands for equal opportunities in education and employment. Military-training exercises were conducted on the steep walls of the Anglican Cathedral to prepare for the next battle with the boot boys and skinheads. In the hot summer of 1976, Colin Jordan and the jackbooted National Front had stirred up trouble in Leeds and Bradford, and fixed Liverpool in their sights for what they thought would be the next easy target, but they were confronted at the Pier Head by the Young Black Panthers and forced to flee for their lives.

By the end of the '70s, Liverpool 8 was officially recognised as an area of social deprivation, akin to the South Bronx in New York, although for most Scousers it was no more dangerous than many other parts of town. Unemployment had led to low self-esteem, despair, anger, insanity and worst of all wasted talent, but there was still a siege mentality in Granby and Abercrombie. Toxteth had become a triangle of misery and was closing in on itself, increasingly bitter, alienated and claustrophobic. The residents slowly started to stick more to the streets where they lived and only mixed with their families and a few trusted neighbours. On the rare occasions they ventured past the Boundary pub and into town, they were ashamed to admit where they came from. Carter Street and Lodge Lane were littered with broken glass, shops started to close down and those that remained resembled fortified banks. The sign at the junction of the tree-lined boulevard of Princes Avenue and the main drag of Upper Parliament Street proclaimed 'City of Liverpool—Toxteth' but the world-class city had begun to disintegrate. As unemployment escalated, 'The 8' had become increasingly invisible and cut off in a city which prided itself on being a friendly, tolerant, welcoming place.

Hopelessness had created a simmering bitterness and frustration but not even the hardened locals could have predicted the events of July 1981.

Friction had been building between the old African black families and the post-war 'alien wedge'. The old Pitt Street crowd blamed the 'chip-on-the-shoulder' attitude of some of the new Jamaicans for the deterioration in community spirit and the hostility on the street. Young black bucks in the rookery of the Falkner Estate, progeny of the potato famine and the slave trade, started to demand their rightful share of the spoils. Some of Granby's old families felt God had deserted them and they in turn started to desert the Church. An area made up of old terraced houses, modern low-rise council developments and a few tower blocks, which had once attracted artists, sailors and drifters, had become a menacing 'no-go' zone. Eric Lynch, a council employee and active black trade unionist, made a speech in 1980 warning that:

> For far too long we have been used by white people in general, for their own amusement. We have been used by the white people of Great Britain for their misfortunes. We have been the handy men and women to do the jobs that no one else wants. We have been the handy men and women to be picked up and dropped at the whim of the white mind. We have been the children to be treated with sweets on occasions, but more often than not to be whipped like dogs when the Master felt like it. No longer are we prepared to be the underling, the plaything.

Granby residents complained of police harassment and racism. Some crooked coppers went farming, planting drugs and stolen items on black youths to increase their conviction rate. The police were likened by the locals to bananas: 'yellow, bent and coming in bunches'.

The battleground was drawn up on the Toxteth streets of former slave captains' homes. Granby was now a garrison for the deprived and marginalised, be they black or white. Criminals prowled the ghetto, mugging and burgling, which the police countered with swoop squads. The windows of the corner shops on Lodge Lane were now guarded by bullet-holed corrugated shutters smeared with graffiti abusing the police. On warm summer nights, groups of T-shirted lads lurked under the Christ on the Cross statue in Mulgrave Street, others in stolen cars led the 'jam-butty' patrol cars a fine dance through the medina. The freckled Showers brothers controlled the closes, the jiggers and the hallways, and random sporadic gunfire could sometimes be heard on Park Road.

Granby Street came under permanent surveillance. The police

intensified their use of the reviled 'Sus' laws and 'Stop and Search Operation Swamp' crime-prevention strategy. Their mantra was that Liverpool blacks refused to follow the laws and mores of England. 'Monkeys go back to the zoo, niggers get your arses back to Granby Street' was an example of the police dialogue in the regular confrontations with black youth. The closure by the plod of yet another shebeen further inflamed the locals and a group of rogue 'Babylonians' was alleged to have taunted the local bucks that they would never have the bottle to 'do a Brixton'.

The touchpaper was finally lit on 3 July in an incident involving the son of a prominent local West Indian who crashed his motorbike in Selbourne Street after a police chase. He was apprehended on suspicion of theft, despite his protestations of innocence. As he tried to struggle free, a crowd gathered, a skirmish then broke out and a youth broke a policeman's nose. While the police waited for reinforcements, the motorcyclist wriggled free but another young man, Leroy Cooper, who objected to the heavy-handed methods of the police, was held and arrested after ramming the police car with his bicycle. The police van fled the scene with three injured policemen in the back as a shower of bricks and stones rained down.

The following night, an anonymous telephone call reporting a stolen vehicle brought the police back to Granby, where an armed mob of around 200 mainly black youths aged between 12 and 20 were waiting with bricks, iron bars and petrol bombs. A police car was pushed into some roadworks and rolled down a hill before being set alight. By dawn, several overturned cars were ablaze and Upper Parliament Street was a picture of devastation. Worse was to follow at the weekend, with a football crowd arriving in taxis from all over the city to give the 'bacon' a hiding. Milk floats and a JCB excavator were used to ram buildings and charge the police. Agents provocateurs and anarchists in balaclavas arrived to marshal and orchestrate the local disgruntlement. Rioting and looting spread into Lodge Lane and Park Road, leaving a trail of charred desolation. Seventy officers were injured and only three rioters arrested. The impromptu tactic of containment with stand-offs behind riot shields and bin lids had proved disastrous for an unprepared police force.

Liverpool's summer sky now glowed an angry tangerine with banks of menacing black smoke drifting above Tiber Street. The Windsor Clock, a watering hole for young blacks, had been torched and the Racquets Club in Upper Parliament Street, the haughty preserve of local retailers, architects and circuit judges, had been razed to the ground. The former

Rialto Ballroom on the corner of Princes Avenue, where the legendary *This is Mersey Beat* albums had been recorded, was another early target. This distinctive domed building, now the home of Swainbanks, a furniture company, had a reputation in the black community for being a poor employer and a 'rip-off joint', and had come to symbolise their exclusion from the mainstream. The launderette, carpet shop and Trustee Savings Bank on Lodge Lane also went up in flames as jubilant looters carried televisions and video recorders away. The animals from the pet shop on Lodge Lane were rescued and taken to a safe haven on Longfellow Street. The roads were littered with shoes, tins and bottles. St Margaret's Church was spared, and the local community also defended the run-down Princes Park Hospital, with its colony of frail, elderly long-stay patients. The post office on the junction of Upper Parliament Street and Princes Road where the rioters cashed their giros also remained unscathed.

The police officers feared for their lives as they tried to neutralise a barrage of unrelenting rage and hatred. Their greatest fear as they crouched under their riot shields was of being isolated from their colleagues. Ambulance sirens, the thud of bricks, whistles and the sound of breaking glass provided the soundtrack for the television cameras. The tactic of 'standing there waiting to be injured' served the 'thin blue line' badly. Hundreds of reinforcements were bussed in from throughout the North of England, with Chief Constable Oxford defiantly stating, 'They won't beat me.' By the next morning, half of Toxteth had been obliterated and at last on Sunday night the order went out for the police to take the offensive. They massed in battle rank, singing 'Men of Harlech', beating out Zulu-like rhythms on their riot shields with sticks and helmets as they launched charge and counter-charge on the brick-hurling, petrol-bombing, gun-toting rabble.

A shout of 'Come on, you black bastards' went up from the police ranks. The rioters responded by banging bits of metal and pickaxes on the ground and shouting abuse. Stand-offs and isolated dog fights took place and some of the trapped looters broke their way into the neighbouring terraced houses to escape.

After three nights of violence and growing fears that the police might be overrun, Chief Constable Kenneth Oxford, a former bomber pilot with a distinguished police record and a tough, no-nonsense approach, was on the verge of phoning the Ministry of Defence when a junior colleague suggested an alternative. As the police were being pushed back down Parly towards Catherine Street, they were instructed to fire gunshots above the crowd and then let salvoes of CS gas loose for the first time on the British mainland. Rioters began to hit the deck, the mob retreated and the initiative was wrested back. These heavy-handed measures by the police had prevented the spread of looting to the city centre. Liverpool had returned from the abyss but skirmishes and pitched battles continued to flare up on Upper Parly and Granby Street for several more days. The insurgents basked in the euphoria of victory while the very few locals with jobs still to go to on Monday morning left home with the smell of smoke in their nostrils and gas fumes nagging at their throats. It felt like the return of the Jerry but the damage was far worse, as their own neighbours were the new enemies.

As gentle rains dampened the fires, Granby slowly returned to some sort of normality but only the drug dealers could look forward to new commercial opportunities. Hundreds of police and rioters had been injured and an estimated £11 million of damage inflicted on an already poverty-stricken community. The Liverpool Liberal leader Sir Trevor Jones, while acknowledging the effect of deep-seated unemployment, considered that the riots were simply due to delinquency on a grand scale, while the Chief Constable blamed black hooligans. Liverpool 8 was now a war zone and the local mongrels were chewing on bricks. In the wake of the mayhem, Margaret Thatcher made an ill-advised dawn visit to Liverpool, where she faced a hostile crowd throwing tomatoes and tin cans. Derek Worlock, the Catholic Archbishop, and Michael Henshall, the Anglican deputy for David Sheppard, informed her that the Church was working for reconciliation. The Iron Lady then enquired, 'Why is there such hatred?', a question to which Archbishop Worlock responded by emphasising the urgent need for compassion. Denis Thatcher turned to his wife and said, 'That's not one of your words, is it?', upon which the Prime Minister replied, 'I find it so condescending.' Worlock and Henshall tried to explain that to suffer with a community that had been deprived of a share in society was a worthy mission but their words fell on deaf ears.

The Prime Minister's team of civil servants rounded up some local officials at the town hall, where they were publicly lambasted by a furious Mrs Thatcher for failing to deal with the disturbance. During her tirade, the Prime Minister's attention was drawn to a black community worker. She stared at the man and asked in a demeaning tone, 'And who are you?' The man pre-empted her: 'Yo Maggie, we're not here about jobs and unemployment. We're here about the race issue.'

The riots were fuelled by a defiant and desperate protest against the heavy-handed tactics of the Merseyside police in a chronically depressed area. Local people felt they had no say in their destiny or affairs and, as Martin Luther King, Jr once said, riots were the voice of the unheard. Mrs Thatcher left town expressing her sympathies to the poor shopkeepers, convinced that Liverpool was a hellhole. The Tories saw 'The Gateway to the Empire' as a pestilential leper colony and a redundant millstone round the country's neck.

The day after the riots, Prince Charles married Lady Diana Spencer to national rejoicing. Many of the rioters hidden away in the Granby favela were holding their own unrelated victory celebrations. Lack of jobs was given as the main reason for the trouble, but festering anger, a breakdown of the social contract, kicks and excitement with an extra bonus of thieving were all probably closer to the truth. No one except Grub Street considered it to be a race riot. A Liverpool 8 local explained the cause to an American news crew: 'If you keep on mithering a dog, no matter how good-natured he is, sooner or later he's going to turn round and bite, and once he's bitten once he'll bite again.'

The following weekend, copycat riots flared in Moss Side, Manchester; Chapeltown, Leeds; Handsworth, Birmingham; and again in St Pauls, Bristol, all inner-city, marginalised areas with substantial Afro-Caribbean minorities. Two dozen other English towns and cities experienced smaller skirmishes. In late July, the first Liverpool 8 fatality occurred when a young, white wheelchair-bound man was accidentally mown down by a police Land Rover. As Granby baked in the hottest summer for years, even the sight of a patrol car triggered an automatic response of a hail of bricks, buckets of boiling water and televisions chucked from high-rise balconies.

When the riots kicked off, I was in Bahia. The pictures of besieged police in visors and with riot shields looked like street theatre. I was in the blackest city in Brazil, a drum port with a history, a place of magic, cloves and cinnamon and supernatural happenings. On the beach guarded by the growling Itapoa rocks, I felt like a snowman melting in Mother Africa's arms. An old Angolan on the beach wall sang the story of a strip of pristine forest in the backlands of Cabo de Santo Agostinho, close to the São Francisco River where the Great Lord Ganga Zumba ruled Macaco, the fortified City of Death and the capital of the maroon Republic of Palmares. Here, the runaway slaves planted the fertile land with vegetables, hunted with bows and arrows, spears and stolen firearms, and stored fruit for the winter. Wild palms made up most of the forest and provided the fugitives with roofing and scaffolding for their houses. 'The Republic' attracted more and more slaves as the plantation owners of Bahia and Olinda were distracted by the Dutch marauders. It also became a haven for hundreds of newly arrived penniless European immigrants. The numbers grew to 20,000 and Palmares would resist Portuguese military offensives for more than half a century. After his family had been captured in Amaro, Ganga Zumba was forced to make a pact with the Portuguese in 1678. The younger slaves, however, refused to give in and Ganga was killed in a palace coup, with power passing to Francisco Zumbi, a man who had been born in the enclave but captured as a baby and sold to Padre Antonio de Melo. The priest had taught him Latin and Portuguese but at 15 Francisco had left, saying he must return to the City of Death. After a series of further frustrated attempts to control Palmares, the Pernambuco Governor João da Cunha Souto Maior turned to the 70-year-old frontiersman Domingos Jorge Velho, who had made his living by enslaving Indians and capturing runaway slaves. After two years of intense fighting, Francisco Zumbi was finally defeated and Palmares razed to the ground. Four hundred Africans were captured, five hundred killed and two hundred former slaves threw themselves to their deaths from Macaco's fortifications. Zumbi escaped and fought a guerilla action against the *bandeirantes* for several more years before finally being betrayed. His disembodied head was paraded through the streets of Olinda but he went into history as the founder of the Zumbi nation with the landless *pretos* and people of the favela celebrating his death each year. I now saw Granby as a *quilombo*, a maroon community that protected its denizens from the harshness, humiliation and penal servitude of a decadent plantation society.

Liverpool's Labour Party demanded Chief Constable Oxford's resignation for the use of CS gas, and Lady Margaret Simey, ex-suffragette and Chairman of the Police Authority, stated that conditions in Liverpool 8 were so appalling that residents had a right to riot. On the streets, the criminal fraternity considered they had fought the law and won. The thrill of victory over the 'bizzies' created a feeling of invincibility and a renewed determination to optimise their criminal ventures. The riot had marked a landmark in relations between the Liverpool 8 black community and the police force.

Reverberations were felt in Whitehall, where fear of further threats to public order led to belated initiatives to tackle the economic and social deprivation in the poorest city in Western Europe. Michael Heseltine was appointed Minister for Merseyside and the Merseyside Task Force was set up specifically to deal with the Liverpool problem. The debonair Heseltine, nicknamed Tarzan, who had just spent £10,000 on nibbles and champagne at his daughter's birthday party, was forced to spend three weeks looking over the polluted Mersey from the dreary Atlantic Towers Hotel while he tried to divine imaginative ways to encourage private-sector investment back into the city. He identified the retreat of Liverpool's business community, the diaspora of the middle class, a failing local authority and the education crisis in Liverpool's inner-city schools as symptoms. The increasing concentration of wealth in London and the City, the decimation of local regional family fortunes to nationalisation and public credit companies, and the failure of capitalist regeneration were key factors underlying urban decay. Liverpool was now a branch office.

In a rare agreement with Militant, the new Minister of Merseyside advocated urban redevelopment at the same time but took control away from the elected local authorities and imposed emergency rule on a defeated tribe. Liverpool council was now compelled to engage with local business and community groups like the Eldonians. The Merseyside Task Force refocused its regeneration measures on tourism, leisure and housing rather than the hope of attracting new private commercial investment. Out of this came the limited successes of the Albert Dock, the now overgrown time-warped brownfield sorry site of the Garden Festival and the 35-acre Wavertree Industrial Park. Like Liverpool's old families, Tarzan's philosophy stemmed from *noblesse oblige*, or as it was now rebranded, 'compassionate conservatism'. Michael Heseltine left Liverpool a wiser man, stating publicly that he had no idea that conditions like the ones he had witnessed still survived in England. The government ordered the planting of caged saplings on Toxteth's main boulevard, Princes Avenue, where the statue of the vandalised William Huskisson in a toga had once stood. The concept of greenery remained central to Englishness and Liverpool's grim asphalt setting was regarded as incapable of nourishing the English soul. Most Scousers disagreed and instead demanded jobs and money to allow them to party, see a show, get on the juice and dance till they dropped.

At one meeting in Liverpool, the men in grey from Whitehall promised that every home would get a bathroom and hot running water. Someone stood up and said, 'Great, but what about the prostitutes? Shouldn't we start with morality?'

What Granby also wanted was its own Law Centre. In the wake of the riots, not a single black barrister or solicitor worked in Liverpool. The

Black Caucus (The Race Relations Liaison Committee) demanded the formation of a central Race Relations Unit, and joined with the local Labour Party in vociferously insisting on Oxford's resignation. Although the Militant Tendency made some concessions, battlelines were quickly drawn. Militant denounced the Black Caucus as a 'self-interested clique of the race-relations industry' and tried to parachute in a black-relations expert from London. In the end, the new friendly ethnic minority cop on Granby Street proved more valuable than all these ideological dialectics. The Moores family also chipped in to secure the future of the Law Centre, which was floundering on inadequate council grants.

Five years after the violence, The Merseyside Community Relations Council travelled to Westminster to give evidence to the House of Commons Select Committee. One in 14 Liverpudlians was now black but they were still invisible in the job sector; out of 10,000 store employees only 75 were black and only 12 of those were working behind the counter. The press were now sensitised to Liverpool as a city of racial tension, and a year after the riots, when 'a reign of terror' broke out in a Liverpool school, an 11-year-old black girl called Sharon Walker was singled out as the ringleader. The *Daily Star* led the next day with a picture of her and the headline 'Big, black and really nasty'.

The nine days of rioting were the beginning of the end for a disinherited society. Eighteen of Granby's forty shopfronts were boarded up and large sections of the ward were a wilderness of litter-strewn dereliction. Many felt forced to get out and follow the Chinese to pastures new. In 1992, a census demonstrated that there were 6,786 black people in Liverpool, just 1.5 per cent of the population, which was about half the estimated figure at the time of the Gifford report a decade earlier.

One man who stayed behind was Leroy Alphonse Cooper, whose arrest had triggered the riots. Cooper, the Spartacus of the uprising, had reinvented himself and was now involved in photography, poetry and dance, and had carved a local reputation as a graffiti artist. Where Princes Road met Parly Street, he painted 'Love life, Love Liverpool', a slogan that he entered for a local newspaper competition. His idea was voted top by the *Echo* readers but was passed over by the judges in favour of another submission with more 'commercial appeal'. Racism, seemingly, remained alive and well in Liverpool.

A series of hate crimes in Huyton culminated in 2005 with the axing to death of 18-year-old Anthony Walker. The murdered youth's mother found it within herself to forgive his murderers but told a newspaper,

'Babies would be calling us niggers and they didn't even understand what they were saying.'

Black O'Reillys, Scouse Somalis, black and white, both shades of brown are still around and Cooper is still painting street signs red, yellow and green in a process described as 'Urban Installation'. As dawn breaks, bleary-eyed Toxteth's morning face uncoils, still a law unto itself. A rare bleeding sun starts to rise above the pink Anglican Cathedral and soon Liverpool 8's future, the children of every colour and creed, will be playing and laughing in the nursery at South Bedford Street. Parts of the original World in One City have even become trendy; web designers and students are moving in and house prices moving up. Regeneration projects are afoot. Lodge Lane still has an edge with its cracked flags, tureen kebabs, discount international food and spices, fancy goods, MFI and DIY, Spendwell and the Horn of Africa green mountain. The 'Pivvy' bingo hall is now joined by the waist with the Rob Roy pub. There are stories of hope too, like the charity Kind on Back Canning Street, started after the riots by Stephen Yip to give disadvantaged children hope, expose them to a structured environment and convince them to make the most of their lives. The Federation of Worker Writers and Community Publishers had also continued to provide a safe space in Liverpool 8. This international initiative grew from the Recife educationalist Paolo Freire's teachings. In his book *The Pedagogy of the Oppressed*, he talks of a culture of silence among the marginalised and submerged, which is born out of economic, political and social domination. The poor could have their eyes opened through the spoken and later the written word, and through a new and modern anti-colonial democratic education the racially oppressed could be freed. Levi Tafari was one of these Liverpool 8 men who rose up out of the riots to become a griot. In *Duboetry* he wrote:

> Cos we might be living inna different country
> But dhe struggle is dhe same where ever we may be . . .
> Word Sound and Power come to set we free! Set we free!

Deggsie

Here there was a family history to be traced:
Martins had merged with the Bank of Liverpool
which years before in turn had joined
the firm of Arthur Heywood who had made
his pile from ships that plied the Gold
and Windward Coasts, Old Callabar, Benin . . .
a thousand leg-irons fixed to their quarterdecks,
those boats were christened with bright abstract names:
Integrity, Providence, Friendship, Liberty.

Extract from 'Inheritance', in *Sky Nails*
by Jamie McKendrick

By the time Derek Hatton came to national prominence in the 1980s, Liverpool had undergone 20 years of job losses and a major out-migration. Two thirds of the dock system lay silent and almost all the big factories had closed. Halewood was still producing Escorts but the labour force had been slashed by the arrival of robots. The city had turned in on herself, lost much of her spunk, and many Scousers were now completely dependent on the safety net of the welfare state. The heyday of Halewood in the early '70s had provided little more than a temporary respite and the large container ships now docked in the east coast ports of Felixstowe and Southampton. Even Dover, Grimsby and Teesside were seeing more ships than the Mersey. The ferry was a pleasure boat that no longer had to weave its way between passing tugs.

Liverpool's population had shrunk from 856,000 in 1931 to less than half a million. Eighty-four per cent of Britain's wealth was owned by just seven per cent of the population. Scousers continued to head down the East Lancs Road in droves aboard the Norman Tebbit Express. The city had become the Museum of Horrifying Example. Beat City had become Beaten City, the Bermuda Triangle of British Capitalism, a no-go area for aspirant politicians, multinational corporations and banks. It was peacetime but as the city became cleaner and emptier, the rhetoric was of sacrifice and siege. Margaret Thatcher and the Tories were not responsible for everything but they considered the city's demise as inevitable and a consequence of uncontrollable global market forces. The Labour Party paid lip service to Liverpool's predicament but offered no solutions and did nothing to resist the Conservative government's neglect. The port's shrinking workforce no longer posed a threat to them as there were no Tory seats to lose. Liverpool was on the wrong side of the country and could not compete with the favoured south. The uneven geography of England was widening and the city island of Liverpool had become a beacon for everything that the English feared: class revolution, squalor and poverty and a threat to the rising political challenge of the middle class. The creation of Red Merseyside, with its monstrous Eastern-bloc civic centres run by men with northern accents, drinking pints of Higson's and Cain's and calling one another 'brother', was anathema to the Conservatives and much of the rest of England.

On the other hand, Mrs Thatcher's corner-shop mentality of snobbishness, thriftiness, self-interest and narrow-mindedness clashed with the Liverpool character. The insincere faces of Whitelaw and Tebbit, with their 'greed is good, get on the property ladder' philosophy, struck fear and indignation into the hearts of Liverpudlians. The Prime Minister's first words on the steps of 10 Downing Street – 'Where there is discord, may we bring harmony. Where there is error, may we bring truth. Where there is doubt, may we bring faith. And where there is despair, may we bring hope' – attributed erroneously by her aides to Saint Francis of Assisi, had proved, by the end of her first term, to be an empty promise. Instead, she pressed full steam ahead with her plans to cut income tax, drastically reduce public expenditure, dethrone the union bosses, and make it easier for people to buy their own homes and invest their savings in the stock market. Consensus was too Latinate a word for her ever to embrace; she saw it as a devious way of dodging hard questions. For Maggie's new yuppie Tories, Beatlemania, Flower Power and the Swinging Sixties had been the start of Great Britain's moral rot. There was no such thing as society. Despite the long years of Tory control, there was also still an ancestral fear in Whitehall of the politicised Liverpool crowd. A monstrous graffiti painted across a Liverpool wall read 'Thatcher's answer to unemployment: CHEAP SMACK!'

The once-great seaport now forced to survive on meagre handouts was a safe harbour for the promulgation of radical politics. The Militant

Trotskyite Left seeded its views through its newspaper and the regular picketing of the besieged docks and the city's last remaining small factories. Two men on Militant Tendency's National Executive, Peter Taaffe and Pat Wall, both had Merseyside backgrounds. They believed investors had bled the port dry then jumped ship, leaving the dockers and their children to face a slow and painful attrition. The city was now a symbol for the Rise and Fall of Capitalism and rocked to the noise of clashing ideologies. If you stood on Everton Brow, the old home of Victorian sea captains, and looked from the ridge down on Scotland Road and Great Howard Street towards the river, all you could see was the wreckage of recently destroyed close-knit communities. It looked as if a meteorite had hit Vauxhall. Militant Tendency's enemies were Britain's middle class and the American Dream, and their rallying cry was 'Better to break the law than the poor'. Liverpool, a city of slavery, would soon become their citadel.

In the same way that individualistic local Toryism had controlled Liverpool for almost a century, Militant Tendency now began to gain a stranglehold in the District Labour Party. The Tory slogan 'You've never had it so good' rang hollow at the mounting dole queues. The Moores and one or two other old families kept faith but they were regarded as sentimental and misguided fools in the City of London. Local politicians and activists were now convinced that Liverpool had no place in the Tory government's new scheme of things. The city had got rid of all its Conservative MPs and just a dozen or so irrelevant councillors now defended the Tories' interests. Liverpool's magnificent heritage had become an enigma beyond all understanding. Her arse seemed to have fallen out and she was acknowledged in Parliament as a basket case. Scousers increasingly felt like outsiders in their own country, building up a defiant siege mentality in the sink estates and North Side terrace rows. There was no feel-good factor for these folk: only a culture of fear.

Militant believed that until the doctrines of Trotsky and Marx were fully implemented the Labour Party would never flourish. Capitalism was failing and a radical new system of reform was needed. In the rotten wards of inner Liverpool, radical left-wing ideologies started to gain a footing among the marginalised and unemployed. Some younger Liverpool trade unionists were attracted to Militant's battling spirit and far-reaching programmes for change. Portrayed by the Tories and the press as dangerous subversives and 'the enemy within', Militant, on the contrary, saw itself as passionate and visionary, standing up for a rejected city. The power behind the Militant Tendency throne in Liverpool was Tony Byrne, a former Jesuit priest and man of absolute conviction, who is alleged to have told Mother Teresa that he had done more for the poor than she ever would and that he strongly disapproved of the voluntary work her Missionaries of Charity had carried out in Seel Street. At the local elections in 1983, a Militant-dominated Labour party swept to power, providing an opportunity for Byrne, Tony Mulhearn and their comrades to carry out a far-reaching urban regeneration policy.

It was not long before the 35-year-old arriviste Derek Hatton ('Deggsie'), newly promoted Deputy Leader of the council, was appearing on peak-time national television. A fiery, mouthy showman with a smart line in double-breasted suits, Hatton walked the walk and talked the talk. He was an only child who had been brought up in a two-bedroomed 'corpy' in Childwall Valley. The Hattons were close-knit, staunchly Protestant and strict, congregating every year for Christmas in the paternal grandparents' home in Wavertree. Hatton's grandfather, a powerfully built blacksmith, used to walk 12 miles to work and back to Formby every day, and his father was a former Coldstream Guards boxing champion and ex-England schoolboy footballer. In common with many Liverpool families, it was Derek's diminutive mother Alma who ran the home and had the most influence on her son.

To the pride of his parents, Derek passed his 11-plus exam and went to the Liverpool Institute, where he made an early decision to rebel against learning and concentrate on football. Early signs of his combativeness occurred when he was banned for life from a local football league for punching a referee. He enjoyed a part-time weekend job at Jackson's, the men's outfitters, and developed an interest in the theatre. In the Liverpool Institute's production of *The Merchant of Venice*, he played Gratiano, with the impresario-to-be and Everton Football Club Chairman Bill Kenwright in the role of Shylock, and the future Tory minister Steve Norris as Portia.

When Hatton left school at 16, Kenwright asked him if he wanted to tour Germany with the National Youth Theatre. His mother blocked the invitation as she had arranged for her son to start an apprenticeship at the Plessey's electrical engineering plant. Uncle Tony, an old-school libertarian Labour supporter, took Derek under his wing and encouraged him to look beyond the headlines to remember that politics was about people. At 17, he followed his father into the fire service and began to witness the appalling housing conditions in many parts of the city. On one occasion, there was a chimney fire in a house in Bedford Street South where 15 Irish men were living in one room on the top floor with a heap of human excrement piled up in the corner.

After four years in the fire service, Derek was ready for further education and jumped at the chance to take a radical course in Community and Youth Work at Goldsmith's College in London. He threw himself into the squats and anti-Vietnam movements and had his eyes opened to a world outside Liverpool. His interest in left-wing politics and particularly housing issues was now established, and on his return to Liverpool he joined the Labour Party and got a job as director of a community scheme. He was ready and equipped to take on the local authority and embrace the radical views of Militant.

Labour had finally got off its knees but the timing could not have been worse for the ordinary people. The other Liverpool, subjugated by the Molyneux in their castle and the Stanleys in their tower, ignored by the old families for so long and despised by the Victorian gentlemen, was about to have its day, ironically at a time when Britain was controlled by a Tory government intent on promoting free enterprise and destroying the nanny state. It was as though the crew were now finally in charge of the brig, with the captain and the first mate being held to ransom.

One of Militant's first actions was to ransack the former office of Liberal leader Sir Trevor Jones and rip his name from the door. The office of Lord Mayor was abolished and replaced by the post of Chairman. Customary consultation process on housing matters was dismissed as an unnecessary bourgeois exercise. Byrne and Hatton had a shared vision that would dominate town-hall policy for the next three years. Five thousand low-rise, low-cost utilitarian council houses would be built in seventeen priority areas. This major programme would provide real jobs in the private building sector and create decent accommodation for the poor. A large plot on the Everton Brow was identified for one project; the propaganda announced spectacular views of the river, unforgettable sunsets and grassy parkland.

The town hall started to resemble a bear pit where policies were forced through by exploitation of the caucus system and peacock politics. Committee meetings rarely lasted more than a few minutes, as agendas were steamrollered through. Moderate Labour councillors were threatened with de-selection if they failed to cooperate.

The dialectics went over the top of most Scousers but Militant's defiance of the government resonated with some. Byrne, Mulhearn and Hatton expressed what Liverpool still wanted to believe. Here was a great city clamouring for recognition, support and, above all, respect. Liverpool had become a working-class-only zone.

Many in the know regarded Derek Hatton's rise to power with wry amusement. To them, he was a one-day wonder, a Scouse megaphone with a stack of confidence and cheek who had wandered into the town hall by chance. To them, Hatton was a born-again bebop Cunard Yank, like the many young Liverpool men who found stewards jobs on the Atlantic liners just after the Second World War. While most of the city was still in demob suits, these Cunard Yanks returned in blue or red zoot suits, button-down shirts and hand-painted ties. They had acquired freewheeling American habits and idioms, brought home washing machines, baby's highchairs, reel-to-reel tape recorders, cine cameras and above all a new-found freedom. The Cunard Yanks could dictate their own terms and were able to travel anywhere in the world. They were poseurs and chancers brimming with confidence who were always one jump ahead. Every family had a Sinbad and every Scouser loved to be on the top deck. Once the cruise ships finally went, this freedom was lost and many of these men of the world found it hard to settle down to jobs on the conveyor belts at Dunlop and Ford.

Boss politics were now back in Liverpool at a time when the city's *raison d'être* had all but disappeared and the Tory government had a vice-like control on the nation's purse strings. Hatton and Byrne's main problem was that swingeing Tory cuts had led to demands for Liverpool to drastically reduce its spending budget, making it impossible for Militant to push forward to build the new estates. Faced with an inherited debt from the Liberals, the Labour council immediately went to war with Whitehall to claw back £30 million of the £100 million they believed had been stolen by cuts in rate-support grants. The council proposed that if the government wanted cuts, they should make them themselves, while Patrick Jenkin retaliated by singling out Liverpool as the bad boys of the overspending league. The council resisted the newly imposed budget and unilaterally proposed a higher, illegal one.

Round one went to Militant, as they increased their majority in the local elections, with the government conceding more money on the unspoken premise that they wanted to finish Arthur Scargill and the miners off first. Twenty thousand people demonstrated in support of the council's stand in December 1983, with the *Daily Mail* proclaiming that Patrick Jenkin had been given two unlovely black eyes. Triumphantly, Militant claimed the government had bottled out in the face-off with Liverpool's working class. Their urban regeneration policy moved forward with the construction of

1,000 traditional new homes with front and back gardens, which became known as 'The Derek Hatton Homes'. Tenements like the squalid Tommy White's Gardens off St Domingo's Road, the Piggeries (Canterbury Heights) and three failed '60s tower blocks on William Henry Street, were demolished and the landscape of Croxteth was transformed by green spaces. The houses were considered of better quality than those being built privately by Barratts. Militant also built sports centres to keep youths off the street, nurseries to help working mothers, and kept rents and school dinner costs down. They provided the elderly with phones and put a race-relations officer in every school. They cleared slums and built a new park.

The Tory government stood firm and the following year Militant was forced to make a tactical withdrawal, borrowing more money from Swiss banks to fund the housing programme and deal with the necessary repairs. The city council called for public demonstrations to protest against the government's treatment of the city. In 1984, Margaret Thatcher was greeted by chants of 'Liverpool, Liverpool, Liverpool' by protesting students in Bandung, Indonesia. The people of Liverpool were estranged and had all but lost touch with the Big Sister's hard-line Britain and the yuppie vision. An insidious corrosion of both family values and faith combined with deprivation had led to a desperate and defiant last stand in a city that had effectively lost its identity. Liverpool was breaking up on the rocks as a sea of hard-line Tory reforms washed over the country.

Hatton's agitprop against Thatcher's Britain continued:

> Comrade Chairman and Comrades, Derek Hatton, Liverpool Broad Green and Deputy Leader of Liverpool City Council. The fury she showed yesterday as she stormed out of that meeting was the fury of her class, which was given a bloody nose by the working people of Liverpool this year.

The national press portrayed Hatton as a Mafia capo who hung on to power by bullyboy politics. There was further criticism of 'Hatton's Army', a platoon of burly security guards whose presence at news conferences and around Mr Hatton acted as a deterrent to full and frank debate. Some moderate councillors claimed they had been spat on and manhandled at Labour group meetings. Deggsie had become a whipping boy for Thatcher's England and a pariah for the middle class. A Fraud Squad investigation was set up to look into his personal finances. Militant's revolution raged on, polarising opinion in the city and leading the media to claim that Liverpool had declared a Unilateral Declaration of Independence.

Although trade union support aided Byrne and Hatton's rise to power, its leaders became unhappy that some Militant Tendency members seemed to be encouraging local shop stewards to usurp their power to solve local issues. As the threats of civic bankruptcy grew and councillors were threatened with jail sentences, the Liverpool bishops also withdrew their support, writing a letter to *The Times* condemning Militant practices and suggesting the money from the housing programme be used to solve the cash crisis. After a special call to prayer for Liverpool by the Church, Tony Byrne invited the clerics to inspect the city council's books. He also chastised them for their hypocritical position, claiming that if they'd all been in Rio de Janeiro, Archbishop Worlock would have been telling the priests to get out on the streets and support the city.

These were uneasy moments in which it seemed as if civil war might break out, with Liverpool leading the revolt against Comfortable Britain. Militant was forced to compromise on finances with Patrick Jenkin, and then two months later made the major tactical error of issuing 90-day notices to all of the council workers in an attempt to gain time for further campaigning. In October 1985, at the party conference in Bournemouth, an exasperated Neil Kinnock announced at the Labour Party NEC that the Liverpool District Labour Party was to be suspended pending an investigation and later, after the NEC had launched an inquiry into Liverpool's finances, stated: 'It is generally recognised that Militant Tendency is a maggot in the body of the Labour Party . . . I want them out.' He regretted Militant's irresponsibility, which had led to the 'grotesque chaos of a Labour council hiring taxis to scuttle round the city handing out redundancy notices to its own workers'. His speech split the conference and although he failed to mention that no member of the council was sacked, he correctly saw Militant and Liverpool as an election disaster waiting to happen and opted for the safer New Labour model of middle-class intellectual and politically correct socialism with something for everyone.

Militant Tendency's reign was terminated by a Labour Party purge and a failed appeal to the Law Lords. In their three-and-a-half-year reign, it was never defeated at the ballot box but equally it never achieved a majority vote from the people. Despite the wind of change blowing through the National Labour Party, Neil Kinnock went on to lose the 1987 General Election. Hatton later defended himself against accusations of financial irresponsibility:

Our only crime is that we are guilty of building houses, of creating jobs, in improving education and nurseries and keeping the rates and rents down and certainly if that's what we are guilty of then we are proud to stand up and say yes we are guilty and do your worst. If there is any sort of justice left, then certainly we should be found innocent.

Wide boy Deggsie had turned out to be Margaret Thatcher's best mate and went on to star in pantomimes and carve out a successful media career. He would also turn out to have more in common with the 'posh' Edwina Currie, his old stablemate from the Liverpool Institute, than he could ever have dreamed. Never afraid to open her mouth, Currie too went on to become a broadcaster and a novelist of political sagas, forever remembered for her comment about salmonella in eggs and the revelation in her published diaries that she had an affair with John Major in the '80s.

Militant had arrived in the town hall with an unshakeable if deluded faith. It dared to fight and challenge authority, and for a few idealists it represented an ephemeral, redemptive, irreverent, passionate triumph for the human spirit. Someone had murdered the city and got away with it. Some of 'Hatton's Army' moved into the dance-music club scene. The hallions were in line for Tory enterprise awards, working hard in their chosen professions of thieving, taking risks and trampling on anyone who got in their way. The city continued to feel unloved and guilty. People went on leaving in droves for Jersey, London and Brighton, where they lived on their wits and screwed the 'soey' (social security). Some even took the 'big trip', emigrating to Australia, New Zealand and North America in search of a new life. Livelihoods had drifted out to sea on the Tory privateer.

Operation Cheetah began in 1990 to investigate newspaper allegations that Hatton had been involved in shady land deals. The police used computer technology designed for murder investigations to sift information and finally swooped at dawn on the homes of a number of Militant councillors, Liverpool businessmen and the Settleside offices, Hatton's public relations headquarters. Derek Hatton, his tailor John Monk and two Militant councillors were charged with conspiracy to defraud the council. The allegations pertained to the granting of an application to Monk to set up a car park on Manesty Lane without Liverpool council putting it out to tender. After an eight-week trial in 1993, costing the taxpayer millions, the case against Hatton and his codefendants was thrown out on the grounds of insufficient evidence. At the press conference, Deggsie chippily commented that the trial 'came down to two scrappy, grotty bits of land which nobody since Adolf Hitler had shown any interest in'. Even today the Militant years create an ambivalence in Scousers, while Deggsie has moved on to be a successful property dealer in Cyprus.

I book in to the Adelphi, that stately establishment where the greats of Hollywood once waited contentedly for their floating palace to set sail. At night, it has turned into a rowdy shebeen playing jaded Motown and Stax. I think of those gowned foxtrotters who cocked a snook at the lost Atlantic trade, the neon-lit town alive with dance halls, cocktail lounges and packed theatres. Off Upper Parly, the Gothic Wedding House holds firm as a symbol of hope and innocence, boxed in by grass verges, empty spaces and freeways heading to the brown river and Toxteth. The desolate, tacky eyesore of Saint John's Beacon and the ugly, treacherous TGWU block reflect a civic meanness that grew out of desertion and neglect. Past glories now contrast with third-generation unemployment, poverty and sickness. A saturnine pot-bellied man with scattergun tattoos passes wearing a sunny Brazil strip. Brotherhood is now Big Brother. There is no one left to lay out the bodies or do a bit of carpentry. The streets seem so tiny, lined by doll's houses too small for habitation and yet once they seemed so wild and monstrous. The fury of the poor who still believe too strongly in miracles lingers, an incurable disease for Christian soldiers. In the chiaroscuro of twilight, the few who have stayed to keep the show on the road bolt down the gullet or head north and east like a defeated army.

People came here to shift things around the world and now there is nothing left to move. The population is shrinking and there are fewer and fewer children. Liverpool has lost her carbon footprint and some Scousers need smack even to appreciate the sanctity of the Stanley Park trees. Why have the fifth generation of unemployed not left in the same way their restless ancestors arrived? What is it that stops them stowing away or jumping a train? What is it that binds them to a neighbourhood and brings them back? Why did their forerunners stay behind and not head out on the ships? What keeps them trapped in the dungeons of Skag City? Liverpool 4 seems afraid to move into the starving unknown but the full moon is reassuring. Those streets, which seemed so threatening, are now on their own. Why can't Liverpool be allowed to die naturally like an old elephant rather than be forced to hang on and pretend it can be something it can never be again?

The Black Rose of Kingston

Our religion kept us from ship-building, our class
And accent tied us slum-bound, yet true
In just two generations we have been absorbed
The lessons of our mongrel history forgotten.
Now, as degradation returns on the ebb-tide
We turn on the underdog. We repeat
The same myth and treason as were spoken of us:
Lazy dog! Dirty dog! Thieving dog!
But in our arsenal of indignity howls
The cold echo chamber of the holocaust:
'Nigger' We carve it with our fangs
On their houses; we bay it
When they dare to walk our streets
Or play in our games. How easily
We claim pedigree and murder memory.

                    Extract from 'Full Circle' by
                    Steve Edwards

A year after Garrincha's death, and with English football racked with self-doubt, the national side beat Brazil 2–0 in the Maracanã. The match was not broadcast live on British television but the 44th minute was shown later on the news. John Barnes received the ball out on the far left, about 40 yards from goal, and set off on a mazy, instinctive run which took him past a frozen Leandro and a petrified Junior. On his own, as would prove to often be the case when he wore an England shirt, he veered ever inwards, shimmied his way into the box and with a final feint deceived Costa, the goalkeeper, and tapped the ball home.

This was a goal fit for Jairzinho and the Brazilian crowd rose to applaud the black man in a white shirt. It was highly praised by the Brazilian television pundits and one Rio newspaper described it as the greatest goal ever scored in the Maracanã. Barnes would later describe it as an 'out-of-body experience'. The more I watched the goal afterwards, the more comical it appeared. Barnesie had brought football back home, at least for a day, and rapped his way into English football legend. He had also challenged the cineaste Pier Paolo Pasolini's maxim that there are just two types of football – prose and poetry. European players were the prose – tough, premeditated, collective and systematic – whereas Brazilians were the poetry – individualistic, balletic, spontaneous and erotic. Before the Rio game, Barnes and another black English player Mark Chamberlain had been taken to Copacabana beach for a photoshoot. Barnes later wrote in his autobiography that they had been embarrassed to see a group of youngsters demonstrate ball skills that far outshone their own. On the return home, the players were forced to listen to a group of National Front racists snarling that England had only won 1–0 because Barnes's goal didn't count.

Barnes was not the usual English player and it showed in his demeanour. Born in Jamaica, he sported an Afro hairstyle, wore hornet yellow every week and played for a suburban family club in Hertfordshire. His father, Colonel Kenneth Barnes, had led the United West Indies Forces in the relief of Grenada and his mother was a television producer. Both were strict disciplinarians and were determined that their son and his two sisters would be brought up in the right way. From an early age, Colonel Barnes also taught his son that industry would be rewarded in white society irrespective of skin colour and made sure he didn't grow up with even a vestige of the ghetto mentality. When his work took the family to London, he also ensured that his 13-year-old son was enrolled at the traditional, middle-class, rugby-playing Marylebone Boys Grammar School. John was good at rugby but lost interest and his father then encouraged him to take up his own game of football. The young Barnes joined Stowe Boys Club on the Harrow Road and was soon in the first team. At Stowe and later with the Middlesex League side Sudbury Court, where he was the only black in the squad, he appeared laid-back to the coaches but he had plenty of application and was able to play to instruction.

The children of the Windrush generation had grown up in England and were trying to make sporting waves. Viv Anderson had become the first black to play for England and Ron Atkinson ('Bojangles') had resurrected the fortunes of West Bromwich Albion with Cyrille Regis, Brendon Batson and the quixotic Laurie Cunningham, a trio affectionately nicknamed 'The Three Degrees' by 'Baggy' fans after the black soul singers adored by Prince Charles. Talented young black players were forcing their way into top-level football and could no longer be denied. It was obvious to the scouts who came to watch John Barnes at Sudbury Court that he had natural talent with exciting rhythm and excellent ball control. He was also popular with his peers because he could take a joke and was respectful to his coaches.

As the Barnes family packed up again to return home to Jamaica, their talented son was being offered professional terms with the upwardly mobile second division club Watford, chaired by their celebrity fan, Elton John. Manager Graham Taylor believed in a professional, workmanlike approach and was forever reminding his players of their responsibilities as role models, and the need to take good care of their bodies. His methods had led to a rise from the lowest echelon of the Football League to the Second Division in four years. The club's new-found success had been founded on physicality and a long pass game. The Jamaican-born Luther Blissett, an imposing black striker who would later taste success in Italian football, was now at the helm and had serious attitude. Cast in the mould of the traditional English bulldog centre forward, he struck fear in many an opposition defence. Taylor had developed organisation into an art form and his no-nonsense, utilitarian approach would lead to Watford's promotion to the English First Division in John Barnes's first season at the club.

Taylor's right-hand man on the coaching staff was the spruce ex-physiotherapist Bertie Mee, who had led Arsenal in the 1970–71 season to the League and Cup double. When interviewed, the elderly Mee likened Barnes's flowing style of play to the earlier uncoached generation of Englishmen like Stanley Matthews and Tom Finney. Taylor on the other hand was ambivalent about his new charge, marvelling at his panache but expressing some concerns about his apparent vulnerability and fickleness. Taylor emphasised the importance of percentage football, which clashed with his enigmatic young winger's artfulness and desire to take opponents on. No amount of cajoling or instruction from his manager could cure Barnes's inconsistency and on unhappy days he seemed to disappear from the game. Despite these perceived shortcomings, Barnes's progress in the game was meteoric and he was soon regular back-page headline news and elevated to the England squad. A strong love–hate relationship grew up between the two men. Barnes resented being talked at like a child but at the same time acknowledged that Taylor had instilled in him the wherewithal to progress and survive in the modern English game.

It was not long before the England boo-boys, the bean-counting apparatchiks of the Football Association and the cynical hacks were all at his throat. After the Maracanã goal he was heralded as a genius but within a few weeks all the old prejudices were back. His face didn't fit and his body language, especially at Wembley, often portrayed discomfort. The negative rumblings of the crowd made him ever more invisible and cautious. It was not that he didn't care or that there was a rebel lurking inside but more that he couldn't adjust his footwork to the unimaginative England system. The small-town England patriots in the crowd felt that he lacked the John Bull spirit and he was just another tricky black winger who felt the cold and couldn't do the business. Bananas were thrown on the pitch by the hard right to the angry cries of, 'There ain't no black in the Union Jack.'

When Barnes played for the first time at Anfield, the terraces were virtually out of bounds for 'niggers'. Some had never been into town despite living within a couple of miles of Bold Street. Even the local black football teams in Liverpool had to play in their own segregated leagues. In film footage of the Kop from the '60s, only one black face can be made out. Ollie was well known amongst Kopites for his permanent smile, fanatical support for the team and his incorrigible optimism. Unlike many of the diehard fans, he never had a chosen spot but wandered around behind the goal. It must have been hell for him when Leeds United came to town. Albert Johannson, a mercurial black South African winger who contributed in no small way to Don Revie's all-conquering champions, was forced to endure chanted insults. Thirty-five years later, Johannson died alone in the South Leeds slums, an alcoholic surrounded by a few pennies and a bus ticket. Ignorance rather than malignant hatred could be blamed. Most Kopites had never lived with black people. There were no blacks in the docks and those who had worked with black sailors on the sea had bought into the old naval stereotype that they were unfit to be trusted with any responsibility.

Caryl Phillips, who in common with my schoolmate Gilbert Browne came to Leeds from the West Indies as a child, describes in his book *The Atlantic Sound* how at the age of eleven he was at Elland Road watching a game between Leeds United and Everton when one of a group of Evertonians standing nearby turned to his mates and asked a question about a Leeds player. Trying to be helpful, Phillips answered, only to be turned on by the group saying, 'Fuck off! We're Scousers and we don't talk to niggers.' When Cyrille Regis made his annual visit to Anfield, he was greeted by chants of 'get back on your jam jar'. Twenty years later, the new multicultural mix of many of England's cities took the travelling Kop by surprise.

This tension finally detonated in 1981 with the Toxteth Riots. The tumult that ensued was emblematic of the need for man to fight for freedom and escape his shackles. Liverpool-born blacks were first of all proud to be black, then proud to be Scouse, but didn't consider themselves to be English at all. Overt hostility now had to be confronted.

Howard Gayle, Liverpool 8 born and young, gifted and black, entered the Anfield crucible on the eve of the riots as the first black player ever to play for the club. Liverpool Football Club now had a trusted formula for success based on denying the opposition the ball and getting stuck in right from the whistle. Shankly's boot room was a shrine of conservatism and superstition. Gayle was a winger with devastating pace who went past people and didn't care too much if an attack broke down. He played only five times for Liverpool but his performance as a substitute against Bayern Munich in the European Cup semi-final is forever rooted in the club's folklore. After a few minutes of the game, Kenny Dalglish limped off and young Howie was thrown on. His penetration and aggressiveness immediately unsettled the opposition and swung the game in Liverpool's favour. The desperate German defenders resorted to fouling the flying winger at every opportunity and when the referee booked Gayle for retaliation, Bob Paisley the Liverpool manager decided to pull him off with 20 minutes still to go. Gayle was later informed that the manager had done it in order to avoid him being sent off.

There was no room for superstars in the Liverpool dressing-room; the senior players used piss-taking as an initiation ceremony and as a form of male bonding. This was a tradition born on the docks, where there was no place for loose cannons. The 'jokes' against Gayle invariably related to his colour and he simply refused to accept them. Malcolm X and Angela Davies spoke to him in the night. Ray Kennedy told me that Tommy Smith, the Liverpool captain, used to call Howie 'my white nigger' because he rather liked him. When Gayle left Liverpool at the end of the season after a derisory offer from the management, most of the squad felt that he had a chip on his shoulder, couldn't take a joke and had failed to settle. He was James Wait, Conrad's 'Nigger of the Narcissus', and in the end it had come down to a question of character. Nonetheless, even the good ship Anfield could not deny his ability. Howie Gayle's subsequent professional career was littered with acrimonious disputes with authoritarian managers until finally he was allowed to sparkle and fulfil his promise under a sympathetic coach at then lowly Blackburn Rovers. In 2000, he was back home, unpaid and still proud, running the Stanley House Youth Project, where he has continued to train teams of local lads in his own academy of football.

Saturday afternoon on Anfield Road still resembled L.S. Lowry's *Going to the Match*, with clans of white working-class matchstick men congregating from all over the city to raise the stadium roof. Closed groups stood on street corners outside pubs before the game, discussing tactics and players with a pint of beer in their hands. Their children were sometimes baptised carrying the names of all 11 Liverpool players. Stanley Park became a scrapyard for visiting coaches. Scallies offered to look after the cars of those who drove to the match but owners knew that however much they paid there was still no guarantee the vehicle would be in one piece when they returned. Taxi drivers observed the fear in the faces of away supporters through their rear mirrors as they drove them from Lime Street to the ground through what was now one of the most deprived stretches of Western Europe.

Finally, in 1987, John Barnes expressed an interest in leaving Watford FC for pastures new. Kenny Dalglish's recent appointment as player-manager had broken the dynastic succession of the Shankly boot room and had been greeted with incredulity by the fans. Dalglish had already targeted Peter Beardsley as a potential replacement for Ian Rush but the canny young Scot felt more signings would be needed and was convinced that John Barnes could bring a new dimension to Liverpool's play. Dalglish had already acquired a reputation for cloak-and-dagger inscrutability and nobody in his squad ever knew what he would do next. He also had a wicked sense of humour and for many at Anfield his interest in Barnes seemed little more than a joke.

Football now nourished and sustained Liverpool and had become the last vestige of civic pride but the Kop was no longer populated by burden-carrying working-class men in ties. It had become complacent, flabby and lethargic. The ball no longer needed to be sucked into the net but went in automatically. The team was sponsored by global multinationals and infiltrated by fly-by-night football tourists from the generation described in Nick Hornby's *Fever Pitch*. A new crowd of shell-suited chameleons had arrived to bask in the club's success. On match day, coaches and charabancs rolled in from the West Country, the Black Country and even the Land of Wool. Planes and ferries arrived from Ireland and Scandinavia. This outbreeding caused the Kop to slowly lose some of its native repartee, the passion became muted and the wit more sporadic. The club was a public limited company and the

Championship was a given. Allegiance was now to Liverpool FC and not to the moribund city.

In one final defiant protest, a rump of hardcore travelling Kopites decamped to the Anfield Road and began to set new trends. Annie Road was suddenly full of fresh-faced smoothies with floppy wedge haircuts and duffel coats, ready to confront the boot boys with their shaved heads and denim. It was left to lad culture and bands like The Farm, with their irreverent forerunner to the fanzine, *The End*, to finally link the Liverpool music scene with footy. These new-wave casuals travelled all over Europe, using the fixture lists as their business plan and returning to Lime Street in Trimm-Trab trainers and effulgent jumbo cords. Peace and love had ironically been replaced by football hooliganism, and one of the favourite Annie Road chants now was:

> Ten past nine is stabbing time, doo-dah, doo-dah
> Ten past nine is stabbing time, doo-dah, doo-dah day.

The custom of pissing in, or 'dipping', a fellow Kopite's pocket had now been replaced by kickings, tomato-sauce defiling of Northern Soul boys and even feather-cut hair burning, where the blow-waved mullets of the opposition would be set alight. These Adidas snorkel boys on the Annie End were made up of Huyton Baddies, the Bennos, the Breck Road crew, the Ant Hill Mob and the Halewood Chains, all 'la's' who liked to sing along, do a bit of robbing and rebound off nightclub walls. Shankly's children had made Liverpool FC their job description. The powerless had discovered the power to scare. Hard cases waited to ambush the enemy in the mazy landings of the tenements in Fontenoy and Gerard Gardens. The sporting nature of Redmen no longer extended to woollybacks foolish enough to try to breach Fortress Anfield.

Liverpool had never had an out-and-out maverick dribbler like Matthews or Best and most of the Kop didn't want one now. Be solid at the back, defend from the front, pass and move, be canny and wear the opposition down was the LFC game plan. Collectivism born in the Shankly days with a dogged no-frills attitude still ruled and there were no superstars. Liverpool players were expected to sweat blood for the team and win trophies without unnecessary ritual. The coaching staff never rested on their laurels and always focused on the next game, irrespective of how well they were doing. Barnes, on the other hand, wore very tight shorts, liked to wiggle his rear and swerve around other players. He also couldn't defend, lacked Howie Gayle's devastating acceleration and wore gloves when it was cold. Poison-pen letters started to arrive at the ground urging the club's directors not to sign 'a coloured player' and vile racist graffiti was daubed on a wall outside the Kop. Barnes garnered advice from trusted fellow black players and waited for other offers to come in from Italy and North London. None were forthcoming and finally Dalglish got his missing piece of the jigsaw for just under a million pounds. The black reggae boy from Jamaica, so different in playing style from his wily boss, was about to experience what playing for Liverpool demanded.

John Barnes's ability to ride racial discrimination was to prove a powerful defence when the monkey chants and banana throwing began. His upbringing had given him the strength to cope with Scouse banter and the laddish humour of the Liverpool dressing-room. At an early training session at Melwood, when the tea lady brought a cuppa for two of Liverpool's seasoned pros and ignored the new arrival, Barnes was able to break the ice with the quip, 'What's wrong, am I black or something?' When he turned up at the Christmas party dressed as a Ku Klux Klan member, he made it clear he was nobody's bitch, but some black people accused him of being an Uncle Tom. By the time he made his home debut against Oxford United in mid September 1987, he had been accepted by the other players and after a faultless performance in front of the Kop he was in for keeps. At Watford, Barnes had been an isolated danger, sporadically destructive but marginalised. At Anfield, his quixotic skills were transfected into the team's DNA, providing exciting new attacking options for the Reds. He had been able to graft the Liverpool way into his play with the result that he dribbled less but saw much more of the ball. The team compensated for his weaknesses by playing to his strengths. Dalglish's class of '87 remained true to the Liverpool way but now they had an exciting new dimension. Barnes in a red shirt was twice the player dressed in white. The conclusion had to be that in some curious way he felt more at home at Anfield than at Wembley.

Barnes eventually forced the Kop to confront its racist bigotry. How could it continue to taunt black opponents without upsetting its new hero? One strategy, of course, was by dissimulation. Garth Crooks, a black player for Spurs, disturbed the Kop in the 1987 season with an early goal. As he moved menacingly in for a second strike at the Kop End, a desperate shout went up, 'Cripple the black bastard!' There was a momentary hush until another Kopite replied, 'Which one, theirs or ours?'

At one home game where Liverpool seemed to be getting all the 50–50 decisions from the referee, the chant came up from the visitors' pen at the Annie Road end. 'Who's the Scouser, who's the Scouser, who's the Scouser in the black?' In a flash came the retort from the Kop: 'Johnny Barnes, Johnny Barnes, Johnny Barnes.' Everton FC, whose ground was just seven minutes' walk across Stanley Park and whose support came from the same back-to-backs and council estates, had no such tensions. A wall of sound greeted Barnes at the derby games with the words 'Niggerpool, Niggerpool, Niggerpool.' A group of Evertonians wearing badges in their lapels saying, 'Everton are White – Defend the Race' were caught trying to smuggle a monkey into Goodison. Barnes was jeered every time he got the ball to the chant of: 'He's black, he's Scouse, and he'll rob your fucking house.' Barnes seemed to take it all in his stride, nonchalantly back-heeling a banana off the Goodison pitch.

'Digger' (named after Digger Barnes, a character in the then-popular American soap *Dallas*) was one of the boys and his girlfriend a nice middle-class white girl. He was also the nearest player Liverpool had ever had to Garrincha, and my dream of seeing a Liverpool player bend a ball round a wall had finally been realised. He had majestic poise, with an ability to coax and tempt wary defenders into foolhardy challenges, push the ball past a full-back, change tack, power forward and instinctively deliver lethal crosses with his left foot or shoot deceptively into the top corner of the goal. Liverpool provided a stable infrastructure that allowed him to consistently express his individual brilliance, and as a consequence the team became wonderful to watch. His skill even managed to tempt some black boys from Toxteth onto the terraces. In Dave Hill's perceptive analysis of the Barnes phenomenon, Digger's glorious rise to acceptance is ironically encapsulated in a quote from one of the Anfield faithful: 'A lot of Liverpool supporters weren't sure at the beginning. But since he's come here he's playing out of his skin.' Barnes had raised the hope that the city of Liverpool's destructive conservatism, bigotry, militancy and judgemental narrow-mindedness could be vanquished, leading to a better game and a decent city.

By the end of the '80s, the carnival was finally over. Respect for the opposition continued, with the Kop giving the Arsenal players generous applause after the Gunners had stolen the 1989 championship from under their noses, but too rich a diet of success had led to ennui and a damaging self-satisfaction. The raving love-thugs and the hooligans-with-feelings now started to pacify the heartless Annie Road Firm. Their older brothers, who had rampaged through England leaving a trail of smashed rail-carriage windows and stolen light bulbs in their wake, had been priced out. The death of the 39 Juventus supporters at Heysel was blamed on a dilapidated stadium, infiltrators from the National Front and the Belgian authorities. Tokens of respect and lasting links with Turin helped the Kop to forget the horror. Hillsborough was a day to remember but Heysel was the day when Liverpool died of shame. Liverpool was now starved of European Wednesday nights and worse was round the corner.

John Barnes would later write that Scousers were passionate and volatile. People had often come up to him in the street and said they loved him. In his autobiography, he relates an incident in 1989 when he was out of the Newcastle United team and back in Liverpool city centre. A man sitting outside a pub said, 'Hey, Barnesie, give us a rap?' to which the player replied, 'Sorry my rapping days are over,' to which the lightning-fast retort came, 'Your football days are over as well!'

On Pancake Tuesday, in the ruins of the faded white Brahma brewery, with the swaying hulk of the Ponto Frio block and the twinkling fairy lights of the City of God coming through the rain, I feel the spirit of the Kop in the regret of a lost moment. I can see Barnes in a red shirt and the nuptials of the Dentons Green ants. As the hot rain eases on Rio, strains of Gerry and the Pacemakers' 'Don't Let the Sun Catch You Crying' drift across the bay from Niteroi:

> Just don't forget that love's just a game
> And it can always come again
> So don't let the sun catch you crying
> Don't let the sun catch you crying, baby
> Tomorrow in the morning light
> Everything gonna be all right . . .

The Sugar Fella

Sugar crystals (the sugar from refineries)
exhibit the most unstable whiteness:
people from Recife know just how much,
and how very little, it will endure.
They know the slightness of how little
the crystals can keep the sugar crystallized
over its ancient past as raw sugar,
the clayish raw sugar that latently seethes;
and they know that anything can break
the slight power of crystals to inhibit,
for that raw-sugar past soon surfaces
when winter or summer melts sugar back to syrup.

Extract from *Psychoanalysis of Sugar*
by João Cabral de Melo Neto

We had once hurried down those sunless streets, past the sombre warehouses and space-age silos to the brutal docks. Amidst the hungry cranes and yellow-funnelled boats, the sugar men still walked and we watched them as they weighed and unloaded the sacks of Demerara molasses. Even now as I trudge alone down the Dock Road towards Gladstone, the juggernauts of Tate & Lyle roar out of the old United Molasses plant, splattering through the oily puddles after a tropical downpour.

Close on to the containers, a night-light vat squats by the deserted silo and the fused Molasses electricity substation. These are dangerous, haunted places. Huskisson was mown down in his prime by the Rocket and lives on only in the silent walls and murky green depths of his dock. The smell of salt and sugar mingle with sewage in Sandon. These days, the Dock Road is a bleak walk haunted by lost jobs and killing moons. I am prowling behind the railway, peering through barbed wire at a sad freighter as it crawls away along the edge of the Irish Sea to the sugar islands. There are no honey pot ants or humming birds searching for nectar.

Tate's remained in family hands, and in 1920 Henry Tate and Company merged with Abram Lyle of Greenock to become Tate & Lyle. Council-owned, walk-up tenement blocks had by now replaced the overcrowded courts around the Love Lane refinery but severe social deprivation remained. The company ran a tight ship and was considered a generous and popular employer by the residents of Vauxhall. The Christmas party was held at the Adelphi Hotel, with free Guinness and a secret raffle for a local orphanage. Tate & Lyle now had operations on five continents and over fifty countries, but unknown to its workers the world of sugar was in flux and storms were building on the horizon.

Parts of 'Sugartown' were flattened by the city council in the 1960s, obliterating hundreds of homes and offices around Scotland Road to make way for the Kingsway Tunnel, but Tate's was still a major employer and Love Lane had an annual output of 500,000 tons. The workers were happy and proud to work for the company and many resisted joining trades unions. Vauxhall still woke every morning to the sugarhouse's shrill whistles and breathed in its cloying fumes. An indelible caramel sweetness tainted the people's lips, clouds of white smoke billowed from the chimneys, and the constant hammering and clanging of the refinery provided the backdrop to neighbourhood gossip. At night, hooters interrupted the sleep of the 'girls from the white stuff' as the Barbados boats were guided in to the North docks. Grey-faced men, determined never to return to casualism, humped bags of sugar sand from the warehouses onto the lorries bound for Love Lane. Sugar was brought to the silo from a conveyor tower and then an overhead rail system distributed the molasses down the whole length of the container. The dawn shift began with the Tate girls sweeping sugar dust from the floor before they started to weigh and pack up the sweet crystals in a powdered snow storm of icing sugar. These jobs were tedious and very tough on a woman's body. Whether in the monstrous Love Lane sugarhouse or in the cane fields around Holetown, a deadly miasma of poverty was left behind in the wake of this white diamond commodity.

Tate & Lyle, the acknowledged mother of all sugar companies, had spent heavily in gaining a national monopoly and her American refineries were performing badly. Sugar prices had risen, investment in new technology had dwindled, and political difficulties with the African and Caribbean affiliates had damaged share prices. After years of growing threat and warnings of closure, Liverpool's 2,000 Love Lane employees fell victim to matricide in 1982, a decision blamed on a surplus of cane sugar caused by the European Community's Common Agricultural Policy. 'Beat city' had been mortally wounded by the mangel-wurzel of sugar beet and a whole community was in danger of being blown away. Vauxhall condemned Margaret Thatcher and Peter Walker (later the Lord Walker who became a non-executive director of Tate & Lyle) for not agreeing to the modest reduction in beet production proposed by the European Community in response to the National Farmers' Union protests. 'Beat the beet, keep the cane,' was the rallying call in the Crystal Club.

Resistance by the Tate workers, their families, local councillors and the Church eventually culminated in glorious defeat as the Tory government refused to intervene. By the time Henry Tate's company followed him out of the city, it had blown all its competitors out of the water and become the largest refinery business in the world. Silvertown had been modernised and Liverpool considered itself to be the sacrificial lamb. Tate girls cried in the streets as the bulldozers and excavators arrived to knock down the beloved Crystal Club. There were no more blue and gold steam lorries chugging out of the refinery to the Uncle Joe's Mint Balls factory in Wigan. Redundant sugar workers joined the already swollen dole queues. The Love Lane refinery was contaminated and polluted and its final closure was to leave further dereliction in the centre of Vauxhall. Tate's had been a good employer and had created a tight, vibrant community but sugar had lost its nobility in Liverpool. Like the city herself, sugar was now a dirty word, linked with tooth decay, dangerous cravings, hyperactivity and attention deficit, obesity and sugar diabetes. Sugar was pure, white and deadly, a harmful anti-nutrient. The sugar wars were a thing of the past, but heart disease and strokes were on the rise. Bagaceira was now a metaphor for Liverpool and her redundant unskilled workforce.

In a short time, Vauxhall became a midden where very few people wanted to live, a wilderness by the sea devoid of profit or potential. The subsequent closure of the British American Tobacco plant on Commercial Road led to a final toll of 30,000 unemployed in and around Liverpool 5. Demoralised locals started to leave to find work in other parts of the city. The city council knocked down more tenements and drew up plans to disperse the remaining families. A group of neighbours from Eldon Street in neighbouring Liverpool 3 continued to resist this break-up of the Tate and BAT family and proposed a regeneration initiative. They had witnessed first hand the disastrous attempts in the '60s to get rid of the slums and break up sectarian divides by transplanting people from different parts of the city into soulless new estates on the fringes. Backed by local priests and councillors and with the support of Prince Charles, Tony McGann and his Eldonians resisted Militant's proposal to municipalise the Portland Gardens Cooperative and knock down the remaining buildings. With the help of several housing grants, they managed to buy the Love Lane site and within 8 years their Housing Cooperative had built 145 new brownfield homes. Their vision centred on a desire to preserve their neighbourhood and at the same time attract community-based businesses with close links to the wider urban economic regeneration of the city. Housing Association status followed with the acquisition of a further 150 shared-ownership homes; and the provision of Athol Village Hall for social functions, a residential care home, a day nursery and an administrative building named The Tony McGann Centre all breathed new life into the area. Mute swans and kingfishers arrived on the canal and the post-Blitz black redstarts held on in the docklands. Even Tate's cavernous old honeycomb sugar silo in Huskisson dock found use as an Orange venue for the music of Shack and Turin Brakes. Out of the rubble of the sugar refinery had come a new start and a society with pride and self-respect. Hardship had reinforced friendship and a sense of belonging.

The jewel in the Caribbean and the most British of the Antilles had become a Creole tourist trap and a sugar lake. Few Bajans now toiled with machetes in the cane fields but they were still behoven to the white masters and their unforgiving God. Freed from the cane, part of Barbados had regained a long-lost pristine beauty, while some former plantations had sprouted pricey condominiums and golf courses geared for successful financiers and returning nationals. Holidaymakers rarely ventured inland to view the ruined chattel houses or taste the unslaked thirst of the choking cane fields. The Bajan 'niggers' who served up the punch and made the music were the progeny of a forgotten shameful commodity. Their dead were dead and were no longer beside them. Their heritage has been bleached and only the whistling frogs of the night sustained a belief in another faraway world beyond the seas.

Travel has failed to ease my hurt as I now wander this invisible, empty city in an effort to recapture an imaginary past. I am a revenant and one-man film crew with an old box camera, choosing to work in shades of gunmetal and charcoal. I am back home in the land of sweet nothings and make-believe. It seems that the passing of time is no more than the shunting of new sensations into a holding account. Liverpool is always elsewhere but she never leaves me alone. She is forever in my dreams and just when I think she has disappeared, finally setting me free, she returns to haunt me once more. Those fond avenues, parkland vistas and seascapes have shrunk to nothing and are as fugitive as each passing year. Painful recollections rise up like the roar of the waves in a dead shell.

In 1988, the Tate Modern opened in the Albert Dock as the vanguard of a heritage vision for stagnant Liverpool. The proceeds of sugar helped create this town and now the old Sugar Fella was trying to revive it. Today in The Holes two decaying giants surrounded by snails lie permanently asleep. One has been chopped in half by an incompetent magician and his tubes of spilled colon left to undulate like dying eels in the abyss. Laurel and Hardy are unrecognisable in their old age. They stare from a canvas that reminds us that time is hard to stop. Sex and death lurk the jiggers of old Sugartown and Liverpool is still sticking to my lapels. Sugar ethanol production produced by fair trade boutique plantations will save the planet and remodel the disaccharide's rank past.

Oh Tell Me Where I'm Going?
Tell Me Where I'm Bound?

> There was so much I ought to have recorded,
> So many lives that have vanished –
> Families, neighbours: people whose pockets
> Were worn thin by hope. They were
> The loose change history spent without caring.
> Now they have become the air I breathe,
> Not to have marked their passing seems such a betrayal.
>   Extract from 'The Betrayal' by Brian Patten

Ten years after the demise of the Mersey Sound, much of the city's dodgily permed and moustached youth were surviving on supplementary and unemployment benefits. Making music was still a respectable alternative to the dole queue and provided a creative channel for the disenfranchised and hopeless. The large number of jobless meant that Beat City no longer featured on the circuit for top international acts. Liverpool was also completely off the planet for the global record companies but hardly any one in town seemed to care.

Peter O'Hallaghan, a former merchant seaman, believed a manhole at the junction of Mathew and Button Streets was bang on an interstellar ley line and that Carl Jung's dream of visiting an unfamiliar, faraway city referred specifically to this junction:

> I found myself in a dirty, sooty city. It was night and winter and dark and raining. I was in Liverpool. The various quarters of the city were arranged radially around the square. In the centre was a round pool, in the middle of it a small island. While everything around it was obscured by rain, fog, smoke and dimly lit darkness, the little island blazed with sunlight. On it stood a single tree; a magnolia in a shower of reddish blossoms. It was as though the tree stood in the sunlight and was, at the same time, the source of light. Everything was

extremely unpleasant; black and opaque – just as I felt then. But I had
a vision of unearthly beauty . . . and that's why I was able to live at all.
Liverpool is the pool of life.

By 1974, most of the cellars where the legendary Cavern Club had once
stood had been flattened to make a car park but, inspired by the magnolia
vision, O'Hallaghan and his brother converted a remaining fruit warehouse
into a downstairs market selling second-hand records and hippy food, and
an arty upstairs called the Armadillo Tea Rooms that soon metamorphosed
into the rather grander Liverpool School of Language, Music, Dream and
Pun. An extraordinary Jungian festival attended by a bewildered Mayor
of Zurich and a performance of the 24-hour-long *Illuminatus Trilogy* by
Ken Campbell were two of a number of memorable happenings. Liver was
now the 'seat of life' and this unique new dream scene that centred on the
Creative Mind underground cinema, the Science Fiction Theatre and the
Liverpool School of Language, Music, Dream and Pun became a focus for
a new generation of artists, poets and musicians. To celebrate this
reawakening and the first import of bananas through the Liverpool docks,
O'Hallaghan jumped into a skip filled with warm custard.

Three years later, after the brothers had closed down and left Mathew
Street to follow a new cosmic dream that would use particle physics to link
mind with matter, the new Liverpool music scene kicked off after a Clash
concert. Under the direction of Twisted Wheel DJ Roger Eagle and the
Deaf School manager Ken Testi, Eric's opened upstairs at Gatsby's in
Mathew Street opposite the old Cavern with an eclectic mix of reggae, jazz
and folk. It then moved downstairs to replace the Revolution Club and
went on to stage many memorable late-night shows by groups such as the
Ramones, Talking Heads, Elvis Costello and the Attractions, The
Stranglers, The Buzzcocks, and Johnny Thunders and the Heartbreakers.
Three out-of-work lads who had supped tea regularly in the Armadillo
Tea Rooms and all cooed over Joe Strummer formed a group called Arthur
Hostile and the Crucial Three. They were determined to make a clean
break from their legacy of the Beatles and pub rock. Each of them would
soon move on to form their own band: Pete Wylie with Wah! Wah! Heat,
Ian McCulloch with Echo and the Bunnymen, and Julian Cope with The
Teardrop Explodes. These pioneers of the new sound were soon joined by
A Flock of Seagulls, Icicle Works and Pink Military. Big in Japan spawned
Frankie Goes to Hollywood and Ian Broudie struck out on his own with
the Lightning Seeds. Liverpool music had become a surreal left-field

fugitive fantasy played out in a ramshackle pisshole. Bill Drummond, owner of the indie record label The Zoo and manager of Echo and the Bunnymen and Teardrop Explodes, linked the ley line in Mathew Street with Iceland and Papua New Guinea. He harboured the dream of standing on the O'Hallaghan manhole and invoking the underworld while Teardrop Explodes played a gig in Port Moresby and the Bunnymen were on stage in Reykjavik. He began to identify his two groups more and more with these two islands. The Bunnymen were grey, honest and dour, with a halo of northern lights. The Teardrops were embodied by Julian Cope, a new spirit with the uncontrollable energy of the jungle, a soul with a thousand masks, dark and devious, light and seductive, an artist charmed by birds of paradise and poisoned by serpents, a soul born, fornicating and dying all at the same time.

This new music, which was cultivated and nourished at Eric's, was defined by a lyrical, mystical, fantastic sound that enveloped the rhythms of the ocean and set Liverpool on a different musical trajectory to the Rainy City 30 miles down the East Lancs Road. It was music devoid of protest with an arty, kaleidoscopic feel. The club was now epitomised by the angelic looks and acerbic tongue of Pete Burns and his much-hated tarts Dead or Alive, and attracted suburban Billy Idol-like poseurs and mascara-heavy punkettes in search of a bit of blow and in-crowd gossip. The audience bounced inches from the low stage and when the music stopped the band members blended seamlessly with the milling crowds.

Liverpool had acquired an escapist interest in psychedelia and The Velvet Underground, and a desire to form her own glam New York scene. Orchestral Manoeuvres in the Dark, the electro pop pioneers from over the water, were one of the few musical bridges between Liverpool and Manchester, and only Echo and the Bunnymen had a strong fan base down the M62. The new scene was all about the dream of the city state of Liverpool. Art for art's sake, being cool, gawping and having the looks overrode musical content.

When Eric's closed after a drugs raid on 14 March 1980, the arty diehards kept the new flame alive in Probe Records, where they leafed through the vinyl racks and reminisced about memorable gigs. After another brief flowering, Liverpool was once more left waiting for her next landfall. Ship Town once more curled in on herself, praying for resurgent inspiration on the Irish tides. The best crack was now to be found in the old Nigerian and Somali joints of Liverpool 8, not in the city centre. Most of Huyton's Girobank tanned beauties had resolutely turned their graceful bare backs on the alternative scene and joined the star-jumping soul set, dancing to the soft-shoe shuffle of Barry White at Annabel's and Tuxedo Junction and smooching to the groovy white-boy soul of the Commodores at the Hollywood and Scamps.

Into the vacuum left by the closure of Eric's came the retro terrace-chic bands like Rain, with their following of unemployed football-loving scallies determined to make a statement. These neophytes, with their Bryan Ferry side partings, straight-legged jeans, Adidas polo tops, button-down shirts and Pod fashions, acknowledged their safety-pin, pogo-jumping, crowd-surfing roots through their love of The Jam, The Stranglers and The Clash but rejected all the piercing and spitting, and challenged the effeminate post-punk dynasty of Eric's. They also kept away from the New Wave Warsaw scene at the Swinging Apple in Wood Street. These smoothies had been reared on their parents' scratched collections of late Beatles, The Who, early Stones, Hendrix, The Byrds, Pink Floyd and Frank Zappa. Their new anthems included Iggy Pop's 'The Passenger', Elvis Costello's 'Oliver's Army', Sham 69's 'Angels with Dirty Faces', Stiff Little Fingers' 'Alternative Ulster', 'White Riot' by the Clash and anything by local eclectic band and Phil residents Groundpig. Much of their weekends were spent at railway stations discussing violence, music and how to get out of Liverpool.

Mike Badger and Lee Mavers formed the La's in Huyton in 1984. The band name came from the elementary musical key note but had a double and uniquely Scouse meaning of 'lads'. Both Badger and Mavers were into Captain Beefheart and the Magic Band, and like its Californian creator Don Van Vliet they elected to strike out on their own, rejecting all current musical trends. With their newly recruited young bassist John Power, they holed up with some grass and a bunch of '60s classics in order to create a fresh raw sound that would reflect the mood and history of Liverpool and wash away all the adulterated chart music they abhorred.

The La's were soon playing to packed houses in the cultural wastelands of Bootle and Walton. They were in your face, awkward, witty, errant and increasingly impossible to ignore. The band's three singles with the indie label Go!, discs entitled 'Way Out', 'There She Goes' and 'Timeless Melody', achieved a ripple of commercial success but by 1988 their street credibility was sky high.

After a few final chaotic live performances, the La's faded into oblivion. In a final interview to the music press before the La's disbanded, 'the little Scouser', as he called himself, urged his inquisitors 'to feel the message in the music and ignore the rest'.

The Stone Roses with their wa-wa pedals now presided over the new influential 'Madchester' scene. Oasis would later burst forth, claiming that they were finishing what the La's had started and with Noel Gallagher claiming that Mavers frightened the life out of him.

'There She Goes' had won some enduring recognition. Its two and a half minutes of repetitive acoustic circling had redesigned my synapses and become a hard-wired chorus with a bridge and momentum that resonated with the Huyton chicken coops. Its fresh, off-beat and unashamedly nostalgic harmonies seemed to me as full of magic as the Beatles' 'There's A Place'. An urban myth grew up that the tune was an ode to heroin. Cover versions appeared from the US evangelical band Sixpence None the Richer, the Boo Radleys and Robbie Williams, and the song was featured on the soundtrack of the movies *Fever Pitch* and *Parent Trap*, employed as both a car and a birth pill advert and later as a popular mobile phone jingle.

The La's lack of commercial success enhanced their cult status in Liverpool, emphasising the city's new ambivalence to the corporate world of big business. The band's failure to deliver on contracts and to refuse to play the game was in the vanguard of a movement in Liverpool where indie bands deliberately refused to venture outside the city's womb. Playing live in the town centre became the be all and end all. It became a standing joke in the music business that Liverpool bands were distinguished by their perverse compulsion to shoot themselves in the foot as soon as they started to walk.

The La's album has worn well and was re-released in 2001, 11 years after it was recorded. Its raw, confessional, silvery, sonic freshness and nursery-rhyme lack of romanticism still appeal to English youth. The band finally reformed in 2006 and Mavers and Power played the Ritz, the Leadmill, the Empire and Glastonbury. Time stood still for a second time.

I am arriving back in Never-Never Land a few years after John Barnes moved north to manage Celtic. I survey the celluloid footage created by the steel framework of the Runcorn Bridge and as we approach Liverpool the honeycomb patterns of the chimney pots stretch across the horizon like a musical score. Edge Hill, with its cuttings and labyrinth of secret rail tunnels carved from soot-stained sandstone, a past hidden in the lost street signs of Chatsworth, Overton, Great Newton, Brownlow, Gill and St Andrews, leaves me with a sense of unfulfilment. The arched cages and dungeons, with their yellow cryptograms and barren trellises, are the portholes of an enslaved city. Blackened, stunted coltsfoot grows out of crannies in the dappled rocks, and high above the track a lone oak marks my entry. Lime Street Station comes into view with its cracked glass roof, grimy platforms and lowering arches, a brooding totem of a golden age, the end of the line and a venerable symbol of the town's decadent past. Liverpool is a city of dark, foreboding tunnels.

Outside on her plateau is the temple of St George circled by the statues of the good and great from the glory days of the Forum. Its biblical mosaics have been embellished with stickers urging support for the dockers. I fall again for her braggadocio, those 16 Corinthian fangs, colossal portico, Minton tiles and sweeping courtyard, but today, as the wind drops out on the river, even the city's gulls seem to have been grounded. The seabirds now hunt like rats around the city's bins; they have forgotten the taste of herrings.

Turning left, I confront the rawness and emptiness of Lime Street, the worse-for-wear Holiday Inn, the sharp, smooth white curves of the crumbling Futurist cinema with its cracked glass and guano stains, the giant Epstein phallus, an ever enlarging row of hoardings and boarded-up shops, The Big House, an abandoned cinema and derelict offices shrouded in a huge drape. In the window of Lewis's, there is a fading nude mannequin staring forlornly at a frosty silver tree adorned with ersatz handbags. A few downhearted second-hand booksellers hang on with the barbers, a discount jug wine off-licence and a mobile phone outlet. The title of one book outside captures my eye, *Perverse Pussy*, but closer inspection reveals a nineteenth-century Sunday School Union guide to raising maladapted cats. I'm out of sight and my intonations have become less defensive and I am at home with this stubborn tattiness.

Down Renshaw is the Rapid Paint Shop and from its upstairs window I look down on the stairs leading to Coleman's the bespoke tailors and then across to Grand Central Hall, former Wesleyan stronghold and now the home for a group of alternative retailers.

On Brownlow Hill, most of the houses are deserted with broken windows and leadless roofs, and there is a dead mongrel in the gutter. I walk a lonely street chasing shadows. Old friends come at me through the rain but I can no longer retain their intimacy or the special ring of their laughter.

Mavers's song infected my nerve cells with a melodic mad-cow-disease sequence, which still interrupts language, distorts reality and evokes solace. It has started to eat into my logic and subvert my memory as it jams its way through the basements of the brain. I put my hands over my ears and see the argent cinematographic boomtown city before me, the river with its wardrobe of jibs and gantries, its rugged semicircle of sublime grandeur. I am hooked and aroused by her senseless, irresistible musical tics and ear worms. These action replays, reveries and reverberating tapes, which synchronise with the sea, carve out unique abstractions, excitations and unexpected oscillations. They break the do-nothing silence and swim against the brain-dead tide of reality television. Mavers, the morose perfectionist, afraid to step back into the harsh, condemning mainstream sunlight, has left a tattoo on my brain. Meanwhile, the city has gone to the dogs instead of the races and someone somewhere in a different time zone has got away with murder.

Valentine

The heart was scarlet satin, sort of stuffed.
I sort of felt it was me own heart, like.
SHE TORE THE STUFFING OUT OF THE SCARLET
HEART
I sort of stuffed and tore her sort of scarlet
I stuffed her, like, and felt her sort of satin.
I sort of felt she'd tore out all me stuffing.

Extract from 'February 15th' by Peter Reading

At a quarter to four on the afternoon of Friday, 12 February 1993 in a Bootle mall, a young mother was queuing in the family butchers when her toddler son strayed from her side. As the panic familiar to all mothers set in and the tannoy announced the missing child's name – James Bulger – the CCTV impassively recorded two young boys, one of whom was holding an infant's hand, as they walked through the shopping centre. When Merseyside Police later released the jumpy silhouettes, their apparent youth raised hopes of a happy ending. A description of the child was released: a month short of three with fair skin, parted light-brown long hair, blue eyes, an engaging smile and a birth mark on his neck. He had been wearing a navy-blue anorak, a blue woollen scarf with a white cat's face, a grey tracksuit and a white T-shirt with Noddy written on the front.

Hopes were dashed on St Valentine's Day when four Walton teenagers, hanging around looking for lost footballs, saw what they thought to be a doll on the freight rail line that runs from Edge Hill to Bootle. As they moved in for a closer look, the dreadful reality dawned on them that it was a child. The discovery of this fragile, lifeless bundle defaced, tortured and severed by a passing train, would soon horrify the nation. James Bulger's face was bruised and bloody and his fair hair was matted with congealed blood. There were blue paint stains on his left eye, neck, ear and fingers. Forensic examination later revealed a strange mark, with an intricate tessellated pattern branded on his face. Some batteries and a tin of blue paint were found close by. Murder seemed likely.

Vulpine journalists from all over Europe tumbled off the Euston trains at Lime Street in anticipation of a good story. The city missed a beat and the tragedy sent ripples of unease across a country increasingly preoccupied with an explosion of juvenile crime. Courtesy, politeness and kindness had become wimpish foibles, and the increasing number of road rage incidents reflected an angry go-getting society. The fuzzy flashbacks now heightened the nation's fears. James could have been anybody's child. Mothers' thoughts flooded back to the relief of tearful reunions, fathers questioned whether their sons were capable of infanticide. The North End shoppers asked themselves why they had failed to see anything wrong. In the mall, close to where a poster of the abduction had been displayed, a mound of wreaths, flowers and teddy bears expressed Liverpool's communal grief. Two miles away on a grass bank at the corner of Cherry Lane in Walton, close to where the child's body had been found, another pile of toys, tributes and mementoes started to pile up. One message read, 'James this is my bedtime bear. You can keep him now for sweet dreams.' Many children brought flowers, including a small boy called Bobby Thompson who laid a solitary red rose.

Over a thousand messages of sympathy, death notices and moving tributes to James Bulger's short life were published in a supplement of the *Echo* with the headline 'We will never forget you' above the child's photograph. A candlelit memorial service was held at St Mary's Roman Catholic Church in Northwood, Kirkby, close to the Bulger home. The Anglican priest at nearby St Mark's spoke of the sadness, the anger and the potential for evil in all of us. The next day, 35,000 stood in silent respect at Anfield before the Ipswich game. A huge banner with the words 'RIP JAMES' enveloped the Kop. The tragedy made front-page news all over Europe. It underscored England's inadequacy in dealing with juvenile crime and the social problems caused by urban neglect. What appeared to most observers as genuine abhorrence, shock and profound loss was interpreted by some sections of the national press as medieval hysteria. Headlines such as 'Self-Pity City' appeared and many Scousers became more afraid of the papers than the emerging horrific facts.

In his 'Letter from Liverpool', published in *The New Yorker*, Blake Morrison tried to outline the scenario to an American audience:

> In a northern working-class environment, where to be thought 'dead

'ard' is a tribute, boys were left to be boys . . . The roads near that part of the route [where the boys walked their victim] have the names of Oxbridge colleges . . . But nothing could be less like Brideshead than this part of Liverpool. To imagine it you have to set aside images of college quads – and of chamomile lawns, bluebell woods, country lanes, mazy rivers, dappled meadows, rolling downs and all the other pastoral myths of southern England – and think instead of a vast tract of brick and concrete. Between Breeze Hill and the railway track where James Bulger died, the only grass to be seen grows between the graves in Walton churchyard . . . The view from the reservoir on top of Breeze Hill is as mean and dispiriting a panorama as you will ever see. The roofs of houses stretch to the horizon: pebble-dash semis, low prefabs, dirt encrusted red-brick row houses, mock Tudors, a handful of high-rises, boarded up shops. A large squat pub called the Mons – 'short for the Monstrosity', say the locals – stands, in its bleak anonymity, as the inverse of whatever cozy virtue English pubs once had. This is a landscape emptied of energy and innovation – a city that no longer knows what to do with itself.

The police investigation started badly with the father of a well-known problem family in Snowdrop Street, Kirkdale, 'shopping' his own son. The sale of toddler's reins rose sharply and mothers started to go shopping in groups. Five anxious days after James Bulger's body was found, the police got their first break. A woman called into a police station saying she was the friend of a family called Venables, whose son Jon had 'sagged off' school with another boy called Robert Thompson the previous week and had come home with blue paint all over him. She also thought she could recognise Jon from the video images. Preliminary enquiries at the children's school confirmed that the boys had not turned up to school on the previous Friday. On the day before the fateful event, a teacher informed them that Jon was very excited and fidgety in lessons as if he knew something was planned for the following day. With a complete media black-out still in force, the police visited the Thompson and Venables family homes early in the morning. Superintendent Albert Kirby, on seeing the two little boys with their nice, innocent voices, found it hard to believe that they could possibly be implicated in such a heinous crime. Both Bobby and Jon denied any involvement at first and burst into tears, but eventually, after patient interrogation, both admitted to taking James out of the shopping centre. Once Mrs Venables had expressed her undying love for her son, Jon finally broke down and confessed that he had been involved in the killing but asserted that Robert Thompson had been the violent instigator. During the first interviews, Robert tried to cover his tracks, denied involvement and blamed Jon for everything. Whereas Robert was guarded, and at times confused and combative, Jon came over to the police as a fantasist in awe of his friend. Both seemed very intrigued by the police investigation, with Jon asking after his fingerprints were taken whether marks are left on whatever one has touched. The forensic scientists had already obtained incontrovertible evidence linking blood and paint on both boys' clothes to the murder scene.

While Jon and Robert were being questioned, a mother who had been shopping at the New Strand Shopping Centre with her young son and daughter came forward with a chilling story. A few weeks before James's murder, two little boys had led her son away. When she finally tracked them down, grabbed her son back and gave the pair a good telling off, they had just laughed and run off. Jon and Robert would later claim that they had originally planned to lure James into the road in the hope a car might hit him. Further evidence of planning and premeditation came from an office worker who regularly lunched in the Strand and identified Venables as one of two boys he had seen a month earlier, trying to lure an infant out of a shop.

When Robert Thompson was finally charged, it seemed to the police as if he couldn't care less, while Jon was tearful and nervy. At the first public hearing, at the end of February in the South Sefton Magistrates Youth Court, a few hundred yards from the Strand Shopping Centre, a raging mob of young mothers with prams, apopleptic men and their hard suedehead sons waited for the police convoy. One man threw himself at the police van shouting, 'Die!' and, 'Hang the Bastards!' and some of the women screamed, 'We've got kids too, you know!' The convoy had in fact been a decoy and the two ten year olds had remained inside the detention area waiting for the incensed mob to disperse. The out-of-town journalists let fly at Liverpool once more, one unkindly claiming the city was 'getting off' on its own mourning and misfortune. There was now also a sectarian slant to the story: 'Two Proddies had butchered an innocent Cogger'.

The circumstances and events that had led up to the murder were now becoming clearer. The two boys in their school uniforms had been in the Strand for some time that day stealing sweets, a Troll doll, blue paint and batteries, and causing a general nuisance to the shoppers. They finally set eyes on a toddler in a grey sweatsuit eating Smarties and Jon enticingly said, 'Come on, baby.' The boys quickly led James out of the butcher's door and within four minutes they had left the mall through Marks & Spencer and walked out into Stanley Road.

James had at first been quite content with his new-found friends, skipping along as the three of them left the precinct. The boys lifted James up, setting him down near the post office, and then pretended to chastise him for running away. They next headed for a bridge by the adjacent Leeds and Liverpool canal where they asked him to kneel down. They joked to each other that they hoped James might fall into the filthy water. When he resisted, one of the boys picked him up like a rag doll and dropped him on his head. Perturbed by his sobs and the large swelling which had appeared on his forehead, the boys ran off, shutting the latch gate from the canal and left James desperately trying to catch them up. A woman spotted the crying child on the towpath and when Jon and Robert saw what was happening they turned round and came back. James took their hands again and innocently walked away with his abductors. When they came back up from the canal onto Stanley Road, they covered James's bruise with the hood of his anorak, crossed an intersection and climbed a wall into the grounds of Merton Towers, where they were picked up on a security camera in Oxford Road. James was now crying his eyes out and resisting the two boys' commands. A passing motorist saw Robert give the toddler what he described later as a persuading kick.

As the walk of death dragged on, the two boys seemed to have lost purpose and direction as they meandered aimlessly past shops and parking lots. They walked on towards the city of Liverpool, making the arduous climb to the top of Breeze Hill. Here, another eyewitness saw the boys swinging James up in the air. At the summit, Thompson and Venables lifted James onto the grassy knoll that covered the underground reservoir, where they rested on a step now a mile and 30 minutes from the Strand. It was at this Station of the Cross that the police would later find a white toy lamb. They crossed the field, where Jon was seen by a witness shaking James by the neck. Some passers-by noticed that James now had two big bruises. When confronted by a concerned woman walking her dog, Robert seemed willing to relinquish James but Jon took control, promising the woman that they would take the lost toddler to the police station. She then gave them directions to Walton police station. Another woman shopper with her little girl who had overheard this conversation was unconvinced by their explanation and challenged the boys. Robert let go of James's hand but Jon once more bluffed it out, saying that the police station was on their way home. The woman was so concerned that she wanted to take the child herself to the police station but this did not happen. The boys carried on leading the now subdued James into a sweet shop and then a pet shop. While Robert looked at a dead fish at the bottom of a tank, Jon gripped James's hand tightly. They then stopped to watch a fire at a bookmaker's shop before crossing heavy traffic to Church Road West. They passed Robert's home, their school and were not far from the Gothic catacomb of Anfield Cemetery. Some older boys who were acquainted with Robert were playing with plastic handcuffs and threatened to use them on him if the boys didn't release James. Tired, cold and aware that they would be in big trouble when they got home, they wove their way through the back streets of Walton into City Road, throwing James's blue anorak hood into a tree. They then crossed to the far side by the railway bridge where they turned into a back alley running parallel to the track. This brought them into Walton Lane and very close to the police station. A man who knew the Thompson family heard one of the boys say, 'I'm fed up with having my little brother. I have him from school all the time. I'm going to tell my mum I'm not going to mind him any more.' A girl saw the boys pushing a laughing James into the road. When she approached, they picked James up, ran off and scrambled up the embankment, squeezing through a gap in the fence, onto the railway line.

After a two-and-a-half-mile walk at around twenty to six in the evening on the deserted rail track near the disused Walton and Anfield station, the two boys finally had the privacy needed to commit their crime. Robert Thompson knew the area like the back of his hand and later that night his mother would go looking for him in his den, close to the crime scene. As they walked over the illuminated white shale towards the line, the boys started to throw paint at the screaming toddler. They pelted him with bricks and finally hit him with a 22 lb railway fishplate, fracturing his eggshell skull in ten places. James kept trying to get up, and Jon later claimed Robert shouted, 'Stay down, you stupid divvie.' James kept crying, 'Don't hurt me,' but the two excited boys ignored his pleas for mercy and removed his shoes and pants and started to kick and stamp on him in a final frenzy of rage. When the toddler stopped moving, they covered him with a pile of bricks and laid him carefully on the railway line. The boys then slid down the bank towards a factory and crossed the road to the house of one of Robert's friends and then on to a video hire shop.

The woman in the shop, who knew Bobby Thompson well, asked them to run an errand and the boys were not found by their parents till much later that evening. Both had been reported missing to the police. When Susan Venables finally found them at the video store, she was so angry that she had struck both Robert and her own son, and then had taken Jon to Walton Police Station. No sooner had Mrs Venables left the station than Ann Thompson arrived, complaining to the officers that Jon's mother had attacked her son.

Exactly when Bobby and Jon decided to kill James will never be known but it seems probable from the course of events that this was not their original intention. The two boys were both familiar with small children and at times protective towards them. As the abduction had dragged on, the boys may have become more and more fearful of the consequences and were unable to work out how to dispose of James without getting into hot water. Their capacity to disengage emotionally, their poor social adaptation and absence of any ability to inhibit each other's actions may explain the shocking end game. Did they place James's body on the rail line in the naive expectation that their crime would be considered an awful accident? Some of the detectives felt that the boys had wanted to create drama through a tragedy. The forensic psychiatrists were drawn to the possibility of sexual abuse, although no signs of sexual interference were ever proved. Thompson later claimed he used James's pants to staunch the blood flow from the child's mouth while Venables would assert that Robert had kicked James in his private parts.

Kirkby, the home of the Bulgers, had begun life as an overspill town for displaced Scousers but by the '90s many young families felt themselves to be Kirkby folk rather than Liverpudlians. Despite factory closures, continuing housing nightmares in the Northwood district and a shrinking population, the town had many things to be proud of. Houses with front doors and gardens leading onto the street had started to replace the hated high-rise tower blocks, its streets were relatively safe for mothers and children, and many hard-working folk struggled to make what they could of the difficult hand they'd been dealt in life. The Bulgers were a close and loving extended family who had ensured that James felt wanted and secure. Denise, who had lost her first child in pregnancy, was considered over-protective by some of her friends and always took James with her wherever she went.

Thompson and Venables on the other hand both came from troubled homes. Robert Thompson was the fifth of seven sons born to abused parents. When Robert was six, his father, Robert senior, a seventh son and violent alcoholic, who had repeatedly thrashed his wife Ann in front of the children, suddenly left home, leaving a five-pound note on the table. He was reputed to have once said, 'See the evil in my eyes, twat?' before giving one of his children a battering. His new partner was a 'family friend', Barbara, a grandmother 18 years his senior, whom the family had met on a caravan holiday in Southport. A week later, the Thompson house had burned down while they were at their nan's; the family were moved to a Toxteth hostel, before being re-housed in a red-brick, bay-windowed terraced house in Walton. Ann had been tanned regularly with a thick army belt by her lorry-driver father and had suffered from bedwetting till she was 15. Both her parents repeatedly told her she was thick, useless and a gobshite. Desperate to get out, she had jumped at the age of 18 into an abusive marriage. Bobby Thompson had been forced to develop defence mechanisms early in his life to survive the frustrated verbal and physical wrath of his depressed and often drunk mother and the constant beatings from his older brothers.

Bobby's eldest brother David was often left in charge and on one occasion he chained, tarred and feathered his brother Philip to maintain order. Life was so intolerable for the Thompson brood that first his younger brother Peter left home at 14 and then David himself requested to be taken into care to protect himself from his mother's violent outbursts. One of Bobby's older brothers became a burglar, sometimes taking a younger brother with him as an accomplice. Another brother became an arsonist and was suspected of sexual abuse, while yet another sibling had threatened his teachers with physical violence. Ann and her son Philip both took drug overdoses and a few weeks before James Bulger's murder, another brother Ian tried to kill himself while in care. All of the Thompson boys were school truants and resented authority. One year before Robert's arrest, Ann had had a further child from a new relationship and seemed to be getting her life slowly back together. Robert tried to gain his mother's approval by babysitting his new stepbrother and helping in the kitchen.

The Venables family lived in a terraced house in a quiet residential block in Liverpool 11 close to the leafy avenues of Norris Green. Neil Venables was a forklift driver but had had long periods of unemployment. When Jon was young, his parents were continually fighting, splitting up and getting back together again. There was also a background of alcohol and violence. Jon's elder brother Mark had a cleft palate and severe developmental problems and demanded a great deal of his parents' attention. He was derided at school and called a divvie and had frequent temper tantrums and volatile behaviour at home. His younger sister had learning problems and went to a special needs school. Imprisoned in her own home with three difficult children, Susan Venables became lonely and depressed and started to go out for an hour or two, leaving the children alone. In frustration, she would also hit Jon. Her childhood had been a battle and she had made two suicide attempts. Her own father, a builder, had been brought up in a drunken fighting family and her mother had worked as a barmaid. In common with Ann Thompson, she too had married very young to get away from a miserable home life.

Despite being the child his parents pinned all their hopes on, Jon was short tempered, jealous and unable to sleep. He was taunted and bullied at school because he had a squint and because of his backward siblings, and was felt by the school psychology services to be a deeply unhappy child. He was a low achiever, overactive and attention seeking and continually complained of being teased and picked on. He sometimes imitated his older brother's rage attacks, throwing chairs around or head butting his desk. Jon choked another pupil with a 12-inch ruler until the boy went red in the face and it took a great effort from his teacher and another woman to pull him off. On another occasion, he hung himself upside down on a coat peg like a dormant bat. His mother reported he was abusive to her at home and that he kept asking to join his brother and sister at the special needs school. She tried to change his diet but his behaviour worsened and he started to injure himself. He was eventually suspended and at the age of nine was transferred to Robert Thompson's school in Walton.

Both boys were placed in a class with children one year younger than themselves and soon forged an unholy alliance after a playground fight. Although his morale improved at the new school, Jon continued to show signs of maladjustment, pretending not to hear teachers' instructions or collapsing dejectedly over his desk as a signal he did not wish to cooperate. When he was made to stand against a wall in the playground as punishment for fighting, he would bang his head against the wall, collapse on the floor and wave his arms around. The teachers considered him an odd little boy, devoid of emotion, with poor eye contact, very easy to wind up, and a child it was easy to feel sorry for. Jon's father was now back on the scene, taking more responsibility for the children and hoping for a reconciliation with his emotionally crippled and controlling wife.

Bobby Thompson was a different character altogether. He was polite, tearful and apologetic when chastised in class but he was deceitful, a stirrer, an accomplished truant, a petty thief and very streetwise. Despite the hard exterior, he was sometimes chided at school for 'being like a girl'.

He was also semi-literate, telling the police, 'I can't read hard words.' At school, he was regarded as sly and quiet rather than a bully. He often hid behind his reputation as a Thompson, leaving his teachers with low expectations and him with very few friends. The Thompsons grew up afraid of each other and of their parents, and Bobby's personality was constructed for the purposes of self-defence. On one occasion, his younger brother Ryan had been found at the Strand Shopping Centre wandering around crying and distressed. He told his teacher later that Robert and another boy had taken him by the canal and punched and kicked him before leaving him on his own to find his way home. Bobby and Ryan would often lie in bed, sucking each other's thumbs or playing with Bobby's troll collection. It was not long before the artful dodger Bobby had persuaded Jon Venables to join him in sagging off from school. There was plenty of time to kill.

James's body was mistaken by the train driver for a doll on the line. Robert liked troll dolls and befriended Jon by giving him one which 'shows you their bum and all that'. The police probed the possibility that one of the stolen batteries had been inserted into either James's mouth or rectum in an infantile attempt to reanimate him. This possibility was fearfully denied by the boys, as was any suggestion of interference with James's penis. Jon may also have had another comically malevolent doll on his mind at the time of the murder. Neil Venables rented a lot of videos and a week or two before the murder, he had got out *Child's Play 3*. In it, the soul of a serial killer inhabits an evil doll called Chucky, who, while only the size of a toddler, runs around slaughtering innocents. Chucky runs without batteries and in the end he is killed on a fairground ghost train. After a battle on the tracks, Chucky, smeared with blue paint, is dismembered. As suggested by Blake Morrison in his book *As If,* Jon may have used the blue paint to dehumanise James and then seen himself as the hero ridding the world of the evil child-doll. Jon may also have watched the horror film *Halloween* at his father's flat. In this film, a six-year-old boy commits murder and years later as an adult escapes from a mental asylum and commits more. In the film, the children call him the boogieman because he won't stay down and keeps getting up. Life seemed to be imitating art.

Robert was prepared to re-enact the murder with the forensic psychiatrist using dolls, a toy railway track and miniature weapons. He demonstrated how the 'Jon doll' hit the 'James doll' and showed how he'd like to kick Jon's face. He also claimed that Jon had said, 'Let's get a kid lost. I haven't hit one for ages.' He then became very agitated and described a recurrent dream in which he was chasing someone and was hit by a car. During the interviews, it became clear to the police that Jon had a vivid imagination and a great deal of suppressed anger. During his confession, he acted out some hostility to his father, particularly when the issue of a sexual assault on James came up. He started punching his father, wailing, 'My dad thinks I know and I don't.' In the secure unit prior to his trial, Jon covered his bed with furry animals to ward off evil and was considered to be deeply in denial by one of the psychiatrists who visited him.

The people of Liverpool were flabbergasted at the age of the suspects. The city was still raw from the shame of Heysel and the tragedy of Hillsborough. Vigilante mobs drove the accused families from their homes. 'Amityville House of Horror' was scrawled over the front of the Thompson home. To many ordinary people, the depravity of the offence meant that Thompson and Venables had lost their right to be regarded as children or even as human. The press revealed a few other horrifying cases of children who had committed murder and rape. The media blamed single mothers, absent fathers, the drop in churchgoing, the oral contraceptive and the loss of discipline in schools. The tabloid headlines clamoured for zero tolerance. This led to John Major's unhelpful comment in response to questioning in the House about the murder: 'We must condemn a little more and understand a little less.' The national press appropriated the memory of 'little Jamie', a name never used by any of the Bulger family. The media continued to accuse the city of maudlin sentimentality, with its excessive shows of chagrin and flowers, and branded the minority of hotheads as Wild West vigilantes.

On Halloween, nine months after James's death, the boys stood trial at Preston Crown Court. A special raised dais had to be constructed to allow them to see above the railings. In court, Jon and Robert were referred to as Child A and Child B. Robert got most of the bad press during the trial and was even accused of staring journalists down like a baby Charles Manson. He appeared hardened and unremorseful in the courtroom and his seemingly unemotional lack of interest as he listened to the litany of police tapes further suggested to the media that he was the ringleader. Jon appeared more distressed, repentant and at times in awe of Robert. Some of the journalists and psychologists considered that both boys had personality disorders but to the jury and most onlookers neither of them looked much like murderers.

Jon took the lead in coaxing the children away and the initiative in deceiving some of the 38 people they had encountered by telling them that James was his brother. Jon maintained that it was Robert who had said, 'Let's get this kid lost outside so when he goes into the road he'll get run over.' It may also have been Robert who had had the idea to take James and lead him to the canal as a way of acting out his anger against his stepbrother Ben. During his denials, Robert had said to the police, 'If I wanted to kill a baby, I'd kill my own wouldn't I?' In one statement, Jon confessed that he had killed James. Robert on the other hand may have been the instigator of the alleged but never substantiated sexual assault. The police believed that James's clothes may have been removed before the murder and that his penis and foreskin had been manipulated. The Bulger family, with the exception of Denise who was now seven months pregnant, attended court every day. Susan Venables tried to keep face while her estranged husband appeared destroyed. As the trial rolled on, a wheezy 41-year-old Ann Thompson also appeared, wearing a bright striped dress with red streaks in her shoulder-length hair and a five-pointed Orange Lodge star round her neck.

Forensic evidence had conclusively linked an imprint on James's cheek to the metal tag of one of Robert's shoelaces. An important aspect of the case centred upon whether the boys knew the difference between right and wrong. In nineteenth-century England, feral children were executed for their crimes until the Victorian concept of *doli incapax* was established to protect them by demonstrating that they were too young to grasp the consequences of their actions. In England, this law is only valid below ten years and both boys were six months over. The defence took the line that this was a dreadful prank which had gone wrong, and the weary boys had not known how to bring their abduction to a happy end.

The trial lasted three weeks. As Robert awaited the verdict, he knitted gloves for his baby stepbrother. As the judge passed the guilty verdict, Robert sat motionless and Jon cried. On passing sentence, the judge called the crime an act of unparalleled evil and barbarity and said that he believed the two boys to be cunning and very wicked. The BBC called it a landmark case. The day after the verdict, the *Daily Star* ('The Newspaper that Cares') had on its front page the photographs of two smiling little boys with the following captions 'Killer Bobby Thompson – Boy A and Killer Jon Venables – Boy B' with the caption underneath: 'How do you feel now, you little bastards?'

After the trial, most of the red tops vilified the boys, branding them as evil freaks and expressing moral outrage. Truant-free zone stickers appeared on shop windows and the government urged parents to limit children's access to video games and be vigilant for any evidence of bullying at school. A minister accused the Church of England of being mysteriously silent in relation to the need to teach children the difference between right and wrong. *The Sun* collected a quarter of a million signatures to protest against the lenient sentence and perhaps as a result the boys' sentences were increased by the Lord Chief Justice from eight to ten years and then by Michael Howard, the Home Secretary, to twenty years, reduced back down to fifteen years. In 1999, the case went to the European Commission of Rights where it was concluded that Thompson and Venables should not have been tried as adults, awarded them both costs and declared the Home Secretary's increased sentence to be illegal. It was claimed that there had been a complete absence of pity for them as children. Ralph Bulger's response to this was to threaten to 'hunt his son's killers down'. Denise, now divorced from Ralph and remarried, commented, 'I feel let down and betrayed by the system.'

Eight years later, the two 'little demons' had made remarkable progress in their ability to appreciate the magnitude of their crime and in their slow quest for redemption. They had been deprived of their liberty, separated from their families, denied the chance of a normal adolescence and yet they had not grown into hardened delinquents. With the help of prescribed institutional parenting, Thompson had become calmer and was now capable of putting the needs of others before his own. Venables had acknowledged the enormity of his offence and had become a pleasant young man with exemplary conduct. Both youths had become role models in the small secure units where they were being held. The psychologists had always been struck by their ordinariness and had never been able to distinguish murderous traits that would single them out from the many other disturbed youths around them. In addition to the enforced protection from a vengeful and vindictive outside world, the killers had also been saved from the numerous unsolicited offers of help from therapists and the flood of letters which could be broadly divided between those spitting anger and threats and others reassuring them that Jesus had forgiven them. They were allowed to play snooker and mix with other inmates and later they were encouraged to start to take bike rides and garden outside. Thompson was allowed to travel for the first time in his life on a bus at the age of 17 and Venables visited Stratford upon Avon and Old Trafford. Some of the media considered that the boys were being kept in an expensive holiday camp with rooms which resembled student pads and cost the taxpayer £2,000 a week.

When the inevitable early parole was finally granted in 2001, a spokesman for James's mother read a statement:

> Denise is absolutely devastated and stunned. There has to be a punishment element for such a crime but all Denise sees is Venables and Thompson being rewarded. It has never been about revenge but about a justice denied. Venables and Thompson are being released back to their families who themselves could only dream of the living conditions they will enjoy. If they had given their children love and support nine years ago James would never have been murdered.

James Bulger's uncle angrily commented, 'Killing's too good for them.' Most people in Liverpool felt parole had come far too soon but very few now believed the boys should be locked away for ever. After the release, the Thompson family were forced to go into hiding after Ann was threatened with her life. Denise and Ralph Bulger had been divorced for some time and the family seemed unable to move on.

On 14 February, I retraced the last journey of James Bulger from the main shopping drag of the cheerless New Strand through the leering streets of Bootle to the plexus of unemployed Walton. It is an area most people would elect to visit only if their plane crashed there. The Strand had not changed, still full of young mothers pushing prams and doing their best on very little. A.R. Tyms was still there but the middle-aged master butchers all had a resigned look as they hacked away at the animal carcases. Next door was T.J. Hughes the discount department store and then the pawnbrokers. Percy Sledge's doleful '60s hit 'When a Man Loves a Woman' was playing and there was a smell of rancid lard. At the end of the mall, past where James had been led, was an exhibition of Old Bootle made up mainly of school photographs. While I was looking at the pictures, teatime shoppers were being advised over the tannoy that if they got separated from their children to meet up at the lower ground exit. Following the signs to Marks & Spencer, I climbed up and out and turned right past the canal. There were a lot of men and women in the streets; others looked down on me from the top of passing buses. A sullen acquiescence and a downtrodden resignation filled the air. I was visiting a land of permanent lottery losses, bungled bank robberies and black dogs. I was observing a people who had missed the boat and now lived on penn'orths of whiskey. The reservoir at the top of Breeze Hill was now a Millennium Park but it was still an unwelcoming place full of distressed trees, forgotten buckets and holes.

It seemed a long and treacherous route for tiny legs to travel as I dodged traffic in the footsteps of Bobby, Jon and James. I recalled the *Times* article from the time asking where had the city's community conscience gone, but this wasn't a case of minding your own business or not getting involved. The murder scene in Cherry Lane was now a storage depot guarded by a pair of formidable gates but there was nothing to remember James. His grave in the chill Kirkdale cemetery is marked by few windswept daffodils, a tree bedecked with a sodden Kanga, a toy plane and a favourite police car, and a fading Christmas memento 'from Mum, Stuart and the boys'. Suddenly I faced the wizened hardness of several pre-teen hoodies whose childhood had been stolen from them. They were on BMX bikes outside a call box, defending their territory and doing dirty work for a drug gang. Their fearless malice made me freeze but then one asked me what I was doing, and his cheeky adenoidal squeaks reassured me. He was not quite a child-man but probably had a knife and perhaps a gun. Eleven-year-old Rhys Jones had just been shot dead through the neck in a car park outside the Fir Tree public house, prompting the *Daily Mail* to recommend that children on Merseyside might be well advised to ask for a bulletproof vest to go with their bicycle in their Christmas stocking. I started to think about *Lord of the Flies* and the interplay between the evil of Roger and the savagery of Jack. Golding believed that without the constraints and authority of family, the basics of right and wrong are lost. Children were now viewed as menacing enemies to society.

YouTube montages and Facebook tributes to James Bulger posted on the web by those who had never met him seemed to epitomise the moral detachment. Jon Venables, now a disturbed, lonely adult with an identity crisis, would soon happily return to custodial care, having been found guilty of downloading and distributing child pornography.

Why hadn't it happened more often? was my overriding feeling as I continued my lonely walk.

Slack Water

We wouldn't have come so close if we'd known
What it was — a barrel shaped hide
washed up on the Mersey shore
and left to rot in peace if peace is to be had
from the tide's corrosive agents, ageless rhythm.
Then we saw the tarnished bones,
the long jaw
jutting out from all the foul jetsam . . .

Extract from 'The Sound of Things'
by Jamie McKendrick

The callused hands of Liverpool dockers had shifted cargoes from the greatest empire the world had ever known for six generations and had left a particular influence on the character of the city. Erratic work patterns, poor pay and the constant risk of serious injury had made family, community and a sense of humour integral to their survival. To work on the waterfront had come to be considered a mark of distinction and by the 1980s the few dockers that were left felt they were fighting not only for their own living but for the lifeblood and regeneration of their city.

The Mersey Docks and Harbour Board which had taken over the running of the docks from the Trustees in 1858 had been reconstituted in 1972 as a limited company and floated on the London Stock Exchange in an effort to raise venture capital for a new container dock at Seaforth. Over the next two decades, £112 million of loans, £200 million of redundancy payments and £37 million of dock regeneration funding from the taxpayer's purse were poured into the docklands. More millions from City Challenge Funding and £13 million of regional development funds from the Common Market were thrown into a bottomless wharf. The docks were the only public utility still benefiting from handouts.

The Mersey Docks and Harbour Company was considered an outstanding model of Tory enterprise. It had grown out of a public body and through the introduction of modern technology had raised its cargo handling tonnage to a record 10 million tonnes per year. It prided itself in running the only unionised port still left in Britain and one that enjoyed a good working relationship with the syndicates and the dwindling number of dock labourers. Within three years, the Thatcher government had provided severance pay to 600 more Liverpool dockers, creating a 41 per cent saving in wages. Lloyd's reported that the Port of Liverpool now had the most productive workforce in Western Europe. Abolition of the National Dock Scheme seemed to have paid off.

The National Association of Port Employers was determined to bring the dockers into line and further modernise working practices. They talked to the Institute of Economic Affairs, lobbied government think tanks and secured the services of a number of Tory MPs to champion their cause in the House of Commons. The financial benefits and new investment opportunities that would result from the removal of restrictive practices in the ports were forcefully argued on radio and television. This culminated in the Dock Work Bill which, after three readings in Parliament, finally received Royal Assent in April 1989. This Bill paved the way for the return of casual labour and would deprive the dockers of their hard-earned right to a minimum wage, holidays and sick pay.

The Trades Union Movement had been disembowelled during the Thatcher years and the TGWU dillied and dallied despite two unanimously approved votes by the membership for a national strike. By the time it finally called for industrial action, unskilled casual labourers were working 12 hours a day for a basic minimum wage in the Liverpool docks, the accident rate had risen and job security had vanished. The registered dockers were on call 24 hours a day and were made to work to finish the job. Workloads were steadily increased, on-call rotas were instituted and men with years of service were given 'final warnings for life'. The threat of forfeiture of a sizeable redundancy package smashed the official July strike almost before it had started. The shop stewards were now under firm instructions from Transport House to maintain a presence on the waterfront at all costs. As the temperature rose on the docks, they sided more and more with MDHC, becoming a duplicitous force in negotiations. Any lingering solidarity in the Port of Liverpool had been cynically dismantled. Large stretches of the increasingly abandoned waterfront were now handed over to property speculators and international bankers, and the feared 'lump' had once more returned to the docks. The world-famous shipping companies had also all but gone. Those that had avoided termination survived as giant combines like the Atlantic Container Line and the Ocean Container Line.

In 1992, industrial relations plummeted further on the Liverpool waterfront following a concerted campaign of macho management. The MDHC had started to ask the shop stewards to agree to what amounted to nothing short of a loyalty pledge or risk being de-recognised by the company. Despite this, the union recommended resistance, which was supported by the rank and file in a secret ballot. By the end of the week, a large advertisement had appeared in the *Liverpool Echo* for applicants to replace the entire MDHC workforce. This resulted in the unreal scenario of hundreds of unemployed 'woolybacks' arriving at the port employer's offices hoping for a job. The threat of mass sackings allowed the company to force through the acceptance of a punitive new deal including the end of overtime payments, flexible 12-hour shifts, and annualised bonuses by five votes. The TGWU later also signed up to an average 25 per cent drop in salary for the dockers. This reinforced the beleaguered Liverpool dockers' view that the TGWU leadership was little more than a cosy outfit serving the aims of the establishment, a dangerous fifth column of the body politic that had led to thousands of men taking voluntary redundancy.

As Christmas 1994 arrived, the North End cranes and derricks were still groaning above their loads of timber but just nine months later twenty men working at the Seaforth Container Basin for Torside, a private sub-contractor, were ordered to complete a job without any prospect of overtime pay. They objected and at the end of their usual shift went to see their shop steward. The first five to arrive were confronted by the managing director of Torside who insisted they return to the ship to finish the job. When they refused, he summarily dismissed them. The rest of the men were also sacked. Torside workers did not receive sick pay or holiday pay and were considered by the registered dockers as a Trojan horse for casualisation.

Over the next few days, the Torside men mounted a wildcat picket that was supported by the last 329 dockers still employed by the Mersey Docks and Harbour Company. Under Margaret Thatcher's new anti-trade union laws, secondary picketing was deemed a dismissible offence and even before an official ballot could be taken the MDHC dockers were all told to 'sling their hooks'. Their P45s were promptly dispatched to their homes by taxis and their jobs advertised in the local press.

Those who lost their jobs included men like Jimmy Campbell whose father had been killed on the docks, and John Morris who had handled cargo from some of the world's great ships for over 20 years. Many of the men with young families had no choice but to find casual dock re-employment and even some of the diehard MDHC dockers felt that the lock-out was doomed to failure. The coal miners had been defeated and their tight-knit South Wales, Nottinghamshire and Yorkshire communities annihilated. The Tories and many of their supporters regarded dockers as a bunch of rogues who had held Britain's ports to ransom for far too long. Old-fashioned dock work was dead in the water and with modern technology and the container revolution, a single man was now able to do what 200 had once done. Cargo turnaround times had reduced dramatically with the mechanised unloading of containers. Most of the dockers, however, clung to the dream that they were still somehow essential and that the working-class movement would come to their rescue. They were a bloody-minded anti-authoritarian lot, eternally bound together by grim tidings, intolerant of faceless authority and determined to win their jobs back.

The creation of Torside and other subsidiaries had allowed the MDHC to dissociate itself from the return of 'The Evil'. The management used jargon like 'downsizing', 'streamlining' and 'retrenchment' to disguise their actions. When dockers refused to cross the picket line, it was deemed illegal, despite the fact that the Torside men had been given their induction training on MDHC premises. Ten days later, when the dockers tried to return to work, they found their jobs had been taken by men from 'off the docks' on contracts which could be terminated without notice. They discovered that some of their comrades had betrayed them and gone back under the new working stipulations while others had accepted the £20,000 severance offer.

The notion of fighting for one's job was an outmoded concept, but in a scene reminiscent of '60s Britain a hundred or so men gathered every evening in front of the empty warehouses, rearing gantries and rusted hulls to scream abuse. To a tirade of whistles, blaring car horns and angry chants of, 'Scabs out, dockers in!', the men who had taken their jobs were escorted by police from the dock. At dawn each day, through that first arctic winter, the sacked men came back to huddle round a lone brazier, waiting for the next confrontation. Their wives, aunts, cousins and mothers would also take their turn, singing 'Stand by your Man' outside the dock gates. These women, many of whom were brought up in traditional waterfront families, had learned to read between the lines before they could write and knew much more about how to win modern industrial disputes than their husbands. Doreen McNally, a docker's daughter and chairman of the support group WOW (Women on the Waterfront), stood outside the 'Joke Shop' (Job Centre) where two strike-breaking agency firms were advertising vacancies on the docks. When two young men came out, she approached them and said, 'Excuse me, those jobs on offer already belong to men who've put their whole lives into the docks. My Charlie was sacked after 29 years' loyal service. Our fathers, uncles and grandfathers fought for those jobs. Look, I'm a picket line, just me.'

The immediate reply was, 'Don't worry, love. We won't pass your line, we understand.'

Doreen's father had been off work for two years after a holster belt he was being hoisted on snapped, then not long after his return to work four bales of cotton slammed into his back. Her first ever speech was delivered on Saint George's Plateau and began with the words, 'I have red hair, blue eyes and flesh and blood and as much right to shelter and nourish my family as yous.'

By the fifth week of the strike, the dispute had been forced to go global, with flying pickets travelling to ports all over the world. Indignation about mean management and inhumane working conditions were shared portside affiliations. Three jet-lagged Scousers mounted a protest in a raging blizzard in Baltimore where MV *Atlantic Companion* was due to arrive from Liverpool. The Maryland longshoremen were offered four times their normal rate of pay to unload the containers but after hearing the men's story turned their cars round and went home. The Scousers were left dancing ecstatically on the snowy dockside. The container ship then sailed on to Norfolk, Virginia, with the three dockers in hot pursuit. Despite being threatened with jail by the District Attorney, the Virginian stevedores mounted a go-slow and the *Atlantic Companion* was forced to sail on again to Newark, New Jersey. Not one of the Puerto Rican American dockers crossed the line. In frustration, the Atlantic Container Company pulled out of Liverpool altogether for a month. The flying pickets headed south and left the port of Miami with a carrier bag stashed to the brim with dollar bills donated by their Floridian comrades. In Montreal, they smuggled themselves into the port and climbed a gantry where they unfurled a banner denigrating the Canadian Pacific-owned container company for employing scabs. When the Quebec police tried to arrest them, a circle of Montreal stevedores protected them until the management agreed to talks. Two Women On the Waterfront members, Collette Melia and Sue Mitchell, travelled to Los Angeles to address 400 sympathetic longshoremen. Their heartfelt appeals later brought tears to the eyes of hardened Seattle dockers.

Jimmy Nolan, a Communist Party member and respected chairman of the stewards who had worked in the docks for 35 years, took the lead in many of these international initiatives, supported by other stewards from the broad left like Jimmy Davies and Terry Teague. As well as this determined direct action, there were also a lot of prayers to St Jude in Vauxhall.

The world's seaports had now become the dockers' picket. Failure to get national backing from traditional allies like the waterway workers, the one-sided nature of the UK labour laws and a complete national media blackout meant that as the strike rumbled on they would be forced to turn more and more to the international fraternity of port workers for support. They also pioneered the use of the Internet to appeal directly to groups of sympathisers all over the world. Their wives petitioned 10 Downing Street, occupied the London boardroom of one of the companies supplying scab labour, and made calls to stockbrokers alerting them to impending blockades. They had also secured support from some local Members of Parliament and the Liverpool clergy and collected money in buckets at Anfield and Goodison. On the day the Newark dockers refused to unload the *Atlantic Companion*, representatives from WOW stood outside the MDHC director's homes in a candlelit vigil, singing, 'New York, New York. It's a wonderful town.' Mike Carden from the Docker's Committee said of WOW, 'The women were like a hurricane of fresh air blowing through the union.'

One of the earliest outside attempts to draw attention to the dockers' cause came from a group of four Glaswegian writers, headed by James Kelman. In a letter to several national newspapers, they alleged a 'conspiracy of silence' with a gentlemen's agreement between John Major and the then-leader of the Labour opposition Tony Blair designed to hush up the whole dispute. Musicians like Noel Gallagher, Paul Weller, Bruce Springsteen and Dodgy also pledged their support for the dockers.

One year into the dispute, hundreds of eco-warriors and anarchists from the 'Reclaim the Streets' movement descended on Liverpool, singing 'The Workers United will Never be Defeated'. Alienated and disenchanted youth empathised with the struggle against wage slavery. As the anarchists scaled the gantries and hoisted defiant banners, the weary white-haired dockers and their families looked on in what will remain as a lasting memory of late-twentieth-century class struggle.

At Anfield in 1997, Robbie Fowler lifted up his Liverpool FC top in front of the cameras to reveal a 'Support the 500 SaCKed Dockers' T-shirt. This attempt to raise the media profile of the dockers' dispute led to a reprimand and fine from UEFA and a threat by Calvin Klein to sue for trademark violation.

Fowler was born in the Dingle, an area of Liverpool 8 bordered by Upper Warwick Street, Aigburth Road, Grafton Street and Princes Road, and named after a brook, which rises at High Park Street and follows Park Road to Toxteth Chapel. It was a traditional residential area of predominantly white Protestants and includes several Victorian terraced streets locally known as the Holy Land. The names of Isaac Street, Jacob and Moses Street, David's Throne, Jericho Farm and the Jordan stream remind us of the area's original Nonconformist seventeenth-century settlement. James Larkin (Seamus O Lorcain) was also born there in 1876, the second son of humble Irish parents. Much of his early childhood was spent with his grandparents in the 'bandit country' of Newry, County Down, but he returned to the Dingle at the age of nine and attended a local Catholic school. He later would claim that it was here he had learned the truth of eternal justice and the fear of God. Jim Larkin became a professional Dissenter constantly at odds with his times and a man who was never afraid to challenge authority. In turn, he was an international trade unionist, Irish Nationalist, German Secret Agent in Mexico, a founding member of the American Communist Party, and a victim of the Red Scare and a delegate of the Comintern. International Socialism was in his blood and he felt no conflict between this and his strongly held Catholic and Irish Nationalist beliefs.

Larkinism was imprinted in the dockers' DNA as they battened down the hatches for what would prove to be their last stand. It was a perverse determination that compelled them to fight on to defend their ancestors' small victories – even when the rest of us were unconvinced a life of hard labour was worth saving. With a stoic, dogged pride and the kind of machismo long associated with manual labour, the dockers battled to save a city which they believed had always belonged to them. For the rest of England, however, their fight was little more than a self-destructive cry for help from a group of losers.

The MDHC was determined to free itself once and for all from this troublesome old workforce, and start afresh with a younger labour force accustomed to a world where no jobs were guaranteed for life. At the beginning of the picket, some of the dockers had been offered individual contracts but refused them. The TUC General Secretary, Bill Morris, a black man born in Jamaica, made a secret visit to Liverpool and in an emotional speech stated, 'I am proud to be with you. Your struggle is so important that our grandchildren will ask where were you at the great moment and you will either stand up with pride and say I was there or you'll hang your head in shame without an answer.' He pledged the union's support and concluded with the words, 'God is on our side,' to rousing cheers from the dockers. At that very moment, the cranes looming out of the gloaming seemed to resemble giant crucifixes.

But there was a hidden agenda. This was a white man's industrial dispute; Granby blacks did not get jobs on the docks. Some of the Liverpool dockers' forefathers may have transported Morris's family unwittingly to the Caribbean. Liverpool dockers had marched in support of Enoch Powell against Asian immigration in the 1960s. The wheel had turned full circle. Although the Liverpool docks was now the only surviving unionised port in Great Britain, the new anti-union legislation had prevented the Transport and General Workers' Union declaring the strike official. Morris and the other TGWU leaders secretly considered the Liverpool dockers to be loose cannons. They were also fearful of further curbs and fines from the Tory government.

Although a vote in support of the dockers' case was won at Transport House, Morris called the strike committee leaders to London and informed them it was the end of the road. They must abandon all hope of getting their jobs back, concede defeat and accept the 'generous' settlement being offered by management. He later claimed his hands had been tied by the draconian anti-union laws. This connivance between the TGWU and John Major's Conservative government finally forced Jimmy Nolan and the rest of the Merseyside Port Stewards Committee to call an end to their long-running dispute in January 1998. Three hundred and fifty dockers were finally given pension entitlements and severance pay in return for renouncing any entitlement on their jobs. New Labour under Tony Blair felt the dockers had brought the defeat on themselves through intransigence and long-standing abuse of monopoly power. England was now the sweatshop of Europe, with politicians keen to suck up to the new entrepreneurial front-runners in the boardroom. Communism was dead, socialism was on the back foot but the dockers had been tied by tradition and a deeply held belief in working-class solidarity.

The two-and-a-half-year Liverpool Dock Strike proved to be the death of a way of thinking. These traditionalists had battled for a way of life as well as a livelihood, determined that their city should remain a general cargo giant. Unfortunately, England had become increasingly self-interested, governed by market forces where people craved freedom of expression, looked after themselves and died alone. The white working class had become an inconvenient relic and the docks were now cenotaphs.

Bob Richie, one of the sacked dockers, defiantly announced that the men were not looking on the dispute as a defeat but an experience, which had greatly raised their awareness and level of consciousness. The Liverpool playwright Jimmy McGovern was contacted by Channel 4 to see if he would write a drama about the dockers' fight. McGovern was busy but suggested Irvine Welsh, the author of *Trainspotting*. McGovern was aware that some of the strikers and their wives had been attending multimedia classes at the Workers' Educational Association and proposed that they write the script themselves under his and Irvine Welsh's mentorship. The dockers' progress was filmed for a fly-on-the-wall documentary and eventually the project was taken up by Ken Loach's film company.

The play was broadcast to great acclaim and the 16 dockers and their wives bought a building opposite the Freemason's Hall in Hope Street with their royalties. Terry Teague, Tony Nelson and a number of other dockers converted it into a non-profit bistro. Now run as a cooperative, The Casa has a free jukebox, there is a small theatre and upstairs a community venture helps advise and retrain the unemployed. Plaques of support from the International Trade Union Movement, a signed poster from Robbie Fowler, and John O'Neill's painting *Resurgence* that depicts three defiant dockers rising naked out of the Mersey hang on the bare walls. The dockers have moved on but their sense of street justice, strong family bonds and a refusal to bow to authority is still felt in this bar. The proprietors continue to be guided by Jim Larkin's words: 'Who is it speaks of defeat? I tell you a cause like ours is greater than defeat can know. It is the power of powers.'

The MDHC had moved on too and announced a £60-million development effort to build two new roll-on/roll-off facilities, an office tower and a portside hotel. Dredgers had replaced freighters in the port and cruise ships were on their way back. Plans were also afoot for the construction of a freight terminal with 860,000 square feet of warehousing and light industrial plant facilities.

Much of the habitat has changed but a few tokens remain; the port continues to feel precarious and deeply disturbing. The men in The Casa have almost forgotten the docks but have not lost faith in the river. Some have joined the long ranks of taxi drivers as independents free to work a lunar day and a hard day's night. Extended families based on close relationships between mother and daughters continue to stabilise their lives. There are still plenty of pirate hauliers in Bootle and ex-boxers running south-side pubs. In the narrow streets, youths still jump over sharp iron railings and kick balls. On rainy, windswept nights, The Atlantic on the Dock Road heaves with scary lads and strong-minded women, trying to forget evil in the smoky intermissions between the gags. Down at the mouth of the Albert Dock amongst the museums, restaurants and souvenir shops, the Roman numerals carved into the sea wall still remind me that the level of the Mersey once controlled this city's working world.

I have left for Shanghai now, searching for surviving river life. The colonial museum pieces on the Bund recall the Three Graces, but the Pudong allotments are buried under an intergalactic, blade-running, post-Cultural Revolution metropolis. The Huangpu is alive with barges, freighters and junks. Shanghai's glassy skyscrapers are full of kept women.

At the end of Old Hall Street heading down to the Mersey I pass a car showroom, a Toys R Us warehouse and signs to Costco. The tide is out and the wreck of the Pier Head lies in the silt. Past the Liver Building and the Isle of Man ferry is the temporary floating liner landing stage. At Roberts Street, I arrive at the old world of Sprague Brothers, with its tumbledown brick facade and its bold spread 'Thousands of castors and wheels always in stock' and those other reassuring industrial accoutrements of toggles, blastgates, jig clamps and ball units. The Scottish streets seem to have changed colour. I am on the empty Dock Road now heading for Bootle, following the rusting tracks of the Overhead Railway and the lost trades of the sea. The trucks and vans keep coming at me but apart from a few sun-helmeted workmen and lads in threes selling tyres I am alone. The right-angled cranes that dangled their hooks over Paradise Street have been replaced by the smaller dock derricks, now motionless like predatory bitterns in the returning reeds.

Riverside station has disappeared, many of the warehouses are levelled and the Lascar House is boarded up. The imposing gateways and the cast-iron fountains embedded in the walls suggest the entrance to a country grange but Waterloo Road is defunct. On the right-hand side, crumbling stores and a chute fronts up Porter but the street is vacant apart from a pig-iron yard, a boarded up chandlers and a car-repair shed. Trafalgar,

Salisbury, Collingwood, Nelson and Bramley-Moore lie silent, and beyond the river gate the beetle-browed Gothic Dockers Clock is suspended on a man-made island between the canal and the Mersey. Each of its six faces tells a different time.

Clarence, the arrival point of the Irish, still has some sporadic activity with its graving docks repairing a few small ships. A new padlock on a rotting door signals renewal. Some of the buildings are burnt-out shells or ruined by years of storms boring through collapsed and open roofs. Grass pushes out from the cracks in the walls and an odd land bird flutters by. On the town side is Stanley Dock with its tall stacks and granite tower abandoned apart from a few dockers' sons moving things in wheelie bins, watched over by sour-faced guards and closed-circuit television. The brick Tobacco Warehouse still has a brooding presence, with its squat funereal King's Pipe clogged with tobacco waste. The closed dock looks as if it is waiting for the ducks, dragonflies and property developers to arrive with the sunshine. It is a place to complete shady deals or dispose of a body. Stanley still has its narrow canal tunnel running inland in a series of steps up the hill under the road and a tangle of locks feeling their way to the Leeds and Liverpool Canal. The conduit traverses the hundred arched viaduct, battle-scarred with repairs and modifications to the sooty brick, interrupted by the gable ends of half-demolished warehouses which once proudly lined the railway track. Bramley-Moore is now a home for sand and stone, and Sandon a sewage-treatment plant. Across the road is a business park linked with London and Cambridge but there is not much to see there and the wind is rising up, forcing me to move on.

Past Huskisson and Canada where boats are moored, heaps of scrap are stacked up and the Dominion pub stands proud with the lumberjack and his dog on its roof. The fulvous Hamburg Süd container stacks wait for clearance. At Nelson Street and Miller's Bridge, the Liverpool Freeport with its robots is guarded by armed police and hidden from the eye of the city. Windmill power has arrived on the sea wall. The wastelands are spreading and the fear is growing. Yet it is the lost medicine of passers-by and the friendship of these new strangers that sustains me in the social laboratory of Vauxhall. It is the kind word at a difficult moment, the generosity of reprobate smokers and the decency of those down on their luck that keeps me alive.

The Cocky Watchman

I'm searching through the streets again
Through the streets of Kenny
I'm looking for the boys again
Can't find Joe or Benny

I don't want a bag
I want a big one
I don't want a bag
I want a big one

I'm searching for the caz again
Through the Streets of Kenny
I'm looking for our joys again
Can't get shit get any.

'Streets of Kenny'
by Shack on HMS *Fable*

In 1959, Curtis Aloysius Warren, a black seaman in the Norwegian merchant navy chancing his luck on the Atlantic trade routes, laid anchor in Liverpool Bay and headed for the fleshpots of Toxteth. There he hit it off with a local girl, Sylvia Chantre, daughter of a shipyard boiler-attendant from St James's Gardens, and they were married a year later at St Vincent De Paul's Catholic Church on the corner of Upper Frederick Street. Both had exotic backgrounds. Sylvia's mother's surname was Baptista and the family hailed from Bird Island in South Africa, while the able-bodied seaman's father was listed as a South American coffee manufacturer. The young couple set up home in rented rooms at 238 Upper Parliament Street and it was not long before their first son, Ramon, was born. Curtis was away at sea for much of the early years of the marriage but with the words of Martin Luther King, Jr's dream echoing through Toxteth and the sound of 'Love Me Do' blaring from the city's jukeboxes, a second child Curtis Francis arrived just over a year later during the Whitsun Bank Holiday.

More and more lads like the Warren children brought up in the Granby Triangle were leaving school in the '70s without even a modicum of social graces or life skills. There were no jobs for them or for their white Liverpool 8 equivalents, and unemployment among school leavers had risen to 80 per cent. Semi-literacy and a congenital paranoia meant that the delivery of a 'Toccy kiss' (head butt) was a common riposte in Liverpool 8 to even the most trivial of frustrations. Kung fu and karate became popular alternatives to boxing as a way of gaining respect and reducing the risk of an early death. The Liverpool police force still broadly accepted the conclusions of the Fletcher Report that mixed-race adolescent males had chips on their shoulders. The 1930s Myrtle Gardens tenement block built on the site of Liverpool's Botanical Institute and close to the Warren home had become a breeding ground for delinquents inspired by the teachings of Malcolm X. The police blamed mixed-race youths for the juvenile crime wave and the Chief Constable declared that if things continued in the same vein the city would soon need an occupying army. In 1978, BBC journalist Martin Young arrived in Liverpool to produce a documentary about the Merseyside Police. His article in *The Listener*, with its reverberations of the Fletcher Report and its sympathetic support for an extension of police powers, was considered in Liverpool 8 to be the opinion of the police themselves. It led, three weeks later, to a protest march through the city centre of about 200 people led by the Liverpool Black Organisation. The most inflammatory passage of the article ran as follows:

> Less poignant, by far, is the other major social problem they face: the half-caste problem. Policemen in general, and detectives in particular, are not racialist, despite what many Black groups believe. Like any individual who deals with a vast cross-section of society they tend to recognize that good and evil exist, irrespective of colour or creed. Yet they are the first to define the problem of half-castes in Liverpool. Many are the products of liaisons between Black seamen and white prostitutes in Liverpool 8, the red-light district. Naturally they do not grow up with any kind of recognisable home life. Worse still, after they have done the rounds of homes and institutions, they gradually realise that they are nothing. The Negroes will not accept them as Blacks, and whites just assume they are coloureds. As a result, the half-caste community of Merseyside – or more particularly, Liverpool – is well outside recognised society.

The young Curtis was a frequent school truant and spent some time in a corrective boarding school in North Wales. Not long after his 11th birthday he was recruited to George Osu's burglary team. His job was to squeeze through narrow windows, then open the front door for the firm's Artful Dodger, the future world kick-boxing champion, Stephen French. French would later earn the nickname 'The Taxman' for his violent methods of extracting money from drug dealers for his own personal gain. Shortly after his criminal career had begun, police found a cherubic brown-eyed child perched in the driving seat of a missing car. Although hardly able to see above the dashboard, Curtis Warren was charged with car theft and placed under a supervision order by Liverpool Juvenile Court. At a time when many South Liverpool youngsters were going on to higher education or starting apprenticeships, Curtis was sent to a detention centre. His peers considered these places as state-funded 'finishing schools', where future gang leaders could acquire new ruses to outwit 'the scuffers'.

His teenage associates included: Stephen Lunt ('Lunty'), a mop top with a scallie grin who could drive a car at 120 miles an hour at night with no lights; the volatile Johnny (Sonny) Phillips; violent street fighter Peter Lair; ex-petrol bomb rioter and karate champion 'AJ' Andrew John; hard boy ram-raider Mark 'Sonny Boy' Osu; and the fearless car thief and burglar Andrew Kasseem. The crew planned their crimes in the International Café on Granby Street and marked their ten-street cage with tags sprayed across walls and windows, but they were still apprentices and the Granby manor remained in the hands of the eloquent Michael and Delroy Showers, the sons of a Nigerian seaman, who had been importing cannabis from Africa for more than a decade. The callous mugging of a 78-year-old woman outside Paddy's Wigwam (the Metropolitan Cathedral) led to the 16-year-old Warren's name hitting the front page of the *Echo* and further charges led to a spell in borstal.

Joyriding and theft were soon replaced by 'rolling', where the punters of prostitutes were robbed with their trousers down. After one desperate 'party' had been forced to seek refuge in a police station, Warren and his associate Johnny Phillips were arrested and charged with blackmail, extortion and violent assault. Shortly after his release from prison, Curtis was involved in a botched armed robbery on Smithdown Road. A brave woman passer-by attacked one of his accomplices and as a result of the skirmish ended up in hospital with a fractured skull. She recovered sufficiently to give evidence in court and Warren went down for a five-year prison stretch.

On the campus of crime, he adhered to the criminal's maxim 'don't serve time, make time serve you'. There he met hoodlums and crooks from all over England's north-west and got to know men from the Liverpool Mafia, like Tommy Comerford (nicknamed Tacker), a larger-than-life Scotland Road character who was one of Liverpool's first international drug smugglers. When he came out, he followed the football casuals and the Croxteth 'Cuckoo Clock gang' to Switzerland for some easy pickings but was arrested again in a shoe shop in Chur after a failed robbery.

In the aftermath of the riots, the nattily dressed Michael Showers had emerged as the self-appointed public spokesman for Toxteth. Although he now lived in Childwall with his Russian-German wife and five children, he still regularly cruised the streets of Granby in his white Rolls-Royce, dispensing advice to young bucks like Curtis. He was appointed a member of the Liverpool 8 Defence Committee and was given a £16,000-a-year job with the Merseyside Immigration Advice Unit, despite two pending police charges for firearms and drug offences. Oozing self-confidence, he demanded Chief Constable Oxford's resignation and delivered an anti-police diatribe to the nation on the BBC's *Question Time*. His brother Delroy had been arrested with Charlie Richardson, former boss of the South London mob and Kray twin adversary, in 1980 and was serving a nine-year jail term.

The Tory government and Merseyside police paid lip service to community policing but after the riots they were forced to turn a blind eye to drug deals in the Triangle. Granby stuck to its traditional cannabis but soft policing was encouraging 'skag' and 'coke' dealers from other parts of the city to investigate new business opportunities. Graffiti like 'Newsflash! This is Toxteth not Croxteth, Strictly Ganja' appeared on walls, a crack house was attacked and the dealers rooted out by a vigilante mob. Michael Showers spearheaded Liverpool 8's campaign against hard drugs but even his own cronies suspected this was little more than a cynical ploy to keep the new cocaine and heroin runners off his patch. It came as no great surprise to Liverpool 8 when Showers was later jailed for 20 years for smuggling 12 kg of 'smack' into Britain from Afghanistan.

Curtis Warren was out of prison by then and working as a bouncer and street-level heroin salesman in the town centre. He had quickly built up a reputation for reliability and was now a well-known face on the strip. The Showers-led vigilantes who had resisted the arrival of smack in Liverpool 8 had been crushed, leaving Granby Street full of shady bottom-feeders trading wraps. 'Slinging rocks' had become the easiest way to nourish a habit so there were plenty of foot soldiers available selling drugs from doorways, secluded walkways and even through the window of a camper van.

A few ex-dockers and fruit shop owners had mysteriously become millionaires in Liverpool and some flashy clubs had sprouted up on the strip. There were also plenty of kids strutting the inner-city streets with expensive trainers and designer tops. On the day Warren started his first jail sentence, Merseyside's Chief Constable Kenneth Oxford had announced in a press conference a new vigorous offensive on hard drugs. Liverpool's barons had greeted his pronouncements and admonishments with derision. The horse had bolted long ago and Liverpool's drug enterprise was on a very solid footing, underpinned by two decades of pot and brown pedigree and a proven business model. The same underhand methods that had allowed Liverpool to become a hub for the handling of contraband over three centuries had helped the city's crime families to become key players in global drug smuggling. She was the English city that had fallen off the back of a lorry.

This new infamy had grown out of a hybrid alliance between the old white Mr Bigs and what the police now referred to as the Black Caucus, a group of violent black and mixed-race Granby criminals. The new generation of commanders in the old white crime families had none of the hang-ups of their fathers about selling drugs and were keen to make strategic alliances in Liverpool 8. These cartels exploited Liverpool's rambling docklands and took full advantage of the international connections stretching back to the city's golden days of Atlantic trading. The old white sugar estates had gone but there was now a new economy of 'brown sugar'. A sophisticated national underworld network of fences, middlemen, hauliers, couriers, 'taxmen' and moneymen, and a black-market banking system were well established. Cannabis, cocaine and heroin were being shifted through England's ports and a cottage industry of 'speed' and LSD manufacture had taken root in the high-rise estates.

Warren learned fast and was soon ready to move into the wholesale business. His earlier adolescent hostility to authority had been replaced with a superficial, sneering friendliness. He addressed police officers politely by their surnames in his soft South Liverpool Scouse accent, never forgetting the name of anyone who crossed his path. He had also developed a rare underworld gift for tact and diplomacy in his dealings. His first big operations were allegedly bankrolled by a businessman called The Banker who lived in a big house in leafy Sandfield Park. He travelled light, didn't smoke or drink, had no credit cards and never signed a cheque. His 'porty', a mobile phone that he regularly changed, and a wad of notes in his back pocket were all he needed to run his business. He moved in a duplicitous, shadowy world of false identities and nicknames. He knew The Bell with no Stalk, the Egg on Legs, the long fella, Tacker and Macker, Lunty, Badger and Boo. Then there was Twit and Twat, the Big Fella, the Werewolf and the L. Fella. His own alias, Cocky, was an abbreviation of the Cocky Watchman, arcane Scouse vernacular for a night watchman, park keeper or concierge, a nickname that recognised his highly developed nose for danger and a photographic memory for names and phone numbers.

Following the Medellín cartel's failure to penetrate the British cocaine market, its Colombian rival based in Cali, with its new crack-friendly merchandise and superior connections, decided to make a determined play. Its senior marketing manager in Europe, under the pay of the Rodriguez brothers, was a 22-year-old Colombian-born Dutch citizen called Mario Halley. Halley, working for a scrap-metal cover operation called the Conar Corporation, met up with Stan Carnall, a senior member of the white Liverpool Mafia, in Amsterdam, and Carnall then brought in Warren. A meeting took place between Halley and another Carnall associate, the flashy 37-year-old Brian Charrington who ran a Bentley, a Rolls-Royce, two private jets and a deep-sea-diving boat from a modest second-hand car sales forecourt. Soon Warren and Charrington left on British visitor passports for Calais, travelled by car to Brussels, from where they flew to Málaga. They then headed for Madrid to catch a plane to Caracas, where they met up with the Conar Corporation executives Halley and Camilo Jesus Ortiz and handed over £6 million to cover the cost of two cocaine shipments. The double-dealing Charrington decided to negotiate a separate deal for himself with Conar but his phone was tapped and in panic he started to drip-feed information about the deal to two officers in the North East Regional Crime Squad. A week later, the MV *Caraibe*, loaded with a cargo of circular lead ingots, came to dock in Felixstowe. Halley slipped back to Manchester to meet up with Warren and oversee the safe delivery of the merchandise. Despite a police tip-off, HM Customs failed to find the drug haul because the bits on their drills were not long enough to penetrate the radio-opaque steel-lined compartments in the centre of the ingots. The failure to find any drugs engendered uncertainty among the Customs officers and after ten days they were forced to let the Venezuelan consignment proceed by rail and lorry to its destination in Aintree. An experienced demolition man called Snowball was waiting in a lock-up to extract the cocaine with a drilling rig and as fireworks lit the November evening sky, the Liverpool crew, covered in cocaine powder, celebrated their harvest.

Contrary to the orders supplied by Halley, the gang decided to try to sell the lead rather than bury it. They approached a former doorman, safe blower and scrap dealer called Paul Grimes, who despite a long criminal record was opposed to drug trafficking. Grimes informed HM Customs and the information he supplied allowed a second consignment of 900 kg of cocaine to be identified in the hold of the MV *Advisor*, a 27,000-tonne ship operated by T & J Harrison Ltd of Liverpool and registered in the Isle of Man. Warren and his gang moved the drugs quickly from the Felixstowe docks to a holding depot in Stoke on Trent, where HM Customs officers were waiting for the extraction process to commence. By this time, MI6 and the CIA had become involved. News came through that Dutch officials had raided a warehouse in Holland and seized 845 kg of cocaine, secreted in identical lead ingots. Ortiz and Halley were later arrested and instructions to 'push the yellow pedal' and abandon the shipment were dispatched urgently from Cali. Warren and his men were forced to return to Liverpool.

Despite the failure to catch the gang red-handed, the Customs officers, operating highly sophisticated equipment used in nuclear plants, confirmed the 32 ingots were hollow. The following March, seven Liverpool men including 'company directors' Warren and John Smith, and Smith's sons Kevin and Colin, were arrested. Charrington was also taken into custody after a raid on his home that revealed £2.4 million of heroin- and cocaine-tainted notes.

At the trial in Newcastle in 1992, it was never revealed that Grimes, who was driven to court every day in a bulletproof car guarded by a tactical firearms unit, was the HM Customs informant, but a major row blew up between the Regional Crime Squad and Customs over how Charrington should be dealt with. The Teesside police offered Charrington £100,000 as a reward for information but HM Customs blocked this, leading to the intervention of the local Stockton South MP Tim Devlin. Devlin, who was Private Secretary to Sir Nicholas Lyell, the Attorney General, tried to cover the whole matter up but the *News of the World* got wind of the story and plastered it over its front page, forcing him to admit that Charrington had been working as a police informer. HM Customs reluctantly agreed to drop charges against Charrington and, following this, the judge concluded that Charrington's evidence was inadmissible and that there was no proof that the MV *Caraibe* had carried a cocaine consignment.

Only one of the defendents, Joseph Kassar, a man with Ghanaian connections, was imprisoned but the Liverpool gang walked free. The Cocky Watchman turned to the Customs officers as he left court and sneered, 'I'm off to spend my £87 million from the first shipment, and you can't fucking touch me.' Charrington headed for Spain and in 1995 was implicated in drug dealing when his yacht was seized off Boulogne by French Customs authorities, loaded with 1.7 tonnes of cannabis resin.

Warren's silence during the trial meant that he could now count even more on full support and cooperation from the Liverpool White Mafia as he built up his new organisation in Liverpool 8. Through the Liverpool Connection, he came into contact with a group of former IRA paramilitaries turned contract killers called 'The Cleaners', operating out of Amsterdam and Marbella. Using the tried and tested methods of the Provos, Cocky divided his gang into autonomous and independent cells, each one with separate responsibilities that included car rental, pager and phone purchase, safe houses, accountancy and distribution. If an arm of the operation failed, he lopped it off and anyone who fouled up was relegated to low-life dealing on the street. Warren enjoyed counting his bundles of money and soon had so much of it he had to use old cars parked in streets far away from Liverpool 8 as surrogate safe boxes.

Operation Crayfish, a new police and Customs joint initiative on hard-drug dealing in the north-west, was now taking a very close interest in the Cocky Watchman and surveillance revealed that he was living in a luxury waterfront pad in Wapping dock. Of great interest to the drug squad was the fact that his girlfriend Stephanie was the daughter of Phillip Glennon Sr, a man well known to the police who had supported Warren throughout the trial from the public gallery. One room of the flat was completely taken over by Stephanie's vast wardrobe crammed full of designer clothes. While she added to her collection, Cocky drove unnoticed through Granby in a Peugeot and circled the Wirral in a Lexus making phone calls. Sometime later, a bag containing £1 million was found hidden under a bed of nasturtiums in Phillip Glennon Sr's back garden.

Warren's skill as a commodity broker earned him great wealth in a very short time and his main challenge was how to launder his loot, a risky step even for his partners in the Cali cartel. Myrmidon money-runners would leave Liverpool for London with grip bags stashed with thousands of pounds. Once the cash had been 'positioned', it was then 'layered' through a number of multinational transactions and fragmented into investments that were repeatedly shifted around until they could be used for legitimate business deals. One of Warren's favourite placement outlets was a small bureau de change in Notting Hill Gate run by a Palestinian nicknamed Sammy the Kurd. Plump wads of £50 notes were exchanged for slim packets of 5,000 Dutch guilders. Taking full advantage of the Big Bang financial deregulation, the couriers would then take the money on to Holland, from where it would be wired to Swiss and Dubai bank accounts and recycled into the property market.

Warren's name now started to appear in the English press. He was listed as the 461st richest man in Britain, where he was described as a trader and property owner with extensive overseas interests. Many of the skinhead doormen who doubled as house dealers on the dance floors were now on Warren's security business payroll. It was also alleged that he owned the Holker Street stadium in Barrow, a Bulgarian winery, properties in Gambia, Morocco, Spain and Turkey, an office block and a yacht. Despite another narrow escape at Burtonwood service station, where he had driven to oversee the delivery of a 250 kg stash of heroin that had been followed from Felixstowe by the police, Warren continued to prosper and rose in four short years from being a run-of-the-mill street dealer to Target Number One for Interpol, stealing a competitive advantage over other ambitious Liverpool foot soldiers. His heroin came from the Taliban's poppy fields via the Turkish babas, his cannabis from Morocco and Senegal, and he ordered his amphetamine and Ecstasy from Europe's top laboratories.

As the police started to close in, Cocky put in an order at Barton Aerodrome for the purchase of a small helicopter but never returned to collect it. By 1994, Liverpool had become too risky and his nose for danger had saved him from almost certain arrest. His moonlight flit ended in a 16-room, sparsely furnished, rented villa in Sassenheim, a nondescript Dutch town between Amsterdam and The Hague. He was used to being hunted and to keeping very cool under pressure. He hid there with another associate called 'Tony Farrell', who was believed to be his linkman to the Colombian cartel. Warren was relieved to be free from the irritation of the Door Wars and his growing conviction that the Merseyside Police were going to shoot him. As one Crayfish Officer later put it, 'He was now like a pig in shit.' His day would start late with a workout on the punchbag and build up to a crescendo of phone calls made as he was driven around by his group of 'joeys'. He would then go for a game of squash, treat himself to a blowjob in one of the local saunas, have a meal and watch some soft porn with Farrell before going to bed.

The drug deals continued unabated in Liverpool but now there was out-and-out warfare between the Black Caucus and the White Mafia. Twenty shootings occurred in one month in 1995, including the shooting of ex-boxer Davey Ungi, a hard man in one of the old Toxteth white gangs. A year later, Warren's old crony Johnny Phillips was shot four times in the chest and stomach as he got out of his red BMW with his daughter. He required major surgery but survived. It was said his blood was so full of anabolic steroids that he hardly bled. 'Fuck off, sausageheads,' was his only comment when two detectives paid him a visit in hospital. Further retaliatory shootings by the Granby mob soon followed, culminating in Mark Osu being brought in by the police after a car chase. He claimed there was a contract on his head and accused the police of siding with the White Clan.

Operation Crayfish next decided to contact their Dutch counterparts, the Prisma team that had been set up specifically to investigate the South American connection. Prisma believed Warren was now doing most of his cocaine business with Luis Botero, a middle-aged Norte del Valle mobster and one of the top ten Colombian dealers who had moved in after the Customs hits on the Medellin and Cali cartels. Life was easy in Bakara and Cocky started to drop his guard. He broke his own rule of never doing business from home and Prisma tapped in to his calls. Tony Bray, a Birkenhead doorman, was Warren's main source of information back in Liverpool. The two shared the same sense of humour and spoke to each other every day on the phone. Unfortunately for the authorities, Cocky's use of Granby back slang and nicknames, and his monosyllabic responses, made it virtually impossible for them to understand anything. One Prisma officer enquired whether there was a place called 'Cafe Buyus' in Liverpool not realising Warren had said 'the cafe by us'. A 'squirt' was a gun, 'goulash' or 'tank' was money, an aeroplane was referred to as a 'paraffin budgie' and drugs were frequently referred to as 'lemon'. His favourite phrase was 'mad innit?' and 'Thingy' was the name for all those without their own alias. Bray told Warren the police were referring to him as the Spigot and that he was now considered to be in the Super League.

'Tony Farrell', Warren's house pal, had now been identified as Stephen Mee, born in 1958 in Manchester and with a criminal record as long as his arm. He was a hardened thief and violent robber who had already served a jail sentence in Holland. Inside, he had made contacts with a number of Colombian drug dealers and on his release had learned how to fly a plane. Although Mee was Warren's only companion in Bakara, a group of associates lived close by in a place nicknamed The Shed, in Waverveen. The Shed was built on a polder and was surrounded by miles of featureless fields, making it impossible to approach unnoticed. This was the temporary lair for the avuncular William Fitzgerald, 'Lancashire Steve' Whitehead (who, to Warren's disgust, had fallen in love with an Ukrainian prostitute), Billy Reilly (in hiding after a stabbing incident in Liverpool), Ray-Ray Nolan (an old friend of Warren's from their car thieving days also on the run after his involvement in a £1.5 million robbery in Huyton), and Mancunian John Farrell (alias Brian Chatterley, a name he had lifted from a tombstone). Mee's immediate contact with the Norte del Valle cartel, a Colombian nicknamed No-Neck, made up the Waverveen crew. Mee returned to Colombia to conclude the shipment of another large cocaine deal using the gang's tried-and-tested method of hiding the drugs inside scrap-metal ingots. The MV *Colombia* would sail from Santa María in Venezuela to Rotterdam in a few days. The ingots would then travel by train to Sofia, where Warren owned a wine warehouse. Once the ingots were secure in Bulgaria, they would be split up into smaller, more manageable lots and returned to Holland.

When MV *Colombia* docked in Rotterdam, it was clear that there had been a major foul-up because the papers showed Rotterdam rather than Bulgaria as the final destination. Warren was forced to intervene, sending a fax to try to get the necessary papers arranged for onward passage. In the early hours of 24 October 1996, Prisma's crack assault team together with Crayfish officers swooped on Bakara and arrested Cocky in bed with an Ukrainian prostitute. A Dutch SWAT team simultaneously arrested the surprised crew in The Shed, and a large amount of cannabis resin, Es, CS canisters and false passports found in the garage were taken away along with large quantities of money and two computers on which one of Warren's gang had been tracking the progress of MV *Colombia* across the high seas. Coordinated raids at 20 addresses in the Liverpool area led to a number of further arrests and the confiscation of several stashes of heroin and hand grenades. A search of MV *Colombia* unearthed 400 kg of super-grade cocaine hidden inside the lead ingots.

Curtis Warren, considered the richest, most successful British criminal ever to be arrested, was kept in solitary confinement for several weeks. His capture led to fall-out all over the world, with the execution of a member of the Russian Mafia in his own driveway, anxiety in the Colombian heartland and the taking of liberties on Liverpool streets. At his high-security trial in The Hague, Warren's defence was nonsensical and unrehearsed but everyone in the courtroom was struck by his imposing presence. He remained icily calm through the prosecution's interrogation and his only show of emotion came when it was suggested that his associates let him win at squash. Warren remained below in his cell when the guilty verdict was announced. He was sentenced to 12 years imprisonment without parole, to be served in the austere Nieuw Vosseveld prison in Vught, a former Nazi prisoner-of-war camp 60 miles outside Amsterdam. Cocky's 20 or so fellow inmates included Brian Meehan, awaiting extradition to Ireland as the suspected motorcycle hit man in the Veronica Guerin assassination. While Warren worked on his appeal, the Crayfish officers had identified more than 200 terraced properties in Liverpool that could be traced to his name, the majority housing DSS tenants. No bank balances were ever traced, although it was suspected that his money was all laundered through Dubai. His only personal luxury had been cars.

In prison, Warren kept fit, learned some Dutch and read a great deal. His fellow captives were impressed by his sharpness, sangfroid and fatalism. True to his nickname, he also kept up with all the gossip in Liverpool 8. On 15 September 1999, Warren was allocated the last exercise period of the day. His companions were the Turkish Kurd, Huseyin Baybasin, a heroin dealer who had been wiretapped planning murders and kidnaps; the Dutch sociopath Henk Ebben, an Ecstasy and cannabis exporter who had killed a courier; and Cemal Guclu, a Turk on a 20-year sentence, who was considered to be mad by the authorities but who had been passed sane by the psychiatrist at his trial. Most of the prisoners in Nieuw Vosseveld kept away from the violent Guclu but the ever-affable Cocky always gave him the time of day. Ebben's support for Feyenoord during a televised football game irritated the mad Turk and he decided to pick a fight with the Dutchman in the exercise yard. Inexplicably, Warren rather than Ebben was hit in the chest and then head butted. Warren retaliated and the Turk fell, hitting his head twice on the floor. He got up and attacked Warren again but Cocky was too strong for him and knocked him down, then kicked him. By the time the guards intervened, Guclu was unconscious. He was rushed to intensive care but died the following day of a brain haemorrhage. It later transpired that the prison's closed-circuit television had not been working during the fight, leading the inmates to conclude that the prison authorities had staged the whole episode. The court partly accepted Warren's claim that he had acted in self-defence but it was judged he had used an excessive level of violence and he was handed out a further four-year sentence to be served consecutively.

No one back in Liverpool had quite assumed Warren's mantle and breadth in drug dealing and many of the foot soldiers believed he was still controlling the Granby streets from his cell. The turf was divvied up among many smaller but equally ruthless gangs using 'postmen' (assassins) to make the hits, and ten-year-old children to work as runners. The outpouring of hopeless anger showed no signs of lessening in Liverpool 8. New faces armed with Tokarefs and Uzis now cruised the avenues in fast cars. Money was their God and the game was now being played for higher, more violent stakes. 'Scrotes' hung around the streets on the lookout for strangers.

In June 2007, Warren was finally released and took the ferry to Harwich, where he was met by an associate who drove him north to visit his beloved mother. After Warren spent a night in a Liverpool hotel, his solicitor made a formal statement saying that his client wanted to spend some time with his family. He was still a marked man as Customs tried to locate his hidden fortune, and just a month later he was arrested in Jersey and subsequently found guilty of planning a million-pound marijuana drug run into the island. Drugs cost much more on the street in the Channel Islands, which explained Warren's chosen target for what he referred to as 'just a little starter'.

Crack was a pestilence in the black ghettos of England and America. The heart had perished and all that was left was a hatred of rich whites and women, and a deadly lust for 'bling' and notoriety. The illiterate underclass who had grown up without fathers, faced with the best straight choice of 'a faggot's wage' were now opting in their hundreds for a gangster lifestyle. The politicians were still not getting told by RiUvEn or taking Kev Teezy's advice to know their postcodes.

Three months after the Cocky Watchman's re-arrest, father-of-five Colin Smith, a former associate of Warren now nicknamed 'the Cocaine King', was gunned down as he walked from Nel's Gym towards his Ford Galaxy parked in Alderwood Avenue, Speke. The European City of Culture opened its celebrations with gunfire and gangland shootings in Norris Green and a narrative of gangland betrayal and retribution. Curtis Warren, the 'Teflon Don', one of the city's most nefarious multinational drug commodity brokers, was behind bars again but pregnant girls were still 'on the gear' and there was still trouble on Liverpool's mean streets. The Bird of Prey and Pancake were now talking to Las Zetas in Ciudad Juárez, Mexico.

A Wrecker's Moon

I walked along the avenue.
I never thought I'd meet a girl like you;
Meet a girl like you.
With auburn hair and tawny eyes;
The kind of eyes that hypnotize me through;
Hypnotize me through.
And I ran, I ran so far away.
I just ran, I ran all night and day.
I couldn't get away.

Extract from 'I Ran (So Far Away)'
by A Flock of Seagulls

In the mid '70s, Les Spaine at The Timepiece on Fleet Street played funk for the Granby crowd and a handful of black American servicemen on the way back from Vietnam. On Monday nights, there was an upfront soul show on Radio Merseyside called 'Keep on Truckin' where Terry Lennaine focused on new US soul imports. One of the classic tracks, which he collected from the parcels depot at Lime Street, was Earth, Wind & Fire's iconic 'Fantasy'. As the funk scene began to die, a few visionary libertines colonised a nest of dives around Merseyside and formed a fringe electro urban underground. The Grafton also hung on through its 'Grab a Granny' Thursday nights where young men had the opportunity to meet '30 to 50 something' divorcees and unite four generations of mambo kings and dancing queens on happy Mondays.

Meanwhile on the woolyback margins, the self-contained grass-roots cult of the obscure had been in full swing for several years and more and more soul boys were living for the weekend. There was a lot of catching up to do now that prized American imports had become more available. A new generation of Ric-Tic, Mirwood and Okeh disciples dedicated their humdrum working week to kindling the soul flame. Many of them also turned into obsessive collectors, snapping up rare seven-inch classic stompers from the trestle-table sales at the all nighters. The best Twisted Wheel disc jockeys were marked by their ability to unearth obscure fast-tempo treasures from the '60s soul vaults. These new stars also pioneered the secretive mystical sequencing of songs to induce highs in their amphetamine-fuelled flock of spinners and flippers. By the early '80s, dialectical clashes between the classicists and modernists started to damage the Northern Soul scene and forced the closure of the Highland Rooms at Blackpool Mecca and Billboard's world number one discotheque the Wigan Casino. The white, anti-punk, snappy-dressing mod somersaulters were now old hat, dance tourism was temporarily on the wane and the musical genre constructed from failures had almost run its course.

In 1982, the State Ballroom opened as an alternative dance venue in an art nouveau building in Dale Street. It rapidly became Liverpool's most fashionable club and hit the national headlines as the set for the club scene in *Letter to Brezhnev*, with its laser beams and girls in tight silver pants, and as the setting for the video feature on Frankie Goes to Hollywood's hit 'Relax'. After the riots, Liverpool doormen were under firm instructions to discourage Toxteth 'stables' and the State was effectively out of bounds for Liverpool-born blacks. The Zumbi nation unleashed their shackles and headed off to the Legend in Manchester where Greg Wilson, who had cut his spurs on the wheels of steel at the Golden Guinea in New Brighton, was now working with new decks and a raw Manhattan electro-funk mix suited for up-town, top-ranking breakdancers, monkey walkers and bodypoppers.

Mrs Thatcher was by now hell-bent on tearing out the innards of Liverpool and hanging them out to dry. The wind whistled through blackened stumps of burnt-out buildings and gutted blocks of flats. The lonely, sallow single mothers, the despairing drunks and gamblers, the pubescent skinny whores, the helpless, the delinquent and the paranoid had come to represent a trapped low-income majority in Liverpool. Most remained locked away from the city centre in corporations of indigence. Their wan children stood on landings, staring from between the lines of nappies down to the deserted exercise areas. Some ran off and drifted into hostels, refuges and prisons or ended up bagged up or boxed over in London doorways. Spray paint messages 'Fuck the Bizzies', 'Class War – Fuck the Law', 'Tookey Grass', or the more pressing 'Kiss it Bitch', inflamed the running sores of the raw red brick. Despairing cries for help like 'Save the Earth – Kill Yourself' or 'Last one out switch off the lights' were scribbled on wasted space. For some, the heavy doors of hopelessness had clanged shut for ever. There were many young suicides but no Beachy Head to allow a finish with a romantic flourish. These ghettos of post-war Liverpool were failed architectural experiments, terminally wounded by a plague of unemployment, ever ready to explode under an intolerable burden of squalor, neglect and marginalisation. Liverpool and its new towns had become a microcosm of economic decline and social disintegration: a hated symbol of the ignored darker side of England. The city was a chamber where positively charged particles generated by the nation's cyclotron collided and self-destructed, emitting wake-up calls for anyone who cared to listen.

In fact, the whole of Lancashire was in free fall, increasingly run down, full of unused buildings and cobwebbed warehouses, and rapidly losing its will to live. The plug had been pulled on the old industries and the radical restructuring had left mill-town communities broken.

At the same time, down the M62 in the land of a thousand puddles, ugly-duckling Manchester had thrown away its plastic mac and become the home of the smiley-faced 24-hour Hacienda party people. The Legend had soon been invaded by white boys and the city had bought into 12-inch Chicago DJ International jack music. This new transatlantic sentiment was encapsulated in the spectral lyrics of Adonis's 'No Way Back', describing loss of control and soul selling, and the angelic Utopia dreamed of in 'Promised Land' by Joe Smooth.

By the late '80s, Ecstasy and acid house had become Manchester's new escapist enterprise culture and jacking had taken on a whole new meaning. Digitally sampled sounds with stuck-in set catch lines created harmony between the inner world and the dance floor. Thatcher's illegitimate children lost themselves in a collective fervour and came to understand the significance of The Dave Clarke Five's '60s hit 'Glad All Over'. A thousand rapturous orchids bloomed in a hurdy-gurdy wonderland where illicit MDMA pollen was the holy sacrament. This was disco for dying cities, a hedonistic, post-monetarist, ketamine soundtrack which transcended power and influence. Manchester's new ravers were as 'mad for it' as the Opium Eater and had also discovered his elusive north-west passage. Ecstasy had created a sense of freedom and a counterpoise to the mainstream preoccupation with style, form, design and packaging.

Scallie ears and feet were also now belatedly primed for house music. Defhouse in Birkenhead, with a dance floor built from paving slabs nicked from Cantril Farm housing estate, kicked the scene off across the water. Strobes brought celebration and a future out of the past; electronic drum trax turned anger and rage into a rare ephemeral beauty. Pete Hooton and The Farm had already calmed the terraces with their scallydelic anthems 'Groovy Train' and 'All Together Now' and the football casuals from the overspills now began to throw away their designer labels and move into hooded tops, long-sleeved shirts, pastel-coloured sneakers and flared jeans. Liverpool was now hot on 'Madchester's' heels as a great venue to take disco biscuits, poppers and 'New Yorkers'. While the south of England concentrated on personal advancement and material growth, the scallies branched out from 'footy' into the rave scene. Liverpool was full of the kind of people who go out on Mad Monday and couldn't care less about Tuesday morning.

The Underground at Ritzy in Victoria Street, The World Downstairs at the Royal Court on Mondays, the mega Saturday Pavilion all nighters at Quadrant Park (The Quad), a converted warehouse in the North End dockland wilderness, all had lasers and smoke machines and ever-improving sound systems and were great places to dream of flying to Mars. Normal transmission was suspended on Daisy Night at the State when a new generation of computerised Moulin Rouge waltzers dressed in kickers and T-shirts relinquished power and lost themselves in a glow of togetherness. Even Manchester had become a lovely place. Lee Butler at the O51 had started to play a more pop-friendly and locally manufactured house music that captured the local vibe. Pezz at 3Beat Records on Slater Street filed these tracks in a separate rack, which he labelled Scouse House. This new techno variant had an uplifting Louisiana bounciness mixed with 'happy ardcore' samples and hip hop. The 'bassline' was distinguished by a pipe/plank 'donk' and a backbeat tachycardia of 150 per second programmed on a Roland 808 drum machine. Scouse House was exceptional, innovative, massive and fun and helped to preserve a sense of community. The Liverpool disc jockeys like Andy Carroll and Mike Knowler were no longer the pack animals of the music business but shamans whose divinations ripped and wrecked. 'It's Over Now' by D'votion and Kaysee, 'Take Me Away' by 4 Strings, and 'Rock to the Rhythm' by DJ Lee Butler and Davy T were three in-demand Scouse House tracks.

Liverpool's bouncy soul sister was also on the slide, with half her Creole population now living below the poverty line. For a while she had managed to extend her usefulness with the discovery of offshore oil but once the docks moved downriver, the Big Easy started to shrivel away. Bayou artisan trades had all but died, the oil boom was quickly over and white businesses were fleeing Louisiana like the plague. The old wards and projects were in terminal decline and the population had shrunk from over a million to half that figure. The old white carnival krewes had long ago left for Jefferson Parish and Covington. New Orleans now smelt of spilt oil, crawfish boils and rising damp, and had turned into a slaughterhouse with a murder rate eight times greater than New York. Louis Armstrong Park was now a killing field at night.

The French Quarter had reinvented itself as a Cajun Disneyworld where in the pounding sultry evening heat, lumbering herds of tight-shorted legionnaires and tipsy-turvy mint-julep hedonists wandered around Faubourg Marigny and Storyville hoping they might get lucky or at least lose themselves for ever. Muffulettas, gumbo, beignets, flea markets and aging funk-jazz horn players tried to maintain the city's image and preserve meaning. Themed museums, casinos and convention centres sprouted up amongst the azaleas and oleanders and a few dodgy new operators were making fortunes. People didn't send postcards home from New Orleans.

In the old wards, Jelly Roll Morton, Fats Domino and the Neville Brothers had been usurped by bounce music, a lascivious form of hip hop based on the call and response of the Mardi Gras Indian chants. 'Take Fo' bounce became the music of the summer block parties using Triggaman beats fused with menagerie noises, funk rhythms, call outs and bass lines to turn up the heat. Tight-skirted bitches like Sissy Nobby 'showed the globe', 'shook da thing like a salt cellar' and 'walked it like a dog'. Verbal tics which included 'break' and 'twerk' were a distinctive feature. The Big Easy was now a brown beat, drag rap 'Nigga Liverpool' with a shared love of life and unshakeable pride in something real but indefinable. 'It must be your pussy cos it aint your face and it must be your money cos it aint your dick' was the '90s characteristic project music catchphrase. Even when Katrina broke the forgotten city's levees, the sassy people in the devastated zones of the Lower Ninth Ward boasted about their heritage. Sentimental and totally unrealistic, the believers remained committed to a moribund port.

By 1992, the Manchester scene had gone sour, with gang wars invading the dance floor and gunshots now part of the Thunderdome soundtrack. 'Madchester' had become cocksure, fallen in love with itself and lost control. James Barton, a former sock salesman and local DJ who launched the Daisy House night at the State, followed his dream and opened a new venue in Liverpool with his friend Darren Hughes. With the help of a council grant, the club rapidly expanded to engulf the courtyard and three-roomed floor space of the Nation in Wolstenholme Square. Hard work and imaginative branding resulted in Cream replacing the Hacienda as the north's most talked about superclub.

Coachloads of shell-suited northerners began to arrive to dance to Planet Perfecto's 'Bullet in a Gun'. The 'Winter of Love' had arrived in the Hurricane Port and many of her neophytes had retreated into this clean-cut, clean-living, safe-parking and tight-security dreamworld. The joy of Folly Fair had returned and Liverpool was bouncing and donking its way to a post-modernist future. Computer technology offered limitless opportunities for do-it-yourself creativity. Cream's 3,000-strong congregation was deeply in love with itself and generated a particular Day-Glo chemistry. The scene revelled in the secrecy and obscurity of its 12-inch vinyls and the experimental virtuosity of its trancemeisters Paul Oakenfold, Sasha, Seb Fontaine, Steve Lawler and Youssef. Tense people and control freaks were not welcome on the dance floor. Talk of the 'footy', Gucci and the ozone layer was out of bounds. The faithful got dressed up to get messed up every night. A Brownian motion of pistol-cock antics and robotic tics swept through the old ammunition warehouse. Lads stripped to the waist performed kung fu and fishy finger programmes to digital bass throbs from 'the scaff' and rapturous pigtailed girls created sinuous aerial patterns in the vortex. High-pitched klaxons, whirring helicopter blades, church organs, bleeps of a nuclear power station, and sub bass manufactured a growing sense of rising tension, which culminated in a post-climactic serenity. For some, dancing had become an all-consuming new religion that led to permanent estrangement from the nine to five world, and a rite of passage to the House Nation. The music went straight to the bones and caused the knees to fizz. Despite this, 'Livercool' managed to stay a cuddly venue where ordinary people could have a good time undisturbed by the old, damaging turf wars.

Within two years of opening, Cream had become a corporate brand with franchised Millennium Eve Parties in Argentina and New Zealand, and its stable of DJs hosting nights in Ibiza and Moscow's Red Square. Its cryptic three-looped logo endorsed a set of profitable compilations with major record labels and retailers. With innovations like its feeder bar Mello Mello, it deliberately tried to distance itself from the typical Liverpool dance and club culture and reach out to the rest of the world. Barton was now a rich man employing 120 staff, including an in-house

Casualty Officer seconded from the Liverpool Royal Infirmary to treat 'raver's foot', acute alcohol poisoning and bad trips.

By the early '90s, acid-house culture with music designed to stimulate neurones had joined the mainstream and become a lifestyle choice with buzzwords like 'sorted' and 'chilled out' entering the Oxford English Dictionary. Middle-class parents could not understand why Liverpool's universities had suddenly become so popular with their children. The Cream quarter was almost singlehandedly keeping Liverpool city centre alive and to a new generation of shiny happy students, dance tourism had become a hardcore career.

Herman Melville's great-great-grandnephew, the original musician Moby, tried to visit Cream but was refused entry even though his hit 'Porcelain' was playing inside. Like *Moby Dick*'s creator, he was struck by the stiletto sexuality of Liverpool's fiesta girls. Cream had brought back the Dionysian dancing rituals of the Locarno and Grafton to a new generation of Merseyside shamblers and shoegazers. Despite Barton's close contacts with Liverpool Health Authorities and Lifeline, concern about the dangers of Ecstasy was mounting and on its tenth anniversary James Barton closed the club down. It had been a flagship for a post-ideological and post-industrial decade in which the old ties of class, family, work and community had come under siege. The scene had now moved on to millenarian gatherings like Creamfields and Ibiza, and the Liverpool clique of trendsetters had eventually rejected it because of its success. Voodoo started to steal the show, jungle was on the up with the students and anonymous instrumental trance music was on the slide. Euphoria gave way to a commercialised come-down and heat stroke. Nostalgia was back again but Barton had proved that 'something good could still come out of Liverpool.'

I leave the cobbles of Pilgrim, the hill of Hardman and the ugly beauty of the bombed-out church in a heavy twilight. A cross-breed lopes across the precinct close to where the elephant's bones were excavated. There is an unnatural, flat greyness about Bold. I start to have flashbacks of solemn bearded patriarchs, enthroned in this unbending city, propelled ever upwards by the jets of steam and the riches of sugar. Now the Dockers Umbrella comes into view and below a group of Shanghai sailors file by The Cocoa Room. The floodgate of Old Europe from whence the restless, desperate and disenchanted left in their millions to live the dream has come to life. Sometimes it seems as if this city is punishing me for returning.

As darkness descends and the ambulance chasers, call-centre

telephonists and insurance clerks flee to St Helens, New Brighton, Warrington and the Wirral, the locked crypts awake like camouflaged moths and unfold their gaudy wings. Systems are dissolved by an unconditional surrender to the feelings of the ocean. In Sleazeville, with its heavy faces, illicit pill-making laboratories and dodgy money, lurks the shadows of a post-Cream Thursday. A new breed of hoods strut the luxury Princes dockside pads playing the same old game. Bladdered lads grope sunbed blondes in micros and a winged fairy in high heels gets her tits out. Furtive knee shakers, weeing in the street and gratuitous violence are part of the happy snapping buzz. Gangsters and footballers top the girls' wish list. Their mothers are on the pull too, dressed in Playboy basques and Wonderbras, soon legless and knickerless enough to fall upon any man. Peacock parties in pyjamas rent Travel Lodge, Dolby and Campanile rooms meant for two and pack in four. The strip is a barbarous bacchanalia for loud hens with throaty sandpaper giggles, a gazpacho of creed and colour, a funk ball for all ages, redolent of the olden days. Carnival rules are in place as a Viking *samba de roda* is acted out on Hardman, Seel, Wood, Slater and on Mathew a man plays a cardboard guitar directly below Arthur Dooley's plaque:

> How lonely is she now
> the once crowded city,
> widowed she who was mistress over nations.
> The princess among provinces
> Has been made a toiling slave
> Bitterly she weeps at night
> Tears upon her cheeks
> With not one to console her
> All of her dear ones
> Her friends have all betrayed her
> And become her enemies
> The old man has abandoned the gate
> The young man his music
> The joy of our hearts has ceased
> Our dance has turned into mourning
> Lead us back to you O Lord
> That we may be restored
> Give us anew such days as we had of old.
> We need a start.

Everyone still wants to choreograph this heartbreak city and above the urinal in Ye Cracke some wit has scrawled, 'the large print giveth and the small print taketh away'.

Bulge Waves

Every day I walk this tightrope of tarmac,
blown toppling in the wake of juggernauts.
I walk it to learn the line of the road,
to keep my place on it.
When I was a lad
my dad took me to a strange part of town
left me to find the five miles home –
a stiff task that taught me to trust my feet.
In a car, it's all distortion,
one landmark smudging the next:
fast food, do-it-yourself
a field with corrugated sheds and a scruffy horse.

Extract from *No Man's Land: Poems
from the Central Reservation of the East
Lancashire Road* by Jean Sprackland

In 1982, an article about Liverpool appeared in the *Daily Mirror* that accurately reflected the current opinion: 'They should build a fence around it and charge admission, for sadly it has become a "showcase" of everything that has gone wrong in Britain's major cities.'

The Banana Republic on the Mersey was now stuck in a groove and the Liverpolitans who had stayed put were trapped in the headlights of a new-order juggernaut. The media portrayed the former Second City of the Empire as a brooding, persecuted freak show, a flagship for the world's redundant ports, living off past glories. On the football terraces, the most cutting and durable opposition chant was, 'Sign on, sign on, you'll never get a job' to the red side of Liverpool's anthem 'You'll Never Walk Alone'. This was sometimes accompanied by a hurtful improvisation of the Spinners folk song 'In My Liverpool Home':

In your Liverpool slums,
You look in the dustbin for something to eat,
You find a dead rat and you think it's a treat,
In your Liverpool slums . . .
You speak in an accent exceedingly rare,
You wear a pink tracksuit and have curly hair,
Your mum's on the game and your dad's in the nick,
You can't get a job 'cos you're too fucking thick.

The baiting often continued with a sardonic rendering of 'You are my Sunshine':

You are a Scouser,
An ugly Scouser,
You're only happy,
On giro day,
Your mum's out thieving,
Your dad's drug dealing,
So please don't take my hubcaps away . . .

To the chattering and twittering south, Liverpool was now a paranoid theme park full of false pride and strident protest. It was an audacious cloud cuckoo land for the great unwashed, England's Beirut where the glass was always half empty, and an aggrieved place that specialised in wringing apologies out of politicians. In Margaret Thatcher's home town of Grantham, a property developer applied to the council for permission to change the name of Liverpool Close to Ipswich Gardens because house sales were much lower than in the surrounding streets. To Manchester, Liverpool seemed to be taking a bloody-minded pleasure in her predicament and, to borrow from their bard Morrissey, she 'bore more grudges than lonely high court judges'.

Scouse jokes were all the rage and had replaced the traditional Paddy put-downs in Lancashire. Ireland was cool, racial jokes were taboo and those hated, mouthy, scrounging Scousers were a soft target: 'Why does the River Mersey run through Liverpool? Because if it walked it would be mugged'; 'What's the difference between a Scouser funeral and a Scouser wedding? One less drunk.'

Liverpool had become the biggest village on earth, a journalist's paradise and a celluloid strip, never out of the national spotlight. In the eyes of the tabloid editors, she now stood for everything that was wrong with modern Britain, a brooding freak show full of the progeny of feckless Irish and 14-year-old girls who dropped their knickers for the price of a Mars bar. The *Sunday Times* columnist Brian Appleyard related how every time he got off the train at Lime Street he immediately felt the deep-seated anomie. Scousers were not witty but threatening and dangerous. He went on to describe how some years earlier he had walked into town at night and bumped into a figure lurking in the shadows of Mathew Street. Convinced he was about to be murdered, he only relaxed when he realised his assailant was the bronze statue of John Lennon.

In response to a suggestion by a young Conservative Iain Picton that the 1981 riots might have been a reaction to chronic unemployment, Norman Tebbit responded with, 'I grew up in the 1930s with an unemployed father. He did not riot. He got on his bike and looked for work and he went on looking until he found it.'

Centuries of hardship had led to the deeply held conviction in Liverpool that the best way to endure poverty and deprivation was to keep your extended family intact and stick together. The city resisted the prevailing Tory view that there was no such thing as community spirit. Many Scousers resented the fact that they were now being told to leave home and seek work in the south. They felt their country had let them down and those who reluctantly followed the Chingford Bovver Boy's advice were back on the coaches north every weekend to unite with friends and family. Scousers had always worn adversity as a peculiar badge of honour and Norman Tebbit's remarks were a further spur to resistance in the touchy, corrupted silo that Liverpool had become.

A story went round that a Mori poll had asked Londoners which was Britain's second city. Most gave the expected answer Birmingham, with its population of over a million. Mori then asked Glaswegians the same question, where Glasgow was the most frequent response. In Manchester, the reply was Manchester. When people in Liverpool were questioned, the inevitable cocky reply was London! It was a place where people were very proud to say they came from but few who had options to leave elected to stay there. The few sentimentalists who stayed behind were secretly considered to be deranged. The apocryphal swagger of scousers was still alive but now hid a new fragility and defensiveness. Liverpool had become watchful, waiting to see what the next hurricane would dump on her shoreline.

In a *Sunday Times* article he later came to regret, entitled 'Self Pity City', Jonathan Margolis wrote: 'Like blacks in the United States,

Liverpudlians are now on the proscribed list. You publicly find fault with them at your peril.'

In April 1999, on the launch of the government's Crime Reduction Bill and a few days after he had visited Liverpool to learn of a novel crime-prevention plan involving gated properties in Edge Hill, Jack Straw, the Home Secretary, wryly commented to a group of councillors and residents in Milton Keynes, 'I thought, what the devil is this? You know what Scousers are like, they are always up to something.' He then hurriedly added, 'Please do not repeat the comment to anyone from Liverpool.'

Mike Storey, the Liberal leader of Liverpool council, later accused Straw of reinforcing a stereotype and encouraging discrimination. In a belated attempt to defuse the media firestorm, Straw came out with the following reasonable explanation, 'As an Essex man and Blackburn supporter, I often find myself the butt of jokes. My comments were meant to be lighthearted.'

Liverpool-born celebrities were also not slow to express their opinion about the minister's comments. Anne Robinson was first with:

> I think we have such a huge sense of humour, I cannot imagine that anyone could be offended. When I heard he had said that, I just wondered who was offended by it. We are intelligent, witty and self-confident, and Scousers would only be offended if they thought he had said something incredibly funny before they thought of it. I have found it a huge plus coming from Liverpool and I am very proud to be a Scouser.

Stan Boardman, the out-of-fashion stand-up comedian, was not so generous in his view: 'Once again, it's someone in power having a go at Liverpool. It's something you'd expect from a Tory not a Labour minister. In a league table of thieves, Liverpool wouldn't even qualify for Europe.'

Straw's view of the character of Liverpudlians had a long history and may not be without substance. A nineteenth-century ship captain had had this to say for Liverpool:

> It has a good name so far as ports go, though its seamen are reputed to be responsible for more than half the misdeeds and mysterious happenings on board ship. When something goes wrong, or some wrong is done and none comes forward to admit culpability, then it was the Liverpool feller wot done it.

In a similar vein, another British Cabinet minister, dining with Helmut Kohl, sympathised with the German Chancellor regarding the challenge of unifying Germany, commenting that, 'Taking on East Germany must be like inheriting 24 Liverpools!'

Alan Bennett, the Leeds-born playwright, has also written of his dislike of the Liverpool attitude. He considered the city sullen, raw and tight-fisted, devoid of the generosity and kindness of the Lancashire mill towns, and with a nocturne that oozes violence. His mixed emotions on learning of the Hillsborough tragedy reflected his jaundiced view of Scousers:

> I find myself thinking it would be Liverpool, that sentimental, self-dramatising place, and am brought up short by seeing footage of a child brought out dead, women waiting blank-faced at Lime Street and a father meeting his two sons off the train, his relief turned to anger at the sight of their smiling faces, cuffing and hustling them away from the cameras.

The carpet of flowers at Anfield in memory of the dead triggered Edward Pearce to write in his Last Word column in *The Times*:

> There are soapy politicians to make a pet of Liverpool, and Liverpool is always standing by to make a pet of itself. 'Why us? Why are we treated like animals?' To which the plain answer is that a good and sufficient minority of you behave like animals.

For the second time in a decade, a mob of Liverpool supporters had killed people and in Pearce's opinion the only difference between Heysel and Hillsborough was that this time moronic inadvertence rather than vicious intent was the culprit.

In response to the post-Hillsborough press catcall, the playwright Alan Bleasdale tried to fight back:

> 'Sentimentality,' the intellectuals wrote. 'Sickly,' they sniggered. They were wrong. Our actions weren't sentimental but they were full to overflowing with sentiment, with love and respect and sorrow and understanding.

Under the banner headline 'THE TRUTH', drunken supporters who had piled through Gate 2 in the Leppings Lane end of Hillsborough were accused by *The Sun* of attacking paramedics as they tried to resuscitate the victims, picking the pockets of the crushed victims, and assaulting firemen and police officers in the line of duty. A factoid allegedly from an unnamed policeman claimed that a dead girl had been physically abused and Irvine Patrick, a Sheffield MP, claimed the South Yorkshire police had been harassed, hampered, punched, kicked and urinated upon. This was the butt end of Thatcher's Britain, when all football fans were considered mindless thugs to be contained in animal pens for the duration of the match and then frog-marched by police to the railway station. A newspaper that sold three million copies nationwide and two hundred thousand on Merseyside was burned on the streets and as a result of boycotts on its sales saw its regional subscription fall to a mere twelve thousand. Liverpool would never forget or forgive and at every anniversary of the tragedy the placards and lapel badges stating 'Don't Buy *The Sun*' were evident on her streets. On 6 January 2007, during Liverpool's third-round FA Cup defeat to Arsenal, Kopites held up a banner emboldened with 'The TRUTH. MacKenzie Liar' in a protest directed at the paper's former editor who had been invited as a studio guest for the live televised game and who had retracted his original half-baked apology.

In 2004, Ken Bigley, a 62-year-old Liverpool engineer, was kidnapped in Baghdad and despite efforts to save him he was decapitated by a band of fanatical Islamist insurgents. The people of Liverpool publicly expressed their grief at his loss, flags were lowered, wreaths were laid, and the city's footballers wore black armbands as their supporters impeccably respected a two-minute silence. When the authorities tried to repeat the tribute the following week at the England against Wales match at Old Trafford, derisive jeers broke out in less than 30 seconds.

This overflowing of emotion in Liverpool led the colourful Old Etonian Boris Johnson to write an editorial for *The Spectator* in which he stated that 'an excessive predilection for welfarism has created a peculiar, and deeply unattractive, psyche among many Liverpudlians.' Johnson went on: 'They see themselves whenever possible as victims, and resent their victim status; yet at the same time they wallow in it.' Because of their flawed psychological state, he considered Scousers had become the nation's crybabies, indulging their victim status. Liverpool had managed to maintain a sinister hold over its people even in exile, and John Lennon's narcissistic emoting and cosmetic Celtism was blamed for the 'Liverpudlianisation' of England, whose gutters were now full of tears for girls they'd never met.

Johnson backed his view by pointing to the soppy, melodramatic reaction they had exhibited after Hillsborough and reiterated the widely held view that Liverpool was in denial about the part her fans had played in the disaster, 'where more than 50 people died'. He went on to claim that the police had been made the scapegoat and *The Sun* a whipping boy for daring, albeit in tasteless fashion, to hint at the wider cause of the incident.

Once news of his article reached Liverpool, views varied from those who felt he was a buffoon who was better suited to highbrow television comedy than to politics, to those who dismissed his opinion and that of his magazine as irrelevancies. Ken Bigley's brother Paul denounced Johnson as a pompous twit who should get out of public life. In mitigation to the now predictable outcry, Johnson explained that the purpose of his piece had been to criticise the new vogue for histrionics in response to public tragedies that he believed was allied to a culture of victimhood. He was also concerned about the increasing reluctance of people to accept that they may be the authors of their own misfortunes and the growing tendency of people to blame the nation state for their own shortcomings and failures.

This guarded retraction did not go down well with the meek and holy of Liverpool. Middle England mass hysteria and celebrity media frenzy at Priness Diana's funeral was in their opinion a very different phenomenon to the measured response of a beleaguered community. In their support of one of their own, they were in their view fulfilling a duty of care and compassion. One Scouse wag wrote in the local press that he had done a survey of both the Liverpudlians who read *The Spectator* and could reassure the city that the magazine's subscription would never recover!

The press pack camped outside the Bigleys' Walton home, hunting new headlines. Liverpool remained on guard against the Saxon and Teutonic forces of Grub Street that seemed needled by her tribal reaction. In the *Telegraph*, Dr Anthony Daniels rallied to Boris Johnson's support, deploring Liverpool's lachrymose response to a man hardly any of them knew, and went on to blame Tony Blair for jumping on the Scouse bandwagon and encouraging a sentimentalisation of public life:

> The whole panoply of public mourning will be employed in Liverpool in Mr Bigley's case. Flags will be lowered, flowers sent, black armbands worn, including by those most sensitive of souls, professional footballers. Thousands of people, in effect, will work themselves up into a state of grief. But it will only count as true or real grief if they express it in public . . . The politics of the individual case

is the politics of gusts of intense but shallow emotion. It is incompatible with the rational pursuit of long-term interests. There are several words to describe such a politics: immature, dishonest and decadent would do.

Johnson's editorial had also struck a chord in the heart of Lancashire: 'same old Scousers always whingeing'. Liverpool was back in the dock and all those indolent, thieving, cheeky scallywags were rising to the surface. Since the First World War, the English had become less expressive about their grief in public. The lengthy periods of mourning prevalent in Victorian times had been replaced by a stiff upper lip and the obligation to get back to work as soon as possible. The twentieth-century feel of Manchester came from this pragmatic reserve, whereas in Liverpool hot-blooded, rabble-rousing expressiveness had never quite been extinguished. Scousers had maintained an estuarine way of confronting death. Her people were trapped on the wrong side of a dry dock in transition between an idyllic Elsewhere and an oneiric childhood fantasy.

Despite support from many quarters, Boris was pressured to concede his article had been too trenchantly expressed, had misrepresented Hillsborough and reinforced an outmoded stereotype of Liverpudlians. At the insistence of the acting Tory leader and Liverpool FC supporter Michael Howard, Boris Johnson's damage-limitation exercise included a furtive visit to Liverpool and in an article titled 'What I Should Say Sorry For' written in *The Spectator* he began gingerly:

> I am writing this in a cold, damp three-star hotel in Liverpool, and I have to admit I don't want to go out. Not only is it raining, there is also the chance that I will be beaten up. As everyone seems to know, I am on a mission to apologise to the people of this great city, and my heart is in my boots. The operation is bedevilled with difficulty, not least that no one seems to accept my apology. Local Tories have said that they intend to snub me. The Lib Dem officials who run the council have made a meeting all but impossible. The police have said they expect an enormous media circus, which rules out a trip to the museums. There was a plan to sign a book of condolence for the late Ken Bigley, but we have reluctantly rejected it, on the grounds that it will look as if we are playing politics with a tragedy. But what makes Operation Scouse-grovel even more depressing is that I am attacked by my own troops for embarking on it.

An unacceptably high mortality rate in the Bristol paediatric cardio-thoracic unit led to a public inquiry in 1999. During the investigation, it transpired that the organs of 850 children had been retained without parental consent in dust-covered pots in a damp cellar in Alder Hey Children's Hospital in Liverpool. At a National Summit on Organ Retention in London, a dossier of evidence was made available to all the interested parties. Buried within the huge bundle was an email allegedly sent by a technical officer at Sefton Borough Council to the government's Chief Medical Officer after the Department of Health had solicited opinions on the organ retention debate. It put all the blame for the Alder Hey human tissue scandal on a particular Liverpool mentality: 'I am 44 and married with three children. I have a responsible job and no strong political views either way and I believe I represent what I would call the silent and sensible majority.'

The anonymous author goes on to say that having been born and bred in Liverpool he is 'qualified to introduce another angle to the subject'. He continues: 'The Alder Hey scandal is one of three significant examples over recent years that give an insight to the way that many people in Liverpool think and it points to a possible link to intelligence.'

Commenting first on the child murderers of James Bulger, the letter goes on:

> Unfortunately the mentality of Liverpool people would have these two boys stoned to death . . . Many people in Liverpool are brought up to hate authority, especially the police. Additionally an eye for an eye is taken very literally. If someone hits you must hit them back harder, never mind discussion or negotiation. And on top of that we don't like to accept blame for anything; it's always someone else's fault.

The author's assessment of Alder Hey is equally forceful: 'It is my view that it is emotion rather than intellect that rules around here, add to this a sniff of compensation and the irresponsibility of the press and you have a scandal. But above all, never cross a Scouser!'

The Liverpool action group Pity 11 regarded the London Summit as a whitewash. One woman informed the Chief Medical Officer that what had occurred at Alder Hey was akin to the Holocaust. As more and more pathological material was unearthed in different parts of Liverpool University, three further instalments of human tissue were sent out to the families for belated burial. It later became apparent that 'The Liverpool Thing' blamed on one rogue pathologist was just an extreme example of what had been standard medical practice in Great Britain for a hundred years.

To the capital's atheist chic, Liverpool was now a delusional mediaeval place with attitude. The Church, with its odious God squads, contemptible cover-ups and institutional, totalitarian self-righteousness should be made publicly to hang its head in shame. What is there to feel guilty about if you know you are good, rich and always right? The Big Bang is an established fact, wormholes exist and Great Homer Street is now a lonely, decaying freeway devoid of marching Christian soldiers. Liverpool was now firmly on the fringes with her religious sensibility and visionary sense of place.

On 15 April 2009, 30,000 people descended on the city's third cathedral for the 20th anniversary of Hillsborough. The city's church bells chimed 96 times for the people who went to a game of football and never came back. Twenty feet of pavement outside the ground was covered with flowers, scarves, flags, shirts and elegies; ninety-six candles were lit and a similar number of balloons released. A sombre litany of the dead was read out and at 3.06 p.m. the city fell silent for two minutes. Later, when the Minister of Sport, Scouser Andy Burnham, started to speak, pockets of the crowd began to boo and a heartfelt chanting of 'Justice for the 96' broke out from the post-Taylor Kop. It had turned into a shrine for the needlessly dead. Hillsborough had ruined lives, the bereaved and the survivors were still counting the cost in the currency of post-traumatic suicides, divorces and drug abuse, and there was still no one to blame. For some, the fall-out had become a way of life from which they found it impossible to move on. The darkest days for the city were long over but sensitivities remained.

In an interview about his highly acclaimed drama series *The Street*, Jimmy McGovern, in a deliberate effort to avoid a reinforcement of the continuing kitchen-sink trope, explained that he had moved the setting of his drama from a road in Kensington in Liverpool to Manchester. People in Liverpool don't parade their poverty – they hide it in shame.

I was at home listening to the commentary on BBC radio when Hillsborough happened. For a moment it sounded like a pitch invasion and then we were informed that stretchers had arrived to carry the injured to the solitary ambulance. As the numbers of dead came through later that evening, I remember thinking what a terrible waste of life and being overcome by a fear that more blame would fall on Liverpool. A couple of days later, I read the views of Monsieur Jacques Georges, the French

President of UEFA, in the *Daily Post*. Georges had been asked by a radio interviewer whether he felt Liverpool was different in some way, given its football club's recent association with football disasters. Georges had replied that the club's fans seemed to have a particularly truculent and aggressive mentality and that those at Hillsborough were 'like beasts hell-bent on charging into an arena'.

I talk about the tragedy in pubs with the disappointed who have stayed behind and know the city too well, and with the hated deserters, infidels and turncoats, who have become ashamed of their home but can never forget it. I loiter with intent in the biting rain, trying to uncover forgotten shanties and mariner's yarns. I listen to those with old scores to settle and read in a fog of anger the Taylor Report. I have seen it all but still don't know enough. An unrecognisable language plagues the streets. This imperial headline city of dark happenings is everywhere and nowhere, an illegible archive of iconic, forgotten absences, a place of returns. The trade routes of memory are embedded in her empty staircases and the threatening footsteps of her walkways. Her sentiments are still dominated by a waterfront, a terminus at the end of the line where good fortune depends on arrivals from the sea. Perhaps the way football supporters were treated by society, cooped in pens and herded together like mindless sheep, had as much to do with the man-made tragedy of Hillsborough as a police blunder.

The River

But the nearer they got to the house, after crossing the river by ferry-boat, the more they knew that it was *not* that. From the landing stage they walked uphill towards Dock Road, slowly because of the blocked roads and the rubble and glass and smashed woodwork which was strewn over the streets; the trail of wrecked houses and the smell of newly-extinguished fires was a terrible accompaniment to their journey. They did not talk to each other, because the cruel destruction was saying it all for them . . .

Nicholas Monsarrat, *The Cruel Sea*

Once in a Preston Guild at neap tide, the caramel water shudders to a halt and takes on the smoothness of Lancashire cotton. It becomes as quiet as a house with no children. The dim lights of the broken docks and the back-to-backs glow as the river's tranquillity is broken by the wingbeat of gulls. In another place, the iron army on Crosby Beach commands the land and welcomes the steel sea. On rare congealed days like this, the sun never quite lifts that deep melancholy which lingers close to the horizon. There is not a trace of sea wind and not a ship to be seen. The river is defeated, devoid of manatees but still defiant.

Now and again I catch sight of the fishing hamlet on the tidal creek, sheltered by red sandstone with the muddy river streaming past its silver sands, the silent beech trees and Leland's chapel. I am in a desolate gusty place on the edge of Mercia filled with the echoes of kelp tides and the mutterings of the waters. The sheltered sloping Pool founded by Henry's Royal Decree in the bloody campaign to bring Ireland to its knees is in front of me. Benedictine monks unload cheese and ale from a rowing boat on the Sea Lake. The Great Oldfield, Moss Lake and the Brecks bridle a tight grid of seven neatly paved streets. To the south, I can make out low Triassic cliffs sliced open by the Dingle stream at Knotts Hole and the hamlet of St Michael snuggled against the shoreline. Ancient children with freckled physogs are playing among the Calder Stones in the grove of she-oaks, running across Speke's soggy swine pastures and jumping Tiw's mossy brook. I cannot explain what it is about these shipwrecks that make them linger like the sodden leaves of a Sefton Park autumn.

This sea of water on which I look out now had grown from humble beginnings on the black-brown Pennine edge that separates Mercia from Northumbria. The swift-running Etherow and Goyt fused at Marple and then met the Tame in the belly of Stockport. There, so close to Cottonopolis, the ruins of old stone mills grow out of the mossy jungle like Mayan temples; the old Roman Lakes and the Wellington Wheel stand as lasting monuments of the past. The river valley has become the M60 and between motorway and water is the blue crystal of the Valley of the Kings. At Irlam, the Mersey flows into the dark Irwell, a polluted river that no one falls into twice and which serves as the border between Salford and Manchester. After the weir, the river is lost in the Ship Canal. Amongst the rubble of demolished steel works and the oil tanks of Cadishead is a post-industrial wildlife sanctuary. These rural remnants are dwarfed by the concrete ramps of the Thelwall Viaduct, which carries the M60 over the canal. The river has now arrived at Warrington, the Roman crossing between Chester and Wigan and important Tudor staging post. St Helens – Liverpool's long-standing provider of coal, copper and iron, and alkali – is joined to the river by the 'Stinky Brook' and resurgent Sankey Canal with its locks at Widnes. Fiddler's Ferry three miles downstream is the site of a coal-fired power station which fed for so long on the local seam. On the other bank are the ruins of Halton Castle perched on a rocky hilltop, once used as a hunting lodge by John of Gaunt and as a garrison by the Royalists in the Civil War.

From Howley Weir the river is tidal, and at the Runcorn Gap the Victorian rail and road bridges span the widening expanse of water and the proximate canal. The galligoo detritus and soap and ash waste of Spike Island that once found its way into the river, producing a stench of rotten eggs to blend with Widnes's choking fumes, is now all but gone and its rust-belt maze of abandoned chemical factories, rail lines, canal and toxic industrial dockage beloved of the Stone Roses is reclaimed as a woodland wetland. Salmon are jumping again. On the south bank beyond Frodsham Marshes and the little country village of Hale, the elevated walkways, snaking pipes and mesh of cables link the fuel tanks and chimneys of the petrochemical agglomerations of Stanlow, Thornton and Ince. The Weaver brings in brine from its damp salt lands and at Eastham Locks, Lancashire's Ostia, the Manchester Ship Canal and the Mersey mate. It is also at this place the tankers come to discharge their crude oil and Vauxhall builds its cars. Further on is the grain port and across the water the model villages of Port Sunlight and Bromborough Pool.

The Mersey still bothers me. Even the short crossing on 'the most famous ferry in the world' to Seacombe is unsettling. I hear the drowned souls begging for salvation below the elemental bow waves and can smell the muddy river's unpredictable cruelty. When heaven is closed off, the river becomes more and more welcoming. On the *Royal Iris*, looking out on rainswept Tranmere Beach, I can see the Birkenhead church, the monstrous block of the Woodhead ventilation shaft and what little is left of Cammell Laird's. There are still a few token chimneys belching smoke and the stains of arsenic and cadmium. Hawthorne's Spa, the Rock Hotel, the bowling greens and Pierrot concerts are daguerreotypes from a bygone age. Time seems to move more slowly in its effort to create new illusions.

The city displays a different panoptic face when you arrive by sea buffeted on a cantankerous wind with the salt air in your nostrils. I am accompanied by a group of breezy black girls posing erotically as the ferry heads back towards the Tobacco Warehouse and the Victoria Tower. Bathed in an uneasy watery half-light, the river is empty and still. It seems to have momentarily given up. The starboard buoys bob and twinkle on the swirling dark water. Otterspool Esplanade looks like a deserted Coney Island, hungry new cranes helping to build the City of Culture loom above the King's Dock. A lonely barge lies stranded in front of the Great Western Railway depot. The black shadow of a cormorant scuds over the gloomy mudflats, heading for Ellesmere Port and Manchester in search of sustenance. This still feels like Viking territory with those sleek Norse merchant boats. A pale light points the way through a never-ending glacial rice field. The ocean hydras and water nymphs feel very close now. Further out in the bay past Wallasey Town Hall, the choppy sea is a wilderness of sombre glimmering water. The redundant Perch Rock lighthouse and its fort guard Liverpool. The Irish Sea is grandiose, alone and boundless, placid and playful with its gambolling breakers rising and falling, swelling and sinking. Then out of its deeps come rolling avalanches of foam and deadly squalls.

Motion dictates Liverpool in the same way the capricious mighty tides dominate the river, a shifting shoreline where the Gulf Stream meets the ocean and a temperate port encounters a tropical mindset. The South-West Atlantic tides and zephyrs leave vines and pines on the beaches. As sunlight radiates from a full low moon, I see a bronze sea crescent coming out of the deep. It has been created from the oars and mainsails of sunken ships. Similar mechanical creatures have been found in teacups and puddles in Galveston and Valparaiso. Particular rhythms shared with sea cucumbers and other waterfronts create the Mersey Sound.

I am combing for the ghosts of my past in forgotten corners of a windswept water's edge. There is something redolent in the rediscovery of chanteys, the mewling of immature black-backs, a message locked in a periwinkle. These strands of narrative blown in on the angry river provide forlorn clues. Liverpool is a dirty old ship town where each generation has left a fresh pungency. The spectre of the Montagues and Capulets stalks her riverside and the air on the Dock Road has a high-voltage hum. The dock remnants reek of clay, excrement, bitumen, rum and tobacco and death is ingrained below their damp surface. An unrelenting darkness has finally fallen over the river; the port is full of ghosts and washed up bodies. Over the water at Woodside on the Kingsway ventilation shaft is a 35-foot-high spray painting, 'The Pies', heralding the predicted second coming of the legendary La's. Banksy Rat's more downtrodden message is 'Global Meltdown Has Started', while the walls of the Cheapside Bridewell are covered with Franny's etchings: 'One day you will all be free', 'Kilroy one police nil'. When this film-set city feels weary, it is to the river mouth that its folk go to draw strength and inspiration and test their faith. Out in the bay, pushed by strong currents, there is sanctuary and a chance of freedom. My sense of reality and vitality comes from this ebb and flow of the tides. I am looking out again at the river, the Cunard ships are back in the middle of town, the *Ark Royal* has moored at the new liner terminal and there are big container-carrying boats heading south to Garston docks. I have started to look out to sea again and count ships and search for sugar loaves.

The intensity of the cerulean skies and the beauty of that faraway bay remain unchanged. The ocean metropolis, with its tumble-down forts cherished by the Batavian and Huguenot sea sweepers, basks on the sun-drowned hillside. Its streaming streets are still just a concentration of the dry lands beyond. The mulatto sailor, with *Agua dos Meninos* tattooed on his chest, sits beating his drum and singing, 'It's paradise to die at sea.' Iemanja, mother and wife of the waters with her shipwreck eyes, crystal necklace and vanities, punishes the Itapagipe canoemen with her storms. Those who never come back become her lovers, doomed to fight for her favours in the deep. The fireflies on the green sea are her gleaming locks, which disguise her nakedness as she rises up to ogle the moon. Ileana, siren of the ocean who left your beloved Africa to guard the sloops and luggers in the sensual aquamarine waters of Brazil and see the Paraguacu river, I pray to you now for my safe passage home to Liverpool, where this all started. Iemanja come, come out from the waters, come and play on the Sandy Point of Itaparica, the wall of stones, and swing to the rhythms of the Bahian night. In hope of fair winds, I have brought my flowers, fragrant soaps, watermelons and combs to Rio Vermelho. Iemanja, Dona Maria, Inae, Dona Janaina, Princess of Aioca, mother with five names, daughter of the earth and sky, you who came to stay in the nightfall of the earth with the Nago speakers and the Juju, guide me safely through the tropical waters behind the blue line. Ask your two children – Oxumare, who holds fire in his fists and travels in the rain, and Xango, who reveals the secrets of the gale – to carry me home. Virgin Mary, Star of the Sea, banish the flawed temperate enlightenment of the Sun worshippers and make the tides turn.

Tiderip

Ah the morning freshness of one's arrivals
And the morning pallor of one's departures,
When the bowels tighten
And a vague sensation like fear
The ancestral fear of moving off and leaving,
The mysterious ancestral dread of Arrival and the New—
Shivers our hide and torments us,
And the whole of our anxious body feels,
As if it were our soul,
An inexplicable urge to be able to feel this in some other way:
Nostalgia for something else—
A confused tenderness for what vague homeland?
What seacoast? what ship? what dock?

Extract from 'Maritime Ode' by Alvaró de Campos

Time passes through me as I try to stand still. I am trapped between a past I can no longer remember and a future I have ceased to contemplate. The force of forgetting and the selectivity of memory have left few facts that are incontestable. I can no longer summon my past at will but go on hoping that before death I can unlock it by chance encounters with unforeseen emblems of childhood. Now, long after I have forgotten my 21st birthday and John Lennon's death, I still look back fondly on small, inconsequential things I once saw in this Punch and Judy Town. Down the lonely winding road is the imported Enterprise City; new buildings are going up, old familiar edifices are now glistening fresh from a makeover. The trophies of the slave trade and the industrial age have become tourist trails and heritage walks. Classy hotels and luxury waterfront flats surround the Three Graces and the fabric of Victorian urban civic pride is being nibbled away in the great march to a brave new future of shopping precincts. Urban Splash and the Celtic Tiger have bought and built. A new smoke-free, architectural vision is free of clutter, designed for participants who will work an agreed seven hours a day, five-day week in telemarketing, information technology and customer services. Liverpool no longer begs for public handouts and EU parachute payments. Her new buildings are here to make statements and receive awards. The cosmic metropolis creates optimum efficiency through recycling and genetic engineering and offers six weeks' holidays a year for its skilled workforce. There never was through traffic or a rush hour and now there are no dole queues and no strikes. The Hurricane Port is 'made up' and no longer beyond the pale. Day-glo petunias now boldly spell out 'Welcome to Liverpool'. Bournemouth councillors want a northern twin, claiming their seaside town has much to learn from Liverpool's friendliness and creativity. But all this is already in the past.

The Maritime Museum on the Albert Dock tries to awaken the city to its singular identity but there are no seafarers left to be roused from slumber. This is nowhere land, a provider of melodramas, soaps and hard lyrics rife with inflections. I find myself unconsciously involved in a fight over the nature of reality. The city seems to be losing its soul and its meeting places but still cannot be ignored. She has turned her back on the river but still feels under the steely fist of the ferrous sea. The Sisters of Mercy have sold their Garden of Contemplation. The Picket has been relocated and the heritage site sold for flats. The derelict Bryant and May match factory has become a residential refurbishment with a car park packed with Vorschprung durch Technik. The Hard Days Night Hotel on North John reels in the Mathew Street crowd and the aging Beatles generation. The city has joined the education industry and is attracting internationally recognised scientists. The brain drain is slowing and the first Cheshire and London merchant princes are drifting back. Liverpool is no longer the butt of England's jokes. She is in the money again and set to become a model for contemporary urban living. The Racquets Club has been born again in the Hargreaves Building, and the Walker and the Phil are flourishing. St George's Hall, the finest neo-Grecian building in England, has been cleaned up, its golden stone now ready and waiting for a new but yet to be defined purpose. The Brunswick Business Park created out of Harrington, Toxteth and Brunswick docks and Wavertree Technology Park are silicone valleys and Jaguar Halewood is cinematic.

The Cold War is over and the silo mentality long gone. Foreigners in garish yellow tabards have replaced the detested sailors and old-school dockers on the waterfront. Wałęsa's children now receive their orders from the Duke of Westminster. Warsaw was rebuilt in a year and home is where you find your bread. Massive Atlantic Conveyor ships now nestle tightly in Gladstone and the Port is handling 600,000 container units a year. To the north, there are wind turbines with seagulls' wings providing dynamism. That good old me-first-ism and devil take the hindmost is back with big ideas. The old directness without bluntness and smugness is still around. The German cormorants smile benignly on the metamorphosis of the monstrous *Ungeziefer*.

Behind Bold Street in Concert Square and Rope Walks, brash planetary shapes shine out from the dereliction. Hornby Heights and the wood-floored lofts of Beetham Tower have changed the old streets of Tithebarn and Old Hall into foci for city-centre living. Big Bang architecture has arrived with the Echo Arena and the X-shaped museum. The Paradise Project has emerged from behind the hoardings as a post-industrial, New Labour, high-security clone town boasting the usual boring suspects, Harvey Nichols, John Lewis and Debenhams. In this flat, glass, modernist world of empty shops, there are no beggars, pamphleteers or *Big Issue* sellers. The fine-grained textured aerial decks and walkways of the Grosvenor Estate, with its shininess and shrieking concrete leopard skin, blankets out a full 42 acres. The Unity Building inspired by the dazzle ships provides palatial modern office space for sharks in suits. Over-qualified Slovakians and Bulgarians are here to serve seamless-knickered 'cappuccino girls' and frothy 'macchiato boys' on the seven streets. The Palm Sugar Lounge on Kenyon Steps serves Saigon Slings and Bombay Sapphires to Liverpool's new female elite. Pierhead 42 penthouses are Spanish footballer investments and there is even a branch of Coutts. There is a marina for water events and exclusive shady moorings.

Two wretchedly thin 'cougar women' carrying designer bags, whom I recognise by their palsied expressions, swollen glossed lips revealing new enamels, and lactating busts, as members of the new cosmetically enhanced class sail by. This is a shiny, corporate, maple-syrup New World full of plazas and eyes in the sky, which challenge the river. The foreign big-headed ants have arrived with their hundreds of queens, giant corporations and sophisticated pheromones. Their mighty soldiers have left a trail of wings and chewed common black abdomens on the picnic grounds and now have their giant wire clippers round the foundations of the city. In their insatiable drive for growth and productivity, they are changing the landscape and exterminating the locals.

I feel a sea mist clinging to my face, on the other side of which lies the past. There is an Atelier Bow-Wow on Renshaw and through the window of a burnt-out house I can see a joyous sunset, a half-read newspaper and the leftovers of a middle-class breakfast. I have begun to witness the best and worst of times. I have collected an infinite realm of stunted non-truths which are in danger of becoming facts. All I hear are my own footsteps. Has Liverpool lost her guts? What is the function of this repackaging? I feel cut off from who I am and where I have come from, talking into a strong wind. I feel as if I were born yesterday and have become old before my time. I am searching for Alsop's Cloud floating somewhere above the Liver Building. Perhaps the World Discovery Centre, with its electronic catalogues of births and parish records, can rescue me. I seek solace in Murphy's dream of a 180-ft high, hollow Neptune rising out of the sea off the New Brighton coast and my old friend the wandering Superlambanana. The Toxteth hornbeams on the corner of Upper Parly have started to move but the people are rooted.

Liverpool is suffocating me with her new sterile sameness and lack of spontaneity. I feel caught in the city's millennium gossamer and red-top headlines. I fear a new place is being born on the same site with the same name but with no recognition of the old city. Trust is being eroded in this new, disinfected, gated enclave. She has become a film set and theme park controlled from out of town. Unmanned drones patrol the skyline. The new dockside plots have been partitioned to deal with divorce and the need to be free. Gated architecture and zero tolerance are defensible but seem to have brought a different kind of unhappiness. Liverpool is turning into a pasteurised style market with greedy chain stores and supermarkets, coffee houses and cafes with tubular-steel tables, fake Irish pubs, a Marriott, a Radisson, a Hilton, a Jury's and a Crowne Plaza, all of which demand a self-confident, presentable labour force with good interpersonal skills and an accent visitors can understand. She is being repopulated with Blackberried loft-dwellers, PR talkers-up and humourless estate agents, desk-bound, rule-bound profit watchers. Up town is more like Islington N1 with its chic little bistros, wine bars and clubs. There is no room for extra time or the comings and goings of stalkers, just mechanical uploads and downloads and penalty shoot-outs. What is left of the city has become fungible. She is being sold off to the highest bidder in the hope that these new adventurers can help Liverpool sign up to David Cameron's Big Society. The pattern is being licked off her plate.

Sefton Park is out of reach. I jump on the first bus out of St Johns, heading for Old Swan and my hometown. Soon we are out on the Prescot Road, sailing past churches at half-mast and the Old Halfway House.

Kensington is still a tough street with the odd kebab house and a desperate curry inn that piles it high at knock-down prices. A single father walks up a deserted terraced street, clutching a plastic bag. The dead chimneys still dominate the skyline but are now museum pieces. A group of cropped hoodies, with their tracksuit bottoms tucked into their socks, train a bull terrier in the art of savagery on a methadone plot littered with turds. There are a few more nasty-looking takeaways, a soulless burger bar, a boarded-up chippy, a barely alive pound shop and a pawnbrokers. Tanning shops, laundromats, misspelt pizza parlours, off-licences and bookmakers are the only places with an inkling of life.

Clock Face is a reminder of a lost rural, cloth-capped, clogged Lancashire now engulfed by an anonymous aggregation of casualised global call centres and a giant life-saving Tesco. Pocket Nook, Peasley Cross, Sutton Leach and Carr Mill Dam, those childhood dreams of rustic Merseyside now seem as distant as the Vikings. My bus transports two Eleanor Rigbys and a Shirley Valentine and an abused ten year old who spends all day riding in and out of town to escape his mother's fists. Two small-time gamblers get on in the dog-fighting territory of Huyton and three heavily eye-lined girls start to sing along to a Sugababes number. We are moving past cooling towers, gasometers, lunatic asylums and the abandoned coal mines of Old Boston, Ravenhead, Sutton Manor, Bold and Lea Green. A group of John Moores' students pass the journey by reading out loud the lonely-hearts club advertisements in *The Star*: 'Youthful pensioner on Viagra seeks a curvaceous lady friend who enjoys Rugby League and topiary . . .' They switch to the *Echo* and the penny-pinching wool adverts: 'String vest and stained undies, photo of Elvis and size 14 football boots, five pounds the lot, phone Widnes 6875321.' Amongst the several pages of 'In Memoriam' they stumble on: 'Pull yourself together, Stan, you've come through worse than this.'

We pass a large video store, its window festooned with a poster of Daniel Craig, enticing the unemployed to bite on the bargain-basement deals. Two girls get on and ask me where I bought my shoes.

I am trying my best to backtrack down the cut and call back words from the incoming sea. St Helens, my lifeblood that began life as a chapel with only a 'challis and lyttle belle' in a mossy bog, will save me. Out of the earth came light and she became a wondrous sandy place steeped in chivalry and romance. The purr of motorbikes heading down the East Lancs Road past Moss Bank to Manchester, the shipping reports and the litany of football results, once indelible lullabies, start to return.

The bus is dropping down past the former mansions of the Pilks bosses into the hustle and bustle of this sprawling company town where rich people no longer venture. My birthplace, the town with the beautiful name, has become a murderous, peculiarly unhealthy locale, a land of the fully grown, protected by a terracotta army of clay figurines. It is a place of absences, all-day breakfasts and accident claims. I fear for my life, marked out by my soft hands and expensive clothes. I have become a stranger in my own front room. The friendly linen weavers and coal miners with their damaged paws seem so far away; no flat boats carry raw molasses from the docks to Sankeys. Only the grimy Victorian town hall, St Mary's Lowe House and the Co-op are there to calm my nerves. In my end is my beginning. I wind my way through those small, toy-town, gas-lit, cobbled streets and take one last left into Speakman Road. My house stands there on the right, guarded by the domovoys. I tap lightly on the door of my home but no one answers. One or two parked cars and the loss of privet cover are the only change. I start to hammer on the doors in blind panic and am welcomed back by disconnected strangers whom I fully understand. I now see that resilience, otherness and solidarity with new eyes. The old furniture seems somehow out of place. I roll a final tennis ball down the back alley and think how diminutive this world has become. Below ground lie the untapped seams of coal from the primeval forests, above ground the fallen lupins and the sound of breaking glass. Liverpool and the sea as ever beckon to the west.

Those first visits with my father, the magnificence of the waterfront, the crow's nest with its Pantheon, the wedding cake of Saint George's Hall adorned by elephants and blackamoors are still held dear. The Albert Dock crowd has hijacked the bench we sat on by the river and I have been forced to come to rest under a solemn yew at the front of St Anthony's of Egypt. I am incognito. A white horse and carriage is parked in the forecourt backed up by a cortège of funereal sedans. A few untidy sinners hang outside the railings muttering and smoking, ashamed to enter. Next to me is a retired ship builder, born in Falkner Street, who helped to build the Yellow Submarine. He told me how in his youth he had wandered around Toxteth cemetery learning the names of ships' captains and the reasons for their early deaths. One had 'fallen off his perch' and another had 'Lucky me, lucky me' engraved on the back of the tombstone. He then told me a joke about a man who went for a walk in the late evening and came across a cadaverous figure carving away at a headstone. When the man accused the intruder of desecration, the reply came back: 'They've spelt my name wrong and I've popped back to put it right.' We talked as if I had never been away. Both contradictory and awkward in our views and marching against ourselves with a litany of 'my arses', we argued about the Queen and the fortunes of the city: 'Juz because they's fuck'n parasites an they don't give a scewby-do about uz ders no need ter crucify em. The show goes ed in der Pool worever dee throw at us an juz because we're funny it duzzn mean we're unemployable.'

As the mourners started to leave the church, he rose and turned to me, 'Mi name's Gerry Brown and it's been good to talk to yer.' The women were dressed up but not all in black and the men wore their only suits. There were few words and no tears. All had hardship written on their faces and were here to show respect. As the crowd slowly dispersed, Gerry came back, 'Ave ye heard de one about de seven dwarves la'? De sevun dwarves are down in de mines whun thuz a cave in. Snow White runs ter de entrance and yells down ter em. In de distance, a voice shouts out "Manchester United are sound as a pound an gud nuff ter win de league." Snow White looks up and smiles, "At least Dopey's alive!"'

Then I woke up in tears realising that this was all a trick. I had lost my childhood and the city where I felt I belonged. What had happened was a bad dream, which told me that these people were phantoms and there would be nobody else who knew me. It was impossible for me to run all the way home. I consoled myself with my pocket postcard, the one with the unrecognisable view of the Pier Head milling with dockers waiting for the ferry and the corrugated deck and iron viaducts of the Overhead Railway snaking away to the docks.

I started to wonder again, what will become of this irregular anarchic place, which lies in the North West but still is not quite part of it? The city's past and her innate serendipity will surely prevent her from becoming just another global conversion. Will she drum up a few more memorable tunes for those left behind in the glass houses of Maghull and the V streets of Walton? Will the Halewood midden get a shopping centre and a bus service to bridge the Great Divide? Will Liverpool's big day with its treats for the toffs have had a lasting purpose? What will happen to the sons and daughters of the unemployed in Childwall and the unemployable in West Derby and Tuebrook? Will she still preserve her look and pool of talent, her old-fashioned medicine of neighbours, her conscience, her children playing ball in the few remaining cobbled streets, her disruptiveness, her check-in zone, near-death experiences and alien geography? Will she continue to punch above her weight? Will her disparate tectonic plates still trigger seismic cultural shifts? Will there still be decency and dignity? Will her lovelorn women still laugh in the cemeteries? Will her Judies still puncture pretentiousness and dance and kiss in those Legoland streets running down to the river? Will she preserve her vitality and exuberant irrationality, her music, her suicidal lows and manic highs, and that concern and curiosity for strangers? Will she remain in the air, stubbornly contesting boundaries?

For me, Liverpool will always be the redemption between crossings, a tense backwater port screaming for recognition, a place on the edge where women talk to me at bus stops as if I were their lost brother and that place where, when all is said and done, will have to take me in.

I pray now to Saint Cosme and Damian that Liverpool will remain a home for escapists, visionaries, gallivanters, charmers, missing persons and the dissatisfied, a sexy, generous, red lipstick, never-look-back, carnival city full of creative rhythms; that swaggering, fizzy, shared space of my childhood with its two brilliant football teams, still rag-arsed and flabby grey, where I can wait with regret for the last boat to Bahia.

Copyright Acknowledgements

Bibliography

I wish to acknowledge the following books as vital source material for some of the factual detail.

'A Genuine Dicky Sam', *Liverpool and Slavery: An Historical Account of the Liverpool–African Slave Trade*, Liverpool: Scouse Press, 1985.

Acland Armstrong, Rev. Richard, *The Deadly Shame of Liverpool: An Appeal to the Municipal Voters*, London: George Philip and Son, 1890.

Allt, Nicky, *The Boys from the Mersey*, Bury: Milo Books Ltd, 2004.

Amado, Jorge, *Mar Morto*, Rio de Janeiro: Publicações Europa-America, 1997.

Aughton, Peter, *Liverpool: A People's History*, Lancaster: Carnegie Publishing Ltd, 1990.

Azurara, Gomes Eannes De, *The Chronicle of the Discovery and Conquest of Guinea*, trans. C.R. Beazley and Edgar Prestage, vols 95 and 100, London: Hakluyt Society 1st series, 1896 and 1899.

Barnes, John, *The Autobiography*, London: Headline, 1999.

Barnes, Tony, et al., *Cocky: The Rise and Fall of Curtis Warren, Britain's Biggest Drug Baron*, Bury: Milo Books, 2001.

Belchem, John (ed.), *Liverpool 800: Culture, Character and History*, Liverpool: Liverpool University Press, 2006.

----*Merseypride: Essays in Liverpool Exceptionalism*, Liverpool: Liverpool University Press, 2000.

Bennett, Alan, *Writing Home*, London: Picador, 2003.

Beynon, H., *Working for Ford*, London: Allen Lane, 1973.

Boswell, James, *The Life of Samuel Johnson*, London: Penguin, 2008.

----*No Abolition of Slavery: or the Universal Empire of Love: a poem*, Project Gutenberg, 2007.

Brinnin, John Naloola, *The Sway of the Grand Saloon: A Social History of the North Atlantic*, New York: Oslacorte Press, 1971.

Brown, J.N., *Dropping Anchor, Setting Sail: Geographies of Race in Black Liverpool*, Princeton: Princeton University Press, 2005.

Cameron, Gail and Crooke, Sam, *Liverpool: Capital of the Slave Trade*,

Liverpool: Picton Press, 1992.

Carter, Chris, et al., The Polyphonic Spree: The Case of the Liverpool Dockers, London: Industrial Relations Journal vol. 34, Blackwell, 2003.

Carlyle, Thomas, *Reminiscences: A New and Complete Edition*, eds K.J. Fielding and Ian Campbell, Oxford: Oxford University Press, 1997.

Chandler, George, *Liverpool and Literature*, Rondo Publications, 1974.

Chief Medical Officer, Department of Health, *The Removal, Retention and Use of Human Organs and Tissue from Post-Mortem Examinations*, London: The Stationery Office, 2001.

Christian, M., The Fletcher Report 1930: A Historical Case Study of Contested Black Mixed Heritage Britishness, Journal of Historical Sociology vol. 21, 2008.

Clemens, P., The Rise of Liverpool 1665–1750, The Economic History Review: New Series vol. 29, no. 2, 1976.

Clifford, M.L., *From Slavery to Freetown: Black Loyalists after the American Revolution*, Jefferson, NC: McFarland and Company, 1999.

Conrad, Joseph, *Heart of Darkness*, London: Penguin, 2007.

Cooper, P., Competing Explanations of the Merseyside Riots of 1981, London: British Journal of Criminology, vol. 25, 1985.

Cornelius, J., *Liverpool 8*, London: John Murray, 1982.

Costello, R., *Black Liverpool: The Early History of Britain's Oldest Black Community 1730–1918*, Birkenhead: Birkenhead Press, 2001.

Crick, M., *The March of Militant*, London: Faber and Faber, 1986.

Crow, Hugh, *The Memoirs of Captain Hugh Crow: The Life and Times of a Slave Trade Captain*, Oxford: Bodleian Library, University of Oxford, 2007.

Defoe, Daniel, *A Tour Through the Whole Island of Great Britain*, London: Penguin, 1986.

Dickens, Charles, *American Notes for General Circulation*, London: Penguin, 2000.

----*'The Uncommercial Traveller' and Other Papers*, London: Weidenfeld & Nicolson, 2000.

Drummond, Bill, *45*, London: Abacus, 2001.

Du Noyer, P., *Liverpool, Wondrous Place: Music from Cavern to Cream*, London: Virgin 2002.

Duncan, W.H., *Physical Causes of the High Mortality in Liverpool, read before the Literary and Philosophical Society Liverpool*, Liverpool: J. Walmsley, 1843.

----*Report to the Health Committee on the Health of the Town during the years*

1847–50, then annually 1851 to 1860, Liverpool: J. Walmsley, 1843.

Ellis, A.J., et al., *On Early English Pronunciation Part V: The existing phonology of English dialects,* London: Asher and Co., 1889.

Equiano, Oladauh, *The Interesting Narrative of the Life of Olaudah Equiano, or Gustavus Vassa, The African,* ed. Shelly Eversley, New York: Random House, 2004.

Finney, Nicholas, 'Editorial: A Decade of Relative Peace and Productivity', London: *Economic Affairs,* vol. 19, No. 2, 1999.

Fletcher, M.E., *Report on an Investigation into the Colour Problem in Liverpool and Other Ports,* Liverpool: Association for the Welfare of Half-Caste Children, 1930.

Freyre, Gilberto, *The Masters and the Slaves: Study in the Development of Brazilian Civilization,* California: University of California Press, 1987.

Gill, J., *Willy Russell and his Plays,* Birkenhead: Countyvise Ltd, 1992.

Gruneberg, C. and Knifton, R., *Centre of the Creative Universe: Liverpool and the Avant Garde,* Liverpool: Liverpool University Press, 2007.

Harris, J.W., *Days of Endeavour: A First Hand Account of a Voyage Round the World in a Sailing Ship in the Nineties,* London: Heath Cranton, 1932.

Haslam, D., *Manchester, England: The Story of the Pop Cult City,* London: Fourth Estate, 2000.

Hatton, Derek, *Inside Left: The Story So Far,* London: Bloomsbury, 1988.

Hawthorne, Nathaniel, *The English Notebooks,* Newcastle upon Tyne: Cambridge Scholars Publishing, 2008.

Heffer, E., *Never A Yes Man: The Life and Politics of an Adopted Liverpudlian,* London: Verso Books, 1991.

Henri, A., *The Glory that was Rome in Saturday's Boys: The Football Experience,* ed. H. Lansdown and A. Spillius, London: Harper Collins, 1990.

Heseltine, Michael, *Where There's a Will,* London: Hutchinson, 1987.

Hill, Dave, *Out of His Skin: The John Barnes Phenomenon,* London: Faber and Faber, 1989.

Hill, Lawrence, *The Book of Negroes,* London: Transworld, 2010.

Holt, John, *Merchant Adventure,* Liverpool: John Holt and Company, 1959.

Hughes, J., *Liverpool Banks and Bankers, 1760–1837: A History of the Circumstances which gave rise to the Industry, and of the men who founded and developed it,* Bibliolife LLC, 2009.

Johnson, Graham, *The Devil,* Edinburgh: Mainstream, 2007.

----*Powder Wars*, Edinburgh: Mainstream, 2004.

Jones, H., *Henry Tate 1819–1899*, London: Tate & Lyle, 1960.

Jung, C.G., *Memories, Dreams and Reflections*, New York: Vintage Books, 1989.

Kelly, S.F., *The Kop: The End of an Era*, London: Mandarin, 1993.

Kingsley, Charles, *Westward Ho!*, Edinburgh: Birlinn Ltd, 2009.

Lane, Tony, *Liverpool: Gateway of Empire*, London: Lawrence and Wishart, 1987.

Langworth, R. (ed.), *Churchill by Himself: The Definitive Book of Quotations*.

Lennon, John, *In His Own Write and A Spaniard in the Works*, London: Vintage, 2010.

Ligon, Richard, *A True and Exact History of the Island of Barbadoes*, (facsimile of 1675 edition), London/Portland, OR: Frank Cass, 1970.

The Liverpool Echo, Dockers Souvenir Editon, Liverpool: Trinity Mirror NW Publications 2010.

Lovejoy, P.A. and Richardson E., *Fighting the Slave Trade* (Ed Diouf), Athens, Ohio: Ohio University Press, 2003.

McIntyre-Brown, Arabella and Woodland, Guy, *Liverpool: The First 1000 Years*, Liverpool: Garlic Press, 2001.

Mariners' Museum, *Captive Passage: The Transatlantic Slave Trade and the Making of the Americas*, Washington, DC: Smithsonian Institute Press, 2002.

Melville, Herman, *Redburn*, London: Penguin, 1986.

Moffat, A., *The Sea Kingdoms: The History of Celtic Britain and Ireland*, London: HarperCollins, 2001.

Morley, Derek Wragge, *The Ant World*, London: Penguin, 1953.

Morrison, Blake, *As If*, London: Granta, 1997.

Murphy, Michael and Rees-Jones, Deryn (eds), *Writing Liverpool Essays and Interviews*, Liverpool: Liverpool University Press, 2007.

Murray, Nicholas, *So Spirited a Town: Visions and Versions of Liverpool*, Liverpool: Liverpool University Press, 2007.

Neal, Frank, *Sectarian Violence: The Liverpool Experience, 1819 to 1914: An Aspect of Anglo-Irish History*, Manchester: Manchester University Press, 1988.

Norton, M.B., The Fate of Some Black Loyalists of the American Revolution, Journal of Negro History, vol. 58, no. 4, 1973.

O'Connell, Sanjida, *Sugar: The Grass that Changed the World*, London: Virgin, 2004.

BIBLIOGRAPHY

O'Mara, P., *The Autobiography of a Liverpool Slummy*, Liverpool: Blue Coat Press, 1994.

Orchard, B. Guinness, *Liverpool's Legion of Honour*, Birkenhead: B. Guinness Orchard, 1893.

Page, J., *The Brazilians*, Reading, MA: Perseus Books, 1995.

Phillips, C., *The Atlantic Sound*, London: Faber and Faber, 2000.

Power, M., Councillors and Commerce in Liverpool, 1650–1750, Urban History 24:3, 1997.

Priestley, J.B., *English Journey*, London: Mandarin, 1994.

Rathbone, P.H., *The Political Value of Art to Municipal Life*, Liverpool. 1875.

Rediker, Marcus, *The Slave Ship*, London: John Murray, 2007.

Reynolds, S., *Generation Ecstasy*, New York: Routledge, 1999.

Richardson, D., et al., *Liverpool and Transatlantic Slavery*, Liverpool: Liverpool University Press, 2007.

Robinson, Peter (ed.), *Liverpool Accents: Seven Poets and a City*, Liverpool: Liverpool University Press, 1996.

Sala, George Augustus, *Gaslight and Daylight*, London: Chapman and Hall, 1859.

Samuels, Samuel, *From the Forecastle to the Cabin*, Charleston, NC: Bibliobazaar, 2009.

Scott, Walter Dixon, *Liverpool 1907*, Loghcrew, Ireland: Gallery Press, 1979.

Shama, Simon, *Rough Crossings*, New York: Vantage Books, 2009.

Shaw, F., *My Liverpool*, Liverpool: Gallery Press, 1971.

Sheppard, D., *Steps Along Hope Street: My Life in Cricket, the Church and the Inner City*, London: Hodder and Stoughton, 2002.

Smeathman, H., *Plan of a Settlement to be made near Sierra Leone on the Grain Coast of Africa*, London: T. Stockdale, 1786.

Smith, James McCune, *The Works of James McCune Smith: Black Intellectual and Abolitionist (Collected Black Writings)*, ed. J. Stauffer, Oxford: Oxford University Press, 2007.

Tain, H., *Notes on England*, trans. W. Rae, New York: Henry Holt and Co., 1874.

Thomas, Hugh, *The Slave Trade: The History of the Atlantic Slave Trade 1440–1870*, London: Picador, 1997.

Thomas, M., *Every Mother's Nightmare: The Killing of James Bulger*, London: Pan Books 1993.

Utting, F.A.J., *The Story of Sierra Leone, Part 1*, Manchester, NH: Ayer

Co., 1931.

Wade, Stephen (ed.), *Gladsongs and Gatherings: Poetry and its Social Context in Liverpool since the 1960s*, Liverpool: Liverpool University Press, 2001.

Waller, P.J., *Democracy and Sectarianism: Political and Social History of Liverpool, 1868–1939*, (E. Allison Peers Lectures), Liverpool: Liverpool University Press, 1981.

Published articles

Beaumont, Peter, 'Supergrass Drugs Baron Back in Business', *The Observer*, 6 October 1996.

----and Rose, David, 'Revenge is So Sweet for Customs as Target One Tries his Cocaine Smuggling Trick Once too Often', *The Observer*, 27 October 1996.

Daniels, Dr Anthony, 'Our Reaction to Mr Bigley's Death is Immature, Decadent and Dishonest', *The Telegraph*, 10 October 2004.

Johnson, Boris, 'Bigley's Fate', *The Spectator*, 16 October 2004.

----'What I Should Say Sorry for?' *The Spectator*, 23 October 2004.

Margolis, Jonathan, 'Self Pity City', *The Sunday Times*, 28 February 1993.

Morrison, Blake, 'Children of Circumstance', *The New Yorker*, 14 February 1994.

Norton, C. and Burrell, I., 'Straw Says Sorry for Insult to Liverpool: Scousers Answer Back', *Independent on Sunday*, 21 April 1999.

Pearce, E., 'Unpalatable Truth but Here Were the Echoes of Heysel', *The Sunday Times*, 23 April 1989.

Pilger, John, 'They'll Never Walk Alone', *The Guardian*, 23 November 1996.

Prestage, M., 'Scouse Equals Louse in Genteel Bournemouth', *The Independent on Sunday*, 1 September 1991.

Rose, David, 'The Mr Big's Mr Big', *The Observer*, 13 July 1997.

Russell, Sir Edward, 'The Religious Life of Liverpool', *The Sunday Magazine*, June 1905.

Williamson's Liverpool Advertiser, Liverpool, 1756.

Young, M., 'On the Merseybeat', *The Listener*, 2 November 1978.

An archive of press articles about the Liverpool Dockers' strike can be found at:

www.labournet.net/docks2/other/archive.htm.

Index

INDEX